PETER AND CAESAR

PETER AND CAESAR

The Catholic Church and Political Authority

E. A. GOERNER

*For Peter Clark
from an old classmate
Edward Goerner*

HERDER AND HERDER

1965
HERDER AND HERDER NEW YORK
232 Madison Avenue, New York 10016

Library of Congress Catalog Card Number: 65–21945
© 1965 by Herder and Herder, Incorporated
Printed in the United States of America

Contents

patribus meis

Acknowledgments

I wish to express my gratitude to Professor Jerome G. Kerwin for writing the Preface. I must also point out that although he naturally bears no responsibility for my follies, it was he who first interested me in the subject of Church-state relations some years ago. Therefore, if my book has any merits, I will be delighted if he is counted among my fathers.

I also wish to thank the University of Notre Dame and the Relm Foundation. Without their help in providing free time and secretarial assistance, I would still be far from finished.

E.A. GOERNER

The Lilacs
South Bend, Indiana

Preface

How simple it would be if we could solve the ever-present problem of Church-state relations under one or the other of the general classifications ordinarily used: union of Church and state or separation of Church and state! On the contrary, we confront a situation born of the coming of Christianity which gives us two orders of life—one supernatural, the other natural, and while both have jurisdiction in the moral sphere, there is in the final analysis a recognition of the superiority of the supernatural by all who hold to either Christian or Judaic beliefs. "God is to be obeyed rather than man" echoes down the ages. It is the challenge thrown at the feet of every political tyranny wherever Christianity has prevailed. No man owes absolute allegiance to any earthly power. St. Augustine taught this principle; Pope Gelasius confirmed it in letters to the imperial authority. Above the power of man organized in the state there exists a standard by which acts are judged and actions taken. This is the heroic, even the revolutionary, side of the picture. It is indeed a noble principle that runs through western political thought.

But who judges the judge? Who says to religious authority that it must not trespass on man's freedom? Who shall convince it of sin when it, too, becomes organized tyranny? Who unmasks the hidden face of oppression that wears a holy countenance? Above all, who possesses the omnicompetency that permits him to draw with precision the line that separates the two powers? Or is each man's conscience the ultimate norm in judging the things that are Caesar's and the things that are God's?

The tension between the two powers, organized or otherwise, has provided some of the most bitter, some of the most dramatic episodes in history. The problem has occupied the minds of some of the greatest scholars throughout the last nineteen and a half centuries. Yet even the unbelieving have inherited from a Christian past conviction of limited political power derived from nature or popular consensus. Even more rigid are their theories restrictive of religious power. Western man has fought vigorously for the preservation of what the late Charles A. Beard called "a sphere of anarchy" within which he determines the philosophy he will live by and the truths he will hold. While many a martyr has fallen victim because of this belief, so too has many a tyranny crumbled because of its persistence.

Within recent years, the political power, possessing as it does a monopoly on the forces of violence, has received the larger share of attention. But religion still remains a force, and man's greatest fear is that it become an ally of the political power, a mere tool for the purpose of crushing man's freedom. This fear has often had the effect of futile attempts to place religion at such a distance from governmental operation that freedom of religion is itself impaired.

Set forth in the ensuing pages is a careful analysis of ideas on Church-state relationships which have appeared at the high points of tension between political and ecclesiastical authorities. The work is not a history of the struggle; its merit lies largely in a successful endeavor to avoid the historical context and to consider ideas as such. Professor Goerner has learned well the dangers of historicism in a work of this kind.

The controversialists of the past—Giles of Rome, Marsilius of Padua, John of Paris, St. Robert Bellarmine—give us the two extreme answers to the problem, and the replies of writers who occupy the middle ground. The great worth of Professor Goerner's study lies in its careful and objective analysis of the views of these men. With equal care, he considers the answers

12

that John Courtney Murray gives to the question, and since this view is so satisfying to most Americans, a critical judgment does not come easily to most scholars in this country.

Professor Goerner, able political theorist, has courageously and objectively faced the whole complex problem of Church-state relationships. He is aware of the difficulties of applying objective principles to subjective realities and aware that, like many a drama, this particular drama has no finale in time. An understanding of the difficulties, however, provides for reasonable men a *modus operandi* for the better realization of the common good.

Peter and Caesar considers the Church-state issue in the light of the changes brought about in Catholic thinking through the Second Vatican Council. Older writers on this issue will envy the freedom Professor Goerner enjoys in his approach. Like John XXIII, he has thrown open the window on the Church-state question, and has let in the fresh air of present thinking. Not as one reveling in a new atmosphere, but as one judiciously weighing all the factors that challenge laity and clergy alike, the author proposes his solutions. No Catholic writer on the problem can ignore them.

JEROME G. KERWIN

University of Santa Clara

Introduction

IT is common practice in writing about the problems of Church-state relationships to speak of "God and Caesar" from the famous text of the gospels (Mt 22:21; Mk 12:17; Lk 20:25). And common practice is not wholly without reason in this as in other cases. To speak of "God and Caesar" emphasizes the inner character of the problem at hand: the confrontation between ends that transcend history and ends within history, between an order of being that is absolute and eternal and an order of being that is relative, that belongs to time and therefore suffers change. One has only to reflect on the phrase, "God and Caesar," and one remembers that, unlike God, Who is, Caesar dies. He dies as a man and is replaced by another. But even his office suffers change and dies. With its death, the structure of life that is ruled dies and is replaced by another. That is all very true, but it is not the whole truth. There is a central fact that it omits, a fact without which it is impossible even to begin to wrestle with the problems of the relations of Church and state.

The very existence of the "problem of Church and state" is inconceivable without the fact of a singular historical event: the inruption of God into history in the person of Christ Jesus. To be sure, the problem of God and Caesar existed before this time, and was, furthermore, known. Witness the cases of Sophocles' Antigone and of Socrates. But the Incarnation wholly transformed the way in which the problem of God and Caesar

15

presented itself to men. Socrates made no claim to be God even if he was, in his way, a witness to Him. Socrates and his heirs led some men to an experience of divine things. But the encounter of men with Jesus of Nazareth was evidently quite different from the encounter with Socrates. I say "different," not "opposed."

Socrates denies his own wisdom in favor of the divine wisdom.[1] On the other hand, the Christ, the Son of the Living God, affirms himself that he was not only a guide on the way, but the Way itself; not only a teacher of truth, but the Truth itself; not only one who leads to a new life, but Life itself. Well, a fool could see that the consequences must be diverse.

Not only were men confronted with a transcendent God in the flesh of Adam (a God whose very name had hitherto been unutterable)—that was problem enough—but He evidently intended to extend His presence in time until its very ending in an *ecclesia,* a Church, a people of God the continuance and sanctity of which He would guarantee. Although the manner of the divine action whereby that guarantee was to be kept was various, yet as foundation He laid down Peter and his successors who, nevertheless, still bear the weaknesses that Adam's flesh is heir to.

Henceforth, the problem of God and Caesar presented itself in a special fashion. The whole order of temporal existence and ends is now confronted for the first time with a universal and independent representative in time of the relationship of man to an eternal God.

Hitherto, there had been two historical alternatives: sacred kingship and its remnants[2] on the one hand, and, on the other,

---

[1] *Apology* 20–23.

[2] They are clearly visible in the politico-religious structure of democratic Athens. Cf. Fustel de Coulanges, *The Ancient City* (Garden City: 1956); Georg Busolt, *Griechische Staatskunde* (Munich: 1920–1926), vol. 1, pp. 514–587; vol. 2, pp. 783–817, 1168–1176; Martin P. Nilsson, *Geschichte*

the challenge to it raised by Socrates, a private person, in the name of a transcendent divine order. In the first case, the problem of God and Caesar does not properly arise. In the second, he who raises it appears to stand alone against the common good. To be sure, both Christ and Socrates are haled before the public power and condemned, but Christ's encounter with Caesar in the person of Pilate is a quite different sort of affair inasmuch as Christ is Himself a king.[3] Henceforth, the problem of God and Caesar presents itself in a special way in Western history. The way represented by Socrates, the private citizen, in his encounter with the city is not abolished. But there is, in addition, a new way: the confrontation of a representative of a higher kingdom and Caesar, the confrontation of Peter and Caesar.

Greek philosophy directed the gaze of men to a divine order that wholly transcends the historical, impermanent world of birth, growth, and decay. And everyone knows that the depth and breadth of that experience of the divine was enough to produce a fatal encounter between Socrates and his own city. But the character of that encounter and its consequences for Plato and Aristotle brilliantly illuminate the difference between the pre-Christian and post-Christian forms of the problem. The philosophic way to the divine was in principle limited to the few, and therefore the political character and influence of the philosophic experience of the divine was inherently private. That fact was immeasurably deepened by the terribly solitary

---

der griechischen Religion (Munich: 1941–1950), vol. 1, pp. 306–359, 390, 670–683, 691–695; vol. 2, pp. 10–84, 125–174, 311–329, 366–375; *idem, A History of Greek Religion* (Oxford: 2nd revised ed., 1952), pp. 224–262; G. Glotz, *The Greek City and its Institutions* (London: 1929); Paul Vinogradoff, *Outlines of Historical Jurisprudence* (Oxford: 1922) vol. 2, ch. 5; J. Walter Jones, *The Law and Legal Theory of the Greeks* (Oxford: 1956), chs. 5 and 6.

[3] Mt 27:11, 27–30; Mk 15:2, 16–19; Lk 23:2–4; Jn 18:33–38; 19:2–3, 5, 10–12, 15.

character of the highest philosophic act. In spite of its dependence on and thirst for communicability, it was denied communion. As Aristotle put it, Zeus is too far away, and, although it is strange to make the supremely happy man a solitary, he ought nevertheless to strain every nerve to live in accordance with the most divine thing in him and then he is most alone and least in need of friends.[4] Only in the unusual cases of the philosopher-king or of the king who would listen to the philosopher was it possible to suppose that the philosopher's experience of the eternal order might seriously extend its influence into the sphere of political action.

The condemnation of Socrates had shown that, under other circumstances, the revelation of the philosophic truth about the divine order and its implications for action in history produced a violent reaction from the public authority. The reaction was inevitable. It was inevitable not only because the new experience of the divine and its implications threatened a change in the ultimate bases of the common life. That always produces a reaction. It was inevitable not only because every manifestation of the divine provokes a diabolic reaction. But it was also inevitable because the new experience was not accessible to the many. Therefore, it threatened the popular regime because it denied to the many its claim to be the proximate standard of the true and good order of human life. But the philosophers also represented a threat to non-popular regimes, with the exception of the special cases in which a philosopher himself was king or in which a king consented to place himself under the tutelage of a philosopher.

The reaction was inevitable for another reason. Hitherto, the political sphere could be regarded as containing the religious as well as that smaller sphere that we have in mind when we speak of "the political." But the philosopher broke a hole, so

[4] *Nicomachean Ethics* viii. 7. 1159a4–5; ix. 9. 1169b17–22; 7. 1177a12–1178a8.

18

to speak, in the sky of the *polis,* and, without wholly leaving the city, he breathed the air of a universal god, of the infinite sphere of the absolute and the eternal. Henceforth, contact with the divine could no longer appear to the initiated as something proper to the city. Heretofore, the contact of men with the divine had been a matter cared for by public acts and regulated by public authorities.[5] But the philosopher's perception of the transcendent order of reality and the philosopher's way to that order were such that the ancient city was threatened to its very roots.

The philosopher's perception of the divine ultimately denied the particularist gods of the city and thereby transformed the political character of religion. Furthermore, the philosophic way to the divine totally undermined the stability of the religious order of society. The philosopher's critique tended to destroy the old structure of belief, but he was unable to assist more than some few to the contemplative encounter with a transcendent god for which many were not suited. Furthermore, it was not possible (except under the improbable case of the philosopher-king) to organize the philosophers into some sort of priestly body to provide a popular and mythologized version of the philosophic truth about the divine. This was not possible precisely because at its core the philosopher's experience was such that it was not subject to verification by the sort of external rules-of-thumb that are ordinarily available to societies for such purposes (e.g., venerable age, examination in the religious doctrine, and an upright life).

---

[5] There were, of course, family cults which were private vis-à-vis the city, just as the civic cults were private vis-à-vis the rest of the world. But the civic cults were at least patterned on the earlier family cults, if not actual borrowings, and in both cases they were radically closed communities.

Notice that I write "public" rather than "political" acts and authorities. Although the latter usage would have been accurate from the point of view of the Greek city-state, it would inevitably be misleading in English. This shift of language suggests how great has been the shift in common perceptions.

19

And, as if all of this were not threatening enough to the holders of political power, the philosopher furthermore laid claim to a perception of the absolute standard of justice by which every political act ought to be judged. Such a claim, of course, threatened almost every imaginable vested interest and subtle self-deception.

The condemnation and death of Socrates made manifest the depth of tension. Henceforth, the problem of the relation of philosophy to the political order of life became, by practical necessity, a burning question for philosophy. One solution, not necessarily appropriate to all circumstances, is the retreat of philosophy from the agora to academe, since, indeed, the philosophers themselves became aware of the tendency of their new experience to undermine the whole of the existing political order. It was necessary, therefore, to develop a less dangerous exoteric doctrine in order to shield both the city and the philosopher from the disastrous consequences of a simple, public revelation of the new experience of the divine.[6]

But whatever the character of the solutions attempted or envisaged by Greek philosophy, the very nature of the problem is decisively different in important respects for Christianity.

First, the specifically Christian experience of the divine was not limited in principle to a few, as was the specifically philosophic way. The divine was revealed in both cases. But the Christian revelation of the divine is through the Incarnation, the taking on of a human existence by God. It is, in consequence, possible to elaborate a way of human contact with the divine not limited to a few special men, as was the speculative way of philosophy. An affective way of approaching the divine

[6] Aulus Gellius *Noctes Atticae* xx. 5. Cf. Mt 13:1–53; Mk 4:1–34; Lk 8:4–18; Jn 10:1–18; 16:25–29. There is also a certain remote analogy in the Christian distinction between the commandments and counsels of perfection; cf. Mt 19:16–26; Mk 10:17–27; Lk 18:18–27.

20

is now open. Because God appears as a man among men, a concrete rather than a conceptual standard of being is made available to men. And this way of revelation is consistently followed in Christ's teaching by parable rather than speculative discourse. So the Christian way of approach to the transcendent order of reality appears as an approach by way of an imitation of a divine example.

However, two things ought to be made clear in this connection. First, the affective way, the imitation of Christ, does not preclude the intellective or speculative way. Second, the imitation of Christ is capable of a practically infinite variation in respect of depth. Thus, not only is Christianity available to the many, but, by virtue of admitting infinite variations in depth and by virtue of admitting the intellective or speculative way in addition, Christianity does not reintroduce the same sort of tension as that between the many and the few who are philosophers. But, as in the case of philosophy, Christianity, too, breaks open the sphere of the political and introduces man to a transcendent order of being. And, as in the case of philosophy, the political sphere, the sphere of human affairs, now finds itself confronted with a demand to conform itself to a standard that is absolutely transcendent and yet appears in the flesh, and that stands in judgment.

However, in the case of philosophy the stability of the political order was threatened because the many were not capable of the philosophic experience on the one hand, and, on the other, one could not easily institutionalize a priestly caste made up of philosophers who would preach a popular myth that conformed in its general outlines to the moral implications of philosophy. Such an institution could not be erected because the philosophic experience was a personal and private thing for the verification of which legal criteria could hardly suffice. Thus, however clear it may have been to the philoso-

21

phers, from the point of view of the city the relationship between it and the philosophers was singularly confused. The
philosophers could appear to the city only as teachers of new
doctrines, at best, and, at worst, as the launchers of criminal
attacks upon the gods of the city. That is to say, the city was
quite unable to distinguish between philosophers and the
teachers of a variety of other doctrines. Nor could the city distinguish between a true philosopher and someone who merely
chose to employ the name. Thus, the city was confronted with
a variety of individuals with differing doctrines all bearing the
same name. That is to say, philosophy did not confront the
city as an organized body of men.

Catholic Christianity, on the other hand, confronted the city
with a hierarchic priesthood in the service not of the god of
the city, but of the God Who Is, and who has created man,
suffered with him, saved him, and judges him in his cities as in
his secret places. The tension between these representatives of
the divine and the representatives of the city now takes on the
form of an encounter between two organized bodies. Heretofore, the city and its representatives had only been faced with
the individual philosophers and perhaps a few disciples. The
consequence of papacy and episcopacy is that, for the first
time, the breaking open of the political sphere and the introduction of man into the realm of the absolute takes place at
the hands of a clearly defined social organization, the hierarchic
priesthood that, while proper to the realm of the absolute, oc-
cupies a position within history as well. The problems involved
in the relations between the philosopher and the city continue
to exist, and there is added to them the problem raised by the
saint in the city. But, since the spirit blows where it will, the
saint may very well not be a member of the hierarchic priesthood. Therefore, *from the point of view of politics,* he presents
the same sort of problem as does the philosopher. From the

22

point of view of the church, a conflict between the spiritual man and a city is a conflict between the church, of which the spiritual man is necessarily a representative, and that city. But from the point of view of the city, it has the same form as a conflict with the philosopher. It is simply another case of an individual opposing what he claims to be the defects in the city's order on the ground of a conviction that he claims is rooted in his perception of a higher, truer order for man. But to this sort of civic encounter with the divine, there is added the quite new problem of the relations between church, in the narrow sense of its representatives in the hierarchic priesthood, and state, in its ruling representatives. This is what I have chosen to call the relationship between Peter and Caesar.

Plainly, it is not *a priori* impossible that the same man be saint, philosopher, high priest, and king, although one can hardly expect to encounter such a one on every afternoon stroll. Thus, the problem is far more complicated than might at first appear. Were the king to be a great saint and a philosopher as well as a great king, and the pope a notorious profligate, what then? Obviously, Peter and Caesar, in the concrete, would then stand to each other on quite different footings than if the vices were Caesar's and Peter's the virtues. Of course, one of the questions still must be: what sort of footing can each claim simply in virtue of the fact that he is either Caesar or Peter? But to have answered that is not enough. To have answered that is to have answered only one part of an existentially more complex problem. Nevertheless, it is the point of departure because the whole church-state problem seems to first raise itself in an acute form in a way that puts the question first. Whatever else they may claim, both Peter and Caesar claim a moral magistracy, and the course of Christian history has been marked by regular conflicts between them. In some times and places, Peter has felt the attempt of Caesar either to absorb

23

his office or at least to reduce it to subordination. And Caesar, at other times and places, has felt the attempt of Peter to absorb his office or to reduce it to subordination. On occasion, each has suspected the other of the same design, and each step taken in defense only served to convince the opponent of the aggressive designs of the other.

Parenthetically, it should be noted that it is beside the point, for the moment, whether one believes or does not believe any of the assumptions about Christ and the hierarchic priesthood in his Church. The whole of the Catholic world believed and believes it. And that means that the whole of the Western world has been importantly shaped by that belief, even in cases where the body politic is composed of Protestants against one or more aspects of it. Therefore, in any case involving a relationship between an autonomously organized religious body and a political organization, the influence of that belief must be taken into account wherever Western thought has penetrated.

Since this seems to me to be the nature of the case with which we are confronted, I determined to attempt to illuminate the question by undertaking first a set of studies of some classical, yet diverse, attempts to formulate the problem and its solutions. Obviously, I have not attempted to treat exhaustively each of the major theoretical elaborations of the question. I had to choose and I chose. But I chose with a view to setting out the chief alternative ways of presenting the question and its solution within the context of a Catholic view of the Church. And for this purpose, it seemed wiser to employ the work of great thinkers on the question rather than attempt to develop these positions myself, as if no one had thought about the problem before me and as if anything I might write of my own were not beholden to what others have thought and written before. Naturally, this procedure does not provide for the representation of every possible way of seeing the matter, nor

24

even for every way in which it has been seen and written about. The reader will have to judge whether those I have chosen are adequate to the issue, for, having attempted to limn the structure of the problem through their works, I have presumed to append some reflections of my own on Peter and Caesar. Clearly, those reflections are only by way of beginnings. They impose on me the obligation of further words on the relationship of religion to the unity of political action and to the theory of regimes.

Giles of Rome

The Terrible Abyss of Freedom

THERE is a certain vertigo that tends to come over one who reflects on his freedom. Head swimming, he is suddenly aware of a vast and bottomless abyss that has opened at his feet. He seems to be faced with a choice. He may abandon his freedom, sink to the earth and cease to move, become a slave to the bit of earth on which he lies in order to have a *place,* that is to say, to be defined in relation to that bit of earth. Or he may choose to take another step. Henceforth, it seems he will have to define things in relation to himself, since the space into which he has stepped seems to have no limits of its own. And then the question is whether he can do that.

Politics sometimes takes on this abyssal aspect. There may or may not be limits to what one can expect from the company of free men among whom one moves. But, if there are such, they do not reveal themslves in advance of our action. And therefore, everything we do seems to carry with it an element of limitless risk.

There are, of course, divers tricks by which one attempts to overcome vertigo. Everyone knows what to do: "Don't look down!" Even better: "Don't look down! Look at something else!" That is to say, return to the plane world of everyday. That sometimes helps a bit, but it is obvious from the nervous movement of his fingers that the fellow who is so intently studying his neighbor's hat hasn't altogether forgotten that one false step and off he goes. A more sophisticated gesture of the same sort is the attempt to master political phenomena by reducing them to statistical probabilities. "The odds" are not wholly uninteresting, but action does not take place in the abstract world of the odds. Indeed, "the odds" are rather beside the point to the man or the city that must choose death or slavery before the sun sets. In any case, whatever the attractions of distractions (and a good whistler can lend a certain charm to whistling in the dark), there are other solutions to the problem of fear and dizziness before the abyss of human freedom. This first chapter is concerned with one of them, elaborated by a student of St. Thomas Aquinas, Giles of Rome, a member of the Order of Hermits of St. Augustine.[1]

To live in our time, writes Giles, is to live "in this flood, in this deluge of waters and violent winds, . . . in this vast and deep sea where there are not only tempestuous winds but also sea serpents without number, that is, every kind of enemy." In this chaos of our existence, "no one will be saved, no one can make his way to safety" except in one way.[2]

There is, in the midst of this tempestuous and abysmal sea, one safe place: the ark of the new Noah, the pope. Absolute master of his ship, he "is to be feared and his commands are to be observed, because his power is spiritual, heavenly, and divine and is beyond weight, number, and measure."[3] Only in the Church, the ark of the new Noah, will anyone be saved.[4] And to be in the Church is to be under obedience to the pope, whose power is not only beyond measure, but who may indeed

---

[1] Known as Aegidius Romanus and Egidio Colonna. Born at Rome, ca. 1246. Died at Avignon, 1316.

[2] *De Ecclesiastica Potestate* ii. 1. 36. I have used the critical edition of Richard Scholz originally published in Weimar (Verlag Herm. Böhlaus, 1929) and recently issued in a new impression (Scientia Aalen, 1961). Hereafter, references will be abbreviated to *D.E.P.*, followed by the numbers for part, chapter, and page in this edition.

[3] *Ibid.*, iii. 12. 209. [4] *Ibid.*, ii. 1. 36.

be called the Church itself.[5] In this new depiction of Peter and his boat, there is no longer any hint of Christ calming the sea, lest the boat sink, nor is there any evidence of nets to which the spirit of the Lord moves such great schools of fish that Peter must call for help. Peter needs no help. He can do alone whatever he can do with the help of anyone else.[6] Nor is there any need for nets: the smart fish jump right in and thereby escape their enemies and the storm. The storm rages on, yet Peter's boat resists it, the passengers strengthened by an iron discipline based on the fear that their captain may toss them back into the storm—amid the sea serpents, their enemies.

Giles of Rome is not the only Catholic who has viewed the Church in this way. But his is one of the most consistent and extreme formulations of the power of the pope as a solution to the interrelated problems posed by human freedom and evil. A certain emphasis on the visibility and juridical organization of the Church has been common in the Catholic West as compared with Orthodoxy, not to speak of Protestantism. But Giles of Rome went further than most in formulating a doctrine of papal supremacy by means of which the Church was to redeem human freedom from the chaos of evil into which it seemed to plunge the race of man. Still, even his rather simple and robust[7] formulations are not the most extreme that are logically possible. The Catholic tradition compels him to note certain limits to papal absolutism. His peculiar value is that he admits the traditional limits to papal absolutism. He admits the traditional limits to papal power. He admits them and then

---

[5] *Ibid.* iii. 12. 209 and ii. 1. 36.   [6] *Ibid.* iii. 9. 190–191.

[7] More subtle formulations have been made. James of Viterbo, for example, draws virtually the same practical conclusions from a far more delicate and comprehensive theoretical base. See H.-X. Arquilliere, *Le plus ancien traite de l'Eglise de Jacques de Viterbe: de Regimine Christiano* (Paris: 1926). However, few contemporary readers are likely to share (or, perhaps, even comprehend) the rather restricted theologico-metaphysical context within which his argument moves. Giles' argument, by comparison, is likely to be far more accessible.

sterilizes them. He quotes the popes themselves declaring the limits to their own power. He quotes them and then reduces their declarations to near nonsense with a few well-aimed distinctions.

Logically, the most elegant way of drawing out a doctrine of absolute papal supremacy (or of any absolute political supremacy, for that matter) is to ignore the *duo sunt* of Pope Gelasius[8] and begin with the assertion *unum est solum*. However, it is impossible for Giles to achieve that elegance without abandoning the whole tradition which had always insisted on two. Indeed, Giles finds it necessary to devote a whole chapter to defending the doctrine that there are two swords. (Gelasius had spoken of the two not as swords, but as the "sacred authority of the pontiffs and the royal power.") He considers the possibility of one sword only, and then the possibility of a trinity of swords which he develops in some detail.[9] Both are rejected. There are two swords and only two. But the Church has them both.[10] And that, for Giles of Rome, is the same as saying that the *pope* has both swords. For the pope "can be called the Church," since, insofar as there is power in the Church, the pope has the fullness of it. He can do alone everything that could be done with the concurrence of anyone else.[11] Naturally, the question arises: why, if all that is so, does Giles speak of two swords rather than one? An answer to that must begin with a statement of his notions of the nature and functions of the two.

What, then, is the work of the Church? The broad outline of

---

[8] Epist. xii. 2. in Migne, *Patrologia Latina*, vol. LIX, p. 42. Cf. A.J. and R.W. Carlyle, *A History of Mediaeval Political Theory in the West* (Edinburgh & London: 1950), vol. 1, pp. 185–193 (cited hereafter as "Carlyle, HMPT"), and A.K. Ziegler, "Pope Gelasius I and his Teaching on the Relation of Church and State," *Catholic Historical Review*, vol. 27 (1942), pp. 412–437.

[9] *D.E.P.* ii. 13.   [10] *D.E.P.* ii. 4–10.
[11] *D.E.P.* iii. 9. 191–193; iii. 12. 209.

Giles' answer is clear: the salvation of souls.[12] But the specification of that answer is not so clear. There are, he says, two foods provided for man by God: a bodily food and a spiritual food, because man is composed of a body and a soul. But Giles does not argue that the Church is some kind of a divine banquet in which one receives the food of the soul. Rather, the Church appears as the wielder of a sword that drives away "impediments" to the reception of the spiritual food.[13] That is to say, "the Church" is chiefly to be understood, at least in the context of Giles' discussion, as a jurisdictional hierarchy. The work of the ecclesiastical hierarchy is so to arrange the affairs of the faithful that they may readily obtain the food of the soul. And the way in which the prelate orders these affairs is by the terror of his sword. Just as he who does not obey the prince is cut out of the body politic by the sword of the prince which kills the body, similarly, he who disobeys the ecclesiastical prelate (especially the pope) is cut off from the communion of the faithful. But only in that communion can one receive the spiritual food. Therefore, "the soul is killed by [the spiritual] sword."[14] Giles makes it perfectly clear that this is no mere slip of the pen. He elaborates on and repeats his judgment. Furthermore, he returns to it later. The Church "cuts through and slays" [*percutit*] souls. She inflicts "wounds" [*lesiones*] on them by ecclesiastical censure. And this is a sign of her great power, for "to wound the soul is far greater than to wound the body."[15] Of course, Giles was not alone in the Middle Ages in transforming Pope Gelasius' "two" into "two swords." Deusdedit, Honorius, John of Salisbury, St. Bernard,

[12] E.g., *D.E.P.* ii. 12. 108–109.

[13] *D.E.P.* i. 6[7]. 23. There is a discrepancy between the chapter numbers given by the Mss in the table of contents and those in the body of the text for the first part of the work. The first number given corresponds to that in the table and the number in brackets to that in the text.

[14] *D.E.P.* i. 2[3]. 11: "*per talem gladium occiditur anima.*"

[15] *D.E.P.* i. 7[8]. 28

and Gerhoh of Reichersberg, to name only a few, consider the texts of the famous scene of Christ's apprehension in the Mount of Olives as the source of the doctrine of the spiritual and temporal swords. Nor is he alone in saying that the Church has them both.[16] But the use of the sword image is freely chosen and carefully managed by Giles.

Giles devotes a whole chapter to the question of the relationship of the two-swords doctrine to the gospel texts.[17] On first reading, the whole chapter seems arbitrarily contrived. The chapter title reads: "Wherein it is more fully argued how it is that the two swords that are in the Church are referred to the two swords named in the gospel." However, one is struck at once by the fact that, although all four gospels refer to the incident, two of them are not mentioned at all: Mark 14:47 and John 18:10–11. He quotes Luke 22:38, but omits Luke 22:49–51. He quotes the first half of Christ's words in Matthew 26:52 and omits the second part of them in the same verse.[18] This is a singularly selective advertence to the biblical sources. And the selectivity becomes more significant when one compares what Giles included with what he left out.

To begin with, Peter's ridiculous ineptitude as a swordsman[19] is conveniently veiled. After all, if Giles hopes by his tract to induce an efficacious fear of the pope in Christians, it would hardly do to present to a medieval audience so preposterously

[16] Cf. Carlyle, *HMPT*, vol. IV   [17] *D.E.P.* ii. 15.

[18] In addition, all of the Mss to which Scholz refers give incorrect references to Matthew (see p. 137, n.g.). Two of them refer to chapter XXII and two refer to chapter XXVII. This could, of course, be the consequence of a variation in the gospel text to which Giles referred; or to a mistake on Giles' part; or, more likely, to copyists' mistakes. But, given the arbitrary way in which Giles breaks up the text in Mt 26:52, it is not altogether extravagant to suppose that he might have deliberately refrained from giving accurate directions to the scene of the crime.

[19] Mt 26:51; Mk 14:47; Lk 22:50; Jn 18:10. Only John's account identifies the swordsman as Peter, yet Giles nowhere mentions John's gospel, even though in referring to Matthew's account he has the Lord speaking to Peter. *D.E.P.* ii. 15. 137.

inadequate and panicky an archetype of papal swordsmanship. Peter's mastery of the weapon can effect no more than the removal of an ear from the head of one of a multitude of enemies: scarcely a fitting inaugural for Giles' swords that slay bodies and souls and strike terror in the hearts as well as in the ears of his readers.

But Giles' selective exegesis is more curious than that. He simply assumes that the two swords that Luke mentions (22:38) being in the upper room at the last supper are both of them at Gethsemane, and that Peter has them both. Therefore, when Peter draws one to defend Christ, the other must remain in the scabbard. The texts, however, do not speak of Peter having two swords at Gethsemane, nor do they speak of any other disciples having any swords. Giles simply fails to advert to the relevant verses. Furthermore, he is plainly aware of a host of difficulties and objections to his interpretation.

First, the biblical texts can only refer to the spiritual and temporal swords of his argument if they are given a figurative reading. Even on the assumption that there were two swords at Gethsemane, a literal reading leaves one with nothing but two material swords.[20] Second, assuming that Peter had the two swords from the upper room with him at Gethsemane and that he drew one of them and left the other in the scabbard, one is left with the problem of deciding which one is a figure of the spiritual power and which of the temporal. It seems that some regard the drawn sword as the figure of the spiritual power and others regard the sheathed one as the figure of the spiritual power. Giles evidently doesn't wish unnecessarily to alienate anyone who is ready to make all the exegetical concessions so far demanded. Having started on a figurative interpretation, he is prepared to make the most of it. You can have it either way, or, even better, both ways. In one respect, the sheathed sword is

[20] *D.E.P.* ii. 15. 138–139.

a figure of the spiritual power, and in another respect the drawn sword is that figure. And similarly for the temporal power.[21]

Third, and still more important, Giles is aware that there is a reading of the texts that gives a wholly different meaning to the matter of the swords. Luke reports (22:37–38) the following conversation at the last supper: "For I say to you that this which is written must yet be fulfilled in me, 'And he was reckoned among the wicked.' For that which concerns me is at its end." And they said, "Lord, behold, here are two swords." And he said to them, "It is enough." Giles' figurative reading of Christ's reply, "It is enough," is that Christ thereby indicated that the Church had precisely what it ought to have, no more and no less than the spiritual and temporal swords.[22] However, an alternative reading is that Christ speaks "ironically and derisively," inasmuch as Judas will bring out with him a big crowd armed with swords and clubs. That is a good reading of the text, he admits, but it is a literal one. The figurative reading doesn't deny it, but adds a new level of meaning.[23] But the difficulties raised by a literal reading are not as easily disposed of. The disciples had no idea what sort or size of an opposition they would have to fight. Therefore, if Christ is here ironical and derisive, he is so privately, by virtue of a foreknowledge of his arrest by the crowd guided by Judas. The reading of Christ's words as ironic and derisive thus presupposes that one has inspected the texts treating of the arrest in Gethsemane. When one does so and then compares the texts with Giles' excerpt, then the full arbitrariness of his treatment of the gospels becomes clear. He quotes Christ saying to Peter, "Put back thy sword into its place" (Mt 26:52). And from this he concludes that, therefore, the sword must properly pertain to Peter, i.e., the Church,[24] otherwise Christ would presumably have charged Peter to turn it over to its owner. But verse 52 continues: "for all those who take the

[21] *D.E.P.* ii. 15. 139–140. [22] *D.E.P.* ii. 15. 138.
[23] *D.E.P.* ii. 15. 140. [24] *D.E.P.* ii. 15. 137–138.

sword will perish by the sword." Giles leaves that out, and he likewise omits the following two verses that read: "Or dost thou suppose that I cannot entreat my Father, and he will even now furnish me with twelve legions of angels? How then are the Scriptures to be fulfilled, that thus it must happen?" Giles also omits reference to John's account where alone (and not in Matthew) Peter is identified as the one to whom Christ spoke. John 18:11 reads: "Jesus therefore said to Peter, 'Put up thy sword into the scabbard. Shall I not drink the cup that the Father has given me?'" Luke (22:51) reports as follows: "But Jesus answered and said, 'Bear with them thus far.' And he touched his ear and healed him."

There are differences of nuance in the texts, but all reveal a Christ who is alone. His disciples, and Peter in particular, are not altogether without courage. They are ready to strike at his enemies against great odds. But the point of the incident is that they do not have the courage that would spring from having apprehended the nature of his mission and having joined themselves to it. Therefore, he rebukes them. Viewed in this light, the irony of the "It is enough" takes on a far greater depth and amplitude than Giles intimates.

In short, the inescapable conclusion is that Giles' argument does not really proceed from the biblical texts at all except in a very tenuous way. He employs a figure in common use in his time that depended on a rather fanciful piece of biblical exegesis. The figure was to his purpose, and that seems to have been enough to justify its use without any serious attempt to validate it in the texts. Further, this use of Scripture is characteristic of Giles' work. The roots of his argument must be found elsewhere. In order to uncover them, it will be necessary to outline the main features of his doctrine on the juridical relationships between the spiritual and temporal powers, and then proceed analytically to the foundations of the juridical structure.

The spiritual power is prior to and institutes the secular

power, and, having instituted it, the spiritual power controls its action; and, thus, when the action of the secular power is unresponsive or inefficacious, the spiritual power judges it and disestablishes it, replacing it with another, and even establishing and changing the civil laws.[25]

The spiritual power (that is to say, the Church understood as the priestly hierarchy and thus the pope[26]) is prior or superior to the secular power in dignity. Giles uses the comparisons of sun to moon and of soul to body. More important, the spiritual power is concerned with spiritual and divine things, whereas the secular power is concerned with the things of time, material things. The office of the political authority is merely concerned with preparing a material environment of tranquillity within which the spiritual power may concern itself with souls without interruption.[27]

[25] On the priority of the spiritual power, 1) in dignity: *D.E.P.* i. 4[5]. 13–17; ii. 4. 48–54; iii. 10. 197–198; 2) in power: i. 1[2]–4[5]; ii. 4. 48–54; ii. 12. 100–111; iii. 2. 149–157; iii. 9. 190–195; iii. 11. 203–204; 3) in end or object: i. 4[5]. 16; i. 7[8]. 29–30; ii. 4. 48–54; ii. 12. 103–105; ii. 13. 112–114; 4) in time: i. 5[6]. 18–22.

On the power of the Church to institute the secular power: i. 3[4]. 11–13; ii. 5. 54–60; iii. 2. 152–154.

On the modes in which the Church controls the action of the secular power: 1) *"ad nutum"*: ii. 6. 61; ii. 13. 116; iii. 10. 197–198; 2) by exercising either immediate or appellate jurisdiction in temporals as well as in spirituals: i. 7[8]. 29; iii. 3. 157; iii. 7. 185; 3) by disestablishing or transferring political authorities: i. 3 [4]. 11–12; ii. 6. 61; ii. 12. 104–111; iii. 4. 163; 4) by framing, establishing, and interpreting civil laws: iii. 8. 185–187.

[26] Cf. *supra,* pp. 27–28.

[27] Most medieval writers would be prepared to admit a priority of dignity to the priestly power, but most of the followers of Aquinas would say that the political order was not merely directed to the things of the body, but to the perfection of natural human virtue. See below, ch. 3. Although he appears to have been a student of St. Thomas at Paris, he nowhere refers to him in the text, although he refers, directly or indirectly, to St. Augustine thirty-eight times, more than anyone else. This in spite of the fact that he cites Aristotle twenty-six times and even Averroës four times. For Giles' position in respect to St. Thomas in a metaphysical context, see the references in Etienne Gilson, *History of Christian Philosophy in the Middle Ages* (New York: 1955), especially pp. 404–405 and 418.

The spiritual sword is also greater than the temporal in power. It can kill souls, whereas the material sword of the prince can only kill bodies.[28] It collects tithes which are given in recognition of servitude. The priest sacres and blesses the king, and he who blesses is greater than he who is blessed. He institutes the secular power inasmuch as the priestly power was instituted first in the Old Testament and the royal power was then set up by it. And if anyone object that all kingdoms have not been set up by priests, but that kingdoms may exist and did exist under the law of nature, Giles dismisses him contemptuously, citing St. Augustine[29] to the effect that such are no true kingdoms, but mere robberies. Furthermore, the king has power over bodies and bodily things only, whereas the priest rules spiritual things, which, in the great ontic hierarchy, are superior to and rule corporal things. Finally, the Lord did not concede to Peter a limited power of binding and loosing. Rather, the Lord said "*Whatsoever* thou shalt bind," etc. And to that universal power was annexed the divine omnipotence. Thus, Peter and his successors may not only excommunicate: with the guarantee of heavenly confirmation, they may strip any man, including a king, of every right to human association, and thus of any share in any human law, and whoever is outside the human law loses all that is his, for it is only by human law that one can distinguish between mine and thine. In short, the pope, and the pope alone, can deprive a man of his nature in a double way. He denies to a social animal every form of sociality. And he denies to a worldly animal everything in the world, and this not only in law, but in fact, for the pope authorizes the believers to execute his sentence by taking for themselves, by force if needed, the goods of the excommunicate. And, lest anything be left to him, the pope bars the gates of heaven to the animal, whose last and deepest thirst is for salvation. Of course, the pope imitates his

[28] Cf. *supra*, pp. 32–33.   [29] *De Civ. Dei* iv. 4.

divine master. If God were to act toward the sinner as the sinner deserves, he would exterminate him at once. But God gives him a second chance. So, too, the pope, out of his god-like benignity, permits the excommunicate to reflect awhile before he grants license to the faithful to invade the excommunicate's goods and deprive him of all that is his.

One may be permitted to wonder whether a city or a heaven would have lost its savor with the knowledge that your fellow citizens or saints were only waiting for the license to take all that was yours and hurl you into a bottomless pit. But be that as it may, Giles is not done. His extraordinary leviathan may already appear terrifying enough. Nethertheless, it is necessary to close the arch of the argument for the superiority of the spiritual power with a double-faceted keystone.

For polemical closure, Giles constructed a rhetorical and exegetical *tour de force* that claimed to show, against current opinion, that philosophy, history, and authority all concur in asserting that priesthood preceded kingship in time.[30] The most interesting point about the argument is that it manages to cover so astonishingly broad a field in but four pages.

For theoretical closure, Giles repeatedly points out that the spiritual power is concerned with souls and the temporal power is concerned with bodies. Contrary to common opinion and the authority of Aristotle,[31] he ignores the usual judgment that the political order is immediately directed to procuring a natural spiritual perfection or virtue in its members. He assumes that

[30] *D.E.P.* i. 5[6]. For the contrary view, cf. John of Paris, *Tractatus de Potestate Regia et Papali* iv. The text is published in Dom Jean Leclercq, O.S.B., *Jean de Paris et l'Ecclésiologie du XIIIe Siècle* (Paris: 1942).

[31] Cf. John of Paris, *Tractatus* v., referring, of course, to bk. i of Aristotle's *Politics*. James of Viterbo, who arrives at the same practical conclusions as Giles, cannot leave his argument rest on so simple a distinction in contradiction to the authority of Aristotle and the data of political experience. See *De Regimine Christiano* ii. 6–7. Giles is not ignorant of the relevant work of Aristotle, as is clear from his quotations from the *Ethics* and *Politics* in *D.E.P.* i 2[3]. 10; ii. 9. 84; ii. 10. 89–90; iii. 9. 194.

the spiritual perfection of man is solidary, and, under the present divine dispensation, it is under the care of the pope.[32] Kings may once have had a spiritual concern. They were unable to meet its demands. They were unable to elaborate a regime based on justice, and, indeed, their regimes were born of invasion and usurpation whereby they were from their very origin thieves and robbers.[33] They have been replaced by a priesthood at the head of which stands the pope, although, in keeping with their character, they are still permitted to coerce the disobedient by drawing "blood and even by death which is the limit of all terrible things, as is said in the *Ethics*."[34] Since the king rules bodies and the pope rules souls, the power of the pope is prior to and superior to the temporal power, for in the ontic hierarchy everywhere manifested in the universe material things exist for and are subordinated to spiritual things.

Naturally, the question arises as to how the pope, who rules souls, exercises his control of kings, who rule bodies. Or, more precisely, what are the juridical relationships between pope and king? To begin, the firm foundation of the relationship lies in the fact that the pope sets up the royal authority in the first place, and sets it up in order that it may obediently do the work that the Church assigns to it.[35] And, this being the case, the pope is competent to judge whether that work is done well or ill.[36] When he judges that it has been ill done, he may disestablish the regal power and perform its work himself, or he may set up a new king or dynasty. And if the condemned objects and resists, the pope, as a last resort, may excommunicate him and authorize the faithful to strip him of his goods. Within the scope of this ultimate power which rests on reduction of kingship to a papal agency for certain unpleasant but necessary tasks, the pope controls the ordinary actions of the king in a variety of ways that

[32] Cf. Gilson, *History*, p. 418.
[33] *D.E.P.* i. 4[5]. 15.
[34] *D.E.P.* i. 2[3]. 10.
[35] *D.E.P.* ii. 5.
[36] *D.E.P.* i. 3[4].

ensure papal supremacy in fact. The pope may frame, veto, and interpret civil laws. He may, whenever he chooses, exercise appellate or primary jurisdiction in civil cases. And, finally, he may direct the specific actions of the king, who is required to act at the nod ("*ad nutum*") of the pope.[37]

If all that is true, if the political authorities are no more than mere agents of ecclesiastical overlords, then why speak of two powers or swords at all? Does it not seem that the temporal power is no more than a mere department of ecclesiastical power? As a matter of fact, Giles goes so far as to say that the material sword belongs to the Church more than to any earthly power. And, indeed, there is no power in the material sword that is not also in the spiritual sword. The difference, however, lies in this: although the spiritual sword has every power that the material sword has, nevertheless the material sword has one power *in a way* that the spiritual power does not have it. Both swords can "exercise the judgment of blood," but only the material sword can exercise it "immediately." The spiritual sword can also impose the death penalty, but the immediate sentence and execution should proceed from the earthly power and its material sword.[38] Indeed, even when "Caesar" has given to a particular Church lands over which it is not only to have the right of use, but also full power and dominion to punish crimes even by judgment of blood, nevertheless the judgment must be carried out by a "lay person."[39] This is the last step before "*unum est solum*," and Giles stops here. This is all that remains of the Gelasian "*duo sunt*." His reason for retaining this shred of dualism will reveal the root of his doctrine. But it is necessary briefly to postpone an examination of it in order to bring out other limitations on the pope's absolute power according to Giles. It will then be possible to investigate the limitations together.

[37] Cf. *supra,* p. 35, n. 1.
[38] *D.E.P.* ii. 14. 132–134; cf. also: i. 2[3]. 10; i. 6[7]. 26; i. 7[8]. 29.
[39] *D.E.P.* iii. 11. 205.

Although according to Giles the pope can rule the whole world in all its details if he chooses to do so, he forebears. Like God, in whose image the pope's office is created, he usually permits the affairs of the world to take their course without positive intervention. For just as God does not often miraculously interrupt the ordinary operation of specific causes of which he is the universal cause, so too the pope should ordinarily refuse to intervene in temporal concerns. This is the most excellent and serene, because most God-like, way of ruling. Thus, no one has a strict right to appeal from a civil judge to the pope, although the pope may, if he chooses, entertain such appeals.[40] Giles recognized that there was a danger in this position. Under Germanic notions of law in the Middle Ages, secular princes might in the course of time acquire prescriptive rights to powers which the pope had long left unused or perhaps even refused to exercise on a number of occasions. Therefore, two further principles are laid down: first, whereas prescription may add permanently to ecclesiastical jurisdiction even in temporals, prescription never permanently adds to the jurisdiction of a temporal lord to the prejudice of ecclesiastical jurisdiction; second, no act of the pope can prejudice the ecclesiastical power, although secular lords can prejudice the power of their successors.[41]

But, although God and the pope intervene only on rare occasions in the normal course of events because of the excellence of their universal governance, the pope has an additional reason for usually leaving secular affairs alone. Unlike God, clerics do not have an unlimited span of attention. They cannot pay attention to everything at once. And if they are to have leisure to attend to divine things, they must not devote too much time to secular affairs. Therefore, they are content to leave to laymen the day-to-day solicitude for earthly goods that is condemned in the sixth chapter of Matthew.[42] Nevertheless, the pope retains

[40] D.E.P. ii. 13; iii. 2–3.   [41] D.E.P. iii. 7. 182–185.
[42] D.E.P. ii. 1. 38; ii. 13. 113.

the chief overlordship and the power to intervene at any time when he judges it advisable for a variety of reasons, e.g., the temporalities involved belong to the Church, or because there is something pertaining to the Church connected to the temporalities, or whenever a question of sin is involved, or when a threat to peace is raised, or where an oath has been broken, or in the absence or negligence of the appropriate secular lord, or even if the pope sees that a given secular lord will tolerate the exercise of papal jurisdiction in a sphere in which the pope for some reason is interested.[43] This "toleration" leads to a further reflection: plainly there are some secular lords who deny the full extent of the pope's power, and infidels deny it altogether. This is the last important limitation on the pope's power.

De jure, there is no limit to the scope of papal jurisdiction, for his power is beyond weight and measure.[44] However, *de facto* the whole world does not acknowledge the papal plenitude of power, for all do not obey the gospel. Some have never entered the Church by baptism, and thus remain in the illegitimacy of original sin. Others, although they have been baptized, have fallen from their baptismal purity by actual sin. But there is no just dominion whatever except under and through the Church. And both infidels and sinning Christians are, in different ways, separated from the Church. Thus, no infidel and no Christian in sin has any just dominion whatever, public or private.[45] That the pope does not in fact move to deprive every infidel and every sinner of all his possessions is due to two causes, one of which Giles specifies and the other of which he leaves unspoken but implied. First, the pope is benign like God, and wishes to give all a chance to repent. And therefore, infidels and sinners hold whatever is theirs through the "indulgence and permission," at least tacit, of the pope. Second, and more important though unspoken, the means are not always at the disposal of the pope

[43] *D.E.P.* iii. 4–6.   [44] *D.E.P.* iii. 12.
[45] *D.E.P.* ii. 7–11; iii. 2.; iii. 11. 200–202.

whereby he can carry out such a penalty. The way in which the pope executes such a sentence is to grant license to faithful believers to seize the property of the one who is to be dispossessed.[46] But in the case where the infidels or excommunicates constitute a compact and militarily organized body, it may frequently happen that the greed of the faithful believers is not quite up to meeting the risks of an attempted seizure. And within Christendom itself, utter chaos would break out if the pope seriously attempted to deprive every obdurate sinner of all that was his by setting his neighbors on him. Indeed, it is not clear in advance whether the obdurate sinners or the saintly and penitent would win out in such a melee. In short, Giles seems to be content that the pope merely brandish the threat, but limit its execution to severe and obvious cases.

In summary, the limitations on papal power are seen to be five. First, *de facto* he may not have the means ready at hand to carry out a *de jure* authority. Second, out of a God-like benignity he may withhold execution of judgment in order to give the sinner a chance to repent. But neither of these limitations is a consequence of a right in someone else that the pope is obliged to respect. Whenever the pope has the means, he may act if he chooses to. The third limitation is a genuine one, but not as extensive as might at first sight appear. The pope is compelled to delegate authority to perform specific functions to political agents simply because he can't attend to everything. However, this is a personal limitation only, flowing from human limitedness. It is not a limitation on his office, since what is done by an agent is more properly attributed to the principal. Furthermore, no specific person or subject matter is thereby permanently or necessarily outside the pope's immediate jurisdiction and attention. Since a question of sin may be attached to any civil dispute, the pope (and thus subordinate ecclesiastical judges) may exer-

[46] *D.E.P.* ii. 12. 103–106.

cise immediate and executive jurisdiction over all temporalities whatever.[47]

But even this third limitation on the pope's power due to his inability personally to attend to everything is not so much a defect as it is a cause of the pope's more glorious reign. For the fourth limitation on the pope's power is that he ought to imitate the divine governance of the universe which proceeds by leaving to secondary causes a regular sphere of operation without frequent divine intervention. And in this case, necessity compels the pope at least to begin an imitation of the divine model. Of course, the pope alone, among men, judges when intervention is desirable.

Only the fifth limitation restricts the pope in a way that excludes certain actions from the scope of his power, because they appear by their very nature to be incompatible with his office. The first limitation is accidental, circumstantial. The second flows from the pope's free gift. The third and fourth impose only a general limitation that can never provide grounds for anyone claiming a right to resist any specific intervention.[48] But the fifth limitation, with which the discussion of limitations was begun, prohibits the pope and all clerics from executing the judgment of blood. Even when they exercise immediate and executive jurisdiction over ecclesiastical domains that have no secular lord, clerics must find a layman to draw blood in punishment. And, of course, the question is: why?

It would be unfitting, Giles says, for the church (i.e., the priests[49]) to draw blood herself in punishment.[50] But in only

[47] D.E.P. iii. 5. 173–174.

[48] It is true that Giles permits the pope to "destroy" the earthly power and "institute another one and transfer it" only "because of [its] fault or, at least, for cause." But it should be pointed out that, first, for the pope to do so for no cause would be for him to act absurdly and, second, the pope alone, among men, decides whether a cause exists or not. Cf. D.E.P. iii. 4. 163.

[49] D.E.P. iii. 2. 153.

[50] "*Quia quedam indecencia esset, quod spiritualiter presidens per se judicium sanguinis exerceret.*" D.E.P. i. 2[3]. 11.

one place, and there only briefly, does Giles indicate why it would not be fitting to do so:

> But someone will say that these two swords should always be conjoined in one person for, since one sword is directed to the soul and the other to the body and because one human person is always made of a soul and body, it seems that both powers ought always to be left in one man. To this we can answer that a soul intent on spiritual and eternal things does not seem to be in the world. In this connection Augustine says in book IX of the *De Trinitate* that, in the measure that we mentally seize something eternal as much as we can, we are not in this world, and the spirits of all the just even now living in the flesh, insofar as they taste divine things, are not in this world. Therefore, the priests of the new law, having a more perfect status than the priests of the old law, and furthermore almost wholly set apart and given to divine things and thus not existing in this world, ought not to retain unto themselves the judgement of blood but ought to commit it to a mundane and secular power.[51]

At first sight, this does not appear to be an even remotely adequate articulation of the grounds for Giles' repeated prohibitions against clerics punishing under the *jus sanguinis*. And it is not. But it does give a decisive key to the roots of Giles' problem. Put most bluntly: Christ introduced a possibility of escaping further out of this world and further into a divine world than had ever been possible before, but with one major difficulty, namely the full completion of the escape is postponed till death, which one is prohibited from immediately procuring for oneself. In the meantime, while the escapers may not "seem to be in the world" and while they are "almost wholly [*quasi totaliter*] . . . given to divine things and thus not existing in this world," nevertheless this world has not ceased to exist, and those in flight from it remain physically in it. And not only do they remain physically in it, but they are responsible for all those who are in it.[52] And not only are they responsible for those who are in it, but the mass of men who are in it are not in flight from it, but live according to its ways and its judgments, and not according to the ways and judgments of the City of God. For them, death and not sin is the "last of all terrible things."[53] Violence, the threat of death, and death itself, the *jus sanguinis,* must be imposed on them in order to keep them from chaos, which threatens to appear everywhere in this world, which underlies all the regimes of this world, and against which only the spiritual man can defend. We are in the midst of a great storm and flood in which all order threatens to disappear.[54] "All do not obey the gospel."[55] And all regimes not instituted by priests have in fact been based on invasions or usurpations, and thus were nothing other than the *magna latrocinia* of St. Augustine.[56] Nor is it simply the infidels who do not obey the gospel. It is not only the infidels who put their trust too greatly in earthly things. Lay Christians are almost as bad. They are not adequately moved by the love of divine things and the hope of escaping this world into the promised land of heaven. They need to be overawed by the splendor, wealth, and power of the priests. Otherwise, they will scorn the Church, will hold it to be of small weight and moment. Therefore, the priests need temporal goods and temporal power if everything is not to be lost in the inundating waters of chaos.[57] Standing in the midst of ever-threatening chaos, the priests and the priests alone make contact with the divine source of order, peace, and justice. Even so, the mass of men, even Christian men, remain laymen, do not freely follow the way out of the world taken by the priests. In order to save them, the priests find it necessary to take command of the forces of chaos itself, to show the lay masses not the Christ, the Son of the living God, but that the splendor, wealth, and power of this world is in the hands of the priests. One may wonder what sort of a salvation this is. Indeed, it is clearly but a temporal and

[53] *D.E.P.* i. 2[3]. 10.   [54] *D.E.P.* ii. 1. 36.
[55] *D.E.P.* iii. 4. 167.   [56] *D.E.P.* i. 4[5]. 15; ii. 5. 54.
[57] *D.E.P.* ii. 1. 36; ii. 2. 43; ii. 3. 48.

negative salvation. It prevents the mass of men from completing, externally, the denial of Christ that they have already begun in their hearts. From Giles' point of view, this has a double value.

First, since the mass of laymen are prevented from lapsing into an habitual and organized order of blasphemy, sacrilege, and other sins, they are thus kept in an external order that appears to conform in essentials to the demands of the gospel. To be sure, the gospel does not inspire that conformity. Still, when individuals make enough religious progress so that they may fittingly receive the "spiritual food" from the priests (or even become clerics themselves), they will not find themselves in a set of external circumstances where conformity with the demands of the gospel is well nigh impossible. Rather than finding themselves in the midst of a well organized *magnum latrocinium,* they will find themselves in a political order that is at least minimally arranged with a view to the external consequences of the gospel.

Second, and of greater importance in the course of the argument, spiritual men who are intent on eternal things find it impossible to devote themselves wholly to such pursuits. It is necessary to hold in check the whole host of natural forces that express themselves in concerns for the things of time, concerns that came to a point in political organizations. By means of a balanced brandishing of the terrors of death to the soul, death to the body and absolute expropriation, the priests of the New Testament manage to reduce the human order to a merely instrumental infrastructure to their contemplative activity directed to an absolutely other-worldly salvation. The clerical intervention does not pretend to be directed at perfecting the political order. It does not pretend that it is aimed at producing the city of justice. It does not even pretend that it is aimed at getting as close to a city of justice as is possible under any given set of circumstances. It does not claim that it is the institutional manifestation of the divine grace penetrating the order of nature and perfecting it from within, all the while refraining from violating any element of its autonomy, precisely because the order of nature is good in itself, worthy of perfection for its own sake, a luminous manifestation of the overflowing goodness of God the creator.

On the contrary, Giles does not claim a special concern by the priests for the political order. He does not claim that priests (and especially the pope) have a right to intervene in political affairs because they are graced with greater political prudence than statesmen. They intervene, rather, to judge and punish sin, and this is their license to a universal intervention.[58] Their object is a spiritual good, either directly, by correcting the sinner and warning potential sinners, or indirectly, by managing some affair that is of interest to the Church in some way.[59] Indeed, and this is most striking, he does not rest the papal plenitude of power on any claim of personal superiority on the part of the pope.[60] On the contrary, by distinguishing in the opening chapter of the book between the spiritual man according to personal virtue and the spiritual man according to rank, Giles makes quite clear that he does not claim that the pope is personally a spiritual man. It is enough that his official position be at the jurisdictional apex of the ecclesiastical hierarchy for him to be St. Paul's spiritual man who judges all and is judged by none. It is, of course, fitting that the pope also be spiritual personally, but it is not necessary.[61] In short, the pope's interventions in political affairs turn out to be intrusions of the worst sort by one who, by virtue of his office, has no deep concern for working

[58] *D.E.P.* iii. 5. 171–172.

[59] *D.E.P.* i. 6[7]. 26; i. 7[8]. 29; ii. 2. 43; ii. 3. 48; ii. 4. 48–49; iii. 5.

[60] This is particularly interesting since in a political work of his he argues for absolute monarchy on the ground that the best man is superior to the best laws. *De Regimine Principum* iii. 2. 29. But even here, the superiority lies simply in that the laws cannot determine all particulars.

[61] *D.E.P.* i. 1[2]; ii. 12. 101–103; and cf. 1 Cor 2:15.

out a genuine human order in this world and who may not be particularly saintly either. The decisive question, therefore, is this: why is Giles prepared to derive all legitimate rulership from a pope who may be a political fool and a spiritual knave? He gives a number of answers.

To begin with, he makes a brief argument about the circumstances of the papal office itself. Personal spirituality does not provide an adequate viewpoint from which to judge matters of government. Giles seems to understand the transformation that frequently overcomes men who find themselves raised to a position of great importance and decision. Their view of things is altered by their new position. He writes:

> If we speak about perfection and spirituality according to status, which consists in jurisdiction and fullness of power, then he who is in a holier and higher rank will judge many and he will not be able to be judged by his inferiors; for as the Apostle says in 1 Corinthians 4 [:4]: "But he who judges me is lord."[62] And so he who is by status supreme over all and most holy over all is the spiritual man who by his power and jurisdiction judges all, for he is lord of all and is judged by none for no mortal man lords it over him. Now we see obviously that he who would judge others ought to be raised above others; but he who is pushed down and in a pit finds that just as nothing is offered to his eyes so he can judge about nothing. But he who is raised on high, whose sight encounters no obstacle, he can judge about others. . . . He who is perfect and holy and spiritual according to rank and most powerful in the way of prelatial status, he is raised up in jurisdiction and plenitude of power: he judges all, that is he lords it over all and can be judged by none, that is none can lord it over him. But such is the supreme pontiff whose status is most holy and most spiritual. Therefore all ought to call him most holy father and all ought to kiss his blessed feet.[63]

Obviously, the altitude has effects not only on him who is raised up, but also on those who now find themselves at foot

---

[62] The exegetical style is remarked *supra,* pp. 31–35.
[63] *D.E.P.* i. 1[2]. 8.

level.[64] In fact, the motion appears to be two-way: not only is the pope raised up, but the rest seem to be pushed down and set in a pit.[65] However, plainly the whole altitudinal simile is hardly enough to establish the *de jure* universal and absolute monarchy of the pope. More decisive is the argument from divine grant.

"For Christ did not say to Peter: 'If thou shalt bind this or that on earth it shall also be bound in heaven,' but he extended [the power] universally: '*Whatsoever* thou shalt bind on earth.' "[66] The argument is familiar. It is extraordinarily simplistic: Christ had all power in heaven and earth, and he committed it to his universal vicar, Peter and his successors.[67] It requires no serious attempt to understand the mission of Christ and of Peter and the other apostles and their successors. It requires no serious attention to the gospel. It requires only the literal reading of a handful of texts without contexts. "Whatsoever" means "whatsoever" and nothing less, and that's the end of it.

But Giles develops another line of argument that reveals the inner structure of his reaction to the presence of evil. In some way or other, all men seem to experience a certain terror before whatever manifests to them the abyss of nothingness called evil. In Giles, this leads to flight of a peculiar kind, a flight into an illusory ecclesiastical security that, among Christians, seems to be a special temptation for Catholics.

The world of Pope Gelasius was a broken world. Broken by sin. Christ, knowing human weakness, separated the offices of pontiff and emperor in such a way that each might be dependent on the other in some respect. Had he given either one an unlimited independence, the temptation to pride and its terrible

---

[64] Perhaps someone less inclined to a servile reverence than Giles might wonder whether the "blessed feet" might not on occasion be tempted to administer a kick to the kisser, remembering that, personally, they are not especially holy or blessed. And, again, someone else might be struck by the preposterous incongruity of Giles' text with Jn 13:1–17 and Lk 22:24–30.

[65] "*Qui autem est depressus et est in fovea.*"

[66] *D.E.P.* ii. 12. 103; and cf. ii. 5. 58; ii. 8. 78–79; ii. 12. 108.

[67] E.g., *D.E.P.* ii. 4. 50–53; ii. 14. 132–133.

consequences would hardly be resistible. Thus, for Pope Gelasius, while the separation is indeed a consequence of sin, it is so
in the way that a medicine is a consequence of sickness, a medicine whereby the world is to be healed. Before Christ, there were
men who were kings and priests at once, either true types or
Satanic imitations of the perfect king and priest, Christ himself.
Now, however, the elaboration of the salvation wrought by
Christ, the king-priest, requires the separation of the two.[68] But
the world of Giles of Rome needs other medicine.

For Giles, not only is the world of man broken by sin, but it
threatens to fly apart, to succumb to a radical disorder, to disappear in an infinite fragmentation. Against that threat, Giles
summons up a desperately simplified view of the whole order of
creation. The unity and order of the universe springs from and is
in absolute dependence on God. Nevertheless, the divinely established law whereby all beings stand in that dependence is
that the lowest is subject to the highest throughout the intermediate.[69] This law Giles interprets to mean that the temporal
sword must be subject to God by being subject to the spiritual
sword of the pope; and it must be subject in such wise that it
has no motion or action of its own that has not been given it in
some way by the spiritual sword, which may likewise take it
away. And it must be subject in such wise that it acts for the sake
of the spiritual sword, for in no other way can temporal things
be considered good except insofar as they serve spiritual beatitude.[70]

Giles cites Averroës, on *Metaphysics* II.2, to the effect that the
end and the good are the same and that he who removes the end
removes the good. Since our end consists in spiritual goods
"which can exist within the soul and can satisfy the soul," therefore "it is fitting that temporals [which are ontically inferior to

[68] See *supra*, p. 29, n. 8, and especially the text of Gelasius I, *Tractatus*
iv. 11.
[69] *D.E.P.* i. 3[4]. 12   [70] *D.E.P.* ii. 5.

the soul] be not good *in any way whatsoever* except in the measure that they are ordained to spirituals."[71] The obvious consequence of such a position is that the whole universe of material things, of the things of time, are only instrumentally valuable. Were Giles to leave it at that, he could hardly retain any reputation for theological or philosophical literacy by the usual standards of his time. But, curiously, there is no reference to the obvious locus of theological objections, the first chapter of Genesis.[72] But he does find it necessary to admit that temporal goods may be good *"in se,"* even if they are not ordained to spirituals and not subject to them.[73] However, he steadfastly refuses to admit the relevance of that fact and to follow up its consequences.

But if the observation is once made that temporals are good in themselves, a whole new problematic is introduced. Not only does it appear that material goods are not solely related to the last end of all things only through man, but it is plain that the material objects of the world of man do not receive their being or their natural powers from man. Neither does man find himself in a position to annihilate them, although he may use them and transform them in an astounding variety of ways. But all this is so despite the fact that man, in virtue of the sort of soul he has, stands next above them in the ontological hierarchy of the cosmos. In short, the material things of the world have ontic status independently of man's soul, even though an instrumental value can be conferred on them by it. But, if this is the case, then the problem of ontic hierarchy appears to be far more complex and difficult of solution than Giles suggests, because it is necessary to discover, to take into account, and to respect the order of things even if they are also given a share in another order, in this case eternal beatitude.

[71] *D.E.P.* ii. 4. 49, emphasis added.
[72] Especially verses 4, 10, 12, 18, 21, 25.
[73] *D.E.P.* ii. 4. 49.

However, Giles systematically refuses to admit the relevance of the value of temporals *"in se"* to man's final end. That end is an end of the soul, and can exist within the soul. Therefore, material things, including the body, appear practically to be mere means the use of which is temporarily and inexplicably imposed on the human soul. It is enough, here, to note but two major implications of this view. Man appears to have hardly more than an accidental unity, so that it seems more appropriate to speak of *animus faber* than *homo faber*. Further, the Christian belief in the resurrection of the body seems to be unrelated to anything other than the arbitrary decree of the divine will. Thus, when the independent ontic status of material things is rendered irrelevant for human action, the moral issues involved in the soul's relationship with material things, including the body, are reduced to questions as to which modes of control permit minimal expenditures of energy and attention to the sphere controlled. Formulated otherwise, the inner dynamism of the spiritual life that flows from such a perception is that of an escapist asceticism arbitrarily forbidden to attain its logical completion in suicide. But it is precisely such a simplistic view of an ontically impoverished body-soul relationship, as well as of the cosmic order and the sun-moon relationship, that Giles repeatedly employs as analogues of the appropriate relationship between the pope and secular rulers.[74]

But observation of the metaphysical and practical difficulties entailed by such a simplistic view of the relationships of matter and spirit requires one to ask the theological question whether the nature of salvation is such as Giles suggests. Reflection on the problem led others to aver that kings and princes are under the Church spiritually and not temporally, that the relationship

[74] Body-soul analogy: *D.E.P.* i. 6[7], 23–27; ii. 4. 50–52; ii. 5. 57–58; ii. 10. 93; ii. 13. 115; iii. 5. 172. Universal order analogy: i. 3[4]. 12–13; i. 4[5]. 16–17; ii. 4. 52–53; ii. 10. 89–90; ii. 14. 136; iii. 1. 144; iii. 2. 154–155. Sun-moon analogy: iii. 10. 196–199.

is far more subtle than mere derivation of one from the other and its consequent all around subjection to the other. Giles knows of the objections. But he steadfastly refuses to regard them seriously. Without attempting an answer, he simply replies, "Those who say such things don't get the force of my argument. For if kings and princes were only spiritually under the Church, then sword would not be under sword, temporals would not be under spirituals, there would be no order among the powers, the lowest would not be reduced to the highest through the intermediate."[75] Beyond this Giles will not go. The price of peace for him is the suppression of the inwardness, mystery, and variety of creation and of the respect for its integrity shown by God the Savior. In its place is the order of a machine shop.[76] And then, for the terrible responsibility in the face of good and evil, one finds a universal ecclesiastical bureaucracy within which salvation is achieved by virtue of obedience alone to a pope whose power is beyond weight and measure and who is judged by none save only God.

Well, others before and after him have also had a sense for the diluvial character of our existence, have seen our condition as that of castaways in a tempest, and have noted—even described—the closing circle of delta-shaped fins and joined the terrified cry of their companions, drawn under amid a red froth in a furious sea. But, taken alone, that is a description of despair of terrestrial salvation, or celestial salvation, or both. In such a context, the mark of a Christian is that he hopes. And that is the case with Giles. But his hope is minimal indeed.

The substance of Giles' response to the flood of evil is a terrified struggle to escape. Escape, first of all, from the reality of this world in the sense of the world of things, of bodies, and thus of flux, violence, tempests, and of fragmentary particu-

---

[75] *D.E.P.* i. 4[5]. 13.
[76] Indeed, he speaks of *"universalis mundi machina"* (*D.E.P.* i. 5[6]. 16.), though undoubtedly without implying the modern notion of machine.

53

larity.[77] Rather than listening to the murmuring cry for order and a participation in man's salvation that issues from that very world,[78] Giles' concern is only for himself. That is to say, he would escape into a puritanical world of monastic contemplation, into the world of the eternal. And, insofar as that is not altogether possible, insofar as this world remains and he remains in it, then there is an escape from the hungry whirlpools of political responsibility by substituting obedience for justice at the apex of political virtues. And, ultimately, the clerics intervene only so much as is necessary to give the clerics leisure for divine pursuits.[79]

In the philosophic tradition, the philosopher returned to the cave and saved his fellow men as far as he could. In the theological tradition represented by St. Thomas Aquinas, the bishop is greater than the monk because he is not only contemplative, but by virtue of his contemplation he draws from God that which he gives to men.[80] For Giles, the pope is a monk who heads a great and terrible power structure only insofar as that is necessary to escape the very milieu of power structures.

It is, of course, not at all unusual for men to be terrified by

[77] Cf. Peter E. Nash, "Giles of Rome, Auditor and Critic of St. Thomas," *The Modern Schoolman*, 28 (1950–1951), pp. 1–20. Concerning Giles' commentary on the *Sentences* of Peter Lombard, Nash wrote, "Giles' master idea is the primacy of unity, simplicity, and immutability and . . . in perfect consistency with this master idea Giles makes *esse actuale* the determinant of individuality as an accidental act. Quite logically he allows only an aggregate unity to the created existent, for whom existence is the possession by a nature of what it needs to be an individual" (p. 19). Again: his position "allows in the created supposit no unity other than that of a sum" (p. 20).

[78] Anyone who has wondered, for example, at the peculiar beauties of diverse gardens, Persian, monastic, Renaissance, formal, etc., will understand how the world of things is drawn into a vortex of the human spirit and shares its glories and its shames.

[79] Cf. *supra*, pp. 40 and 43–45. Thus, Giles wrote (*D.EP.* ii. 13. 113.): "It was good to institute a second power (i.e., political authorities) that especially presided over bodily matters so that the spiritual power would be able more freely to be at leisure for spiritual things."

[80] St. Thomas Aquinas, "*de perfectione vitae spiritualis*," cap. 18, *Opuscula Theologica*, vol. II, p. 137 (Turin, Rome: 1954).

54

some evil. Nor is it altogether unusual for a whole life to be marked by fear and flight. And one of the peculiar modes in which that fear and flight express themselves is an attempt at a magical suppression of some aspect of reality which induced the fear. Under diverse circumstances, that magic takes different forms. For Catholics, there is a temptation to use the ecclesiastical hierarchy in such a way. It appears to be a ready made instrument of tremendous efficacy, because divinely guaranteed, with which evil can be suppressed. But it is characteristic of such suppression that it is initiated and directed by human fear and will and it is usually directed at others. It is also characteristic of *this* expression of the cowardice of the magician that it has gross political consequences over a wide area inasmuch as the great juridical organization of the Church constitutes the magic wand.

St. Augustine, who didn't mind having the Emperor coerce the Donatists into returning to Catholicism, at least argued that the ex-Donatists were now enthusiastic Catholics, force being needed only to start them on their path.[81] But Giles, an Augustinian who cites Augustine more than he does any other Christian writer except the four Evangelists, doesn't even argue that his coerced Catholics are enthusiastic about the coercion. He is content merely to mass in the hands of the Church enough this-worldly pomp, force, and magnificence to terrify the lay masses from blaspheming, from demanding that Christ come down from the cross, and from laughing that he saved others, himself he cannot save. Well, of course, the question is: inasmuch as Christ did not get down from the cross and strike terror into the hearts of the blasphemers with twelve legions of angels, why must Giles do so? Unlike St. Augustine, Giles' pope is even ready to kill the blasphemers—although the pope has to find a lay hangman to do the dirty work for him. It seems that Giles needs to do what Christ did not do, because

[81] *Epistolae* xciii.

his faith is so weak that he is terribly afraid. Silencing the blasphemers by death if necessary is a symbol of his own desperate attempt to silence his own doubts. He, too, is unable to accept the fact of Calvary, and he, too, is unable to bear the mighty cry of Christ whereby the heavens were shaken: "My God, my God, why hast thou forsaken me?" And he knows that if his secret fears are true, then existence is meaningless—a great, echoing, obscene, and mocking joke—then the abyss of evil will have swallowed him. His response, rather than to pick up his own cross and head for Calvary, is to find a sword and attempt to murder the mockery of the Judas-kiss, and it seems that in some recess of his soul he knows that he is not permitted to do that. So he leaves out the words of Christ's rebuke to Peter for having drawn a sword. But there is no other ground to stand on, for nowhere is it said: Blessed are the executioners for theirs is the kingdom of heaven. Therefore, he insists that the deed be done by a layman who may work out his salvation as best he can.

But whatever the spiritual roots of Giles' argument, the political consequence of such a position is that public order is regularly disturbed by papal attempts to employ the instruments of this world for the solution of spiritual problems—the consequence is a tendency for the political structure itself to break down from its being repeatedly put to uses for which it is not fitted, uses, furthermore, that tend to produce violent excitement in the body politic. Worse still, the papal intervention is occasional. It cannot be predicted in advance. The pope is not regularly concerned in the maintenance of the health of the political structure, but with spiritual concerns for which he periodically employs the political structure as a means, and the pope may not be even minimally prudent in political matters. Indeed, Giles nowhere even raises the question about the political prudence of the pope precisely because he is not concerned with the *political* consequences of papal action except as manifestations of a supra-political concern with the problem of evil.

Needless to say, sooner or later such a doctrine—and the historical reality of Italian politics in Giles' time seems to have come close to it—such a doctrine leads to a reactionary counter-proposal. Sooner or later, someone will assert that peace, justice, and order are genuine goods, and that they are not to be sacrificed, as if of no value, to ill-considered religious concerns that manifest themselves in patently disastrous political interference by the pope and his court.

Whatever the ultimate theological tests whereby this doctrine is to be judged, its political condemnation is its notorious ineffectiveness. That is enough for politics which is concerned with *praxis*. Whatever one may think of turning the mystical body of Christ into a sword, the statement cannot help pointing out that the ecclesiastical swordsman is not truly concerned to do his task well. He who started out attempting to escape evil ends by accepting a victory of appearances if he can get it. If virtue cannot be had, respectability, the appearances of virtue and order, will do. And, at last, it is discovered that Peter's swordsmanship only cuts off ears. That is painful, to be sure, but there are men who will give a life as well as an ear for what they want. Then will Giles' Peter flee. Never truly concerned with politics, he will find his subjects, in the midst of the corruption of their common life, not very concerned to defend his rule.[82] If, when all this is done, he is allowed to remain a prisoner in the Vatican rather than being driven again into the catacombs, then perhaps there is cause for joy and thanksgiving as well as for wonderment. There are some, as we shall see, who would have wrought a harder fate.

[82] How many will still recognize Christ's mission behind that sword is another question.

Marsilius of Padua

The Revenge of Nature

THE practical absurdity of the extreme papalist position could not help but summon up a powerful reaction. The forces of nature that are inherent in every human encounter and that had been denied in the papalist sterilization of politics inescapably produced a resistance to papal action in political affairs and therewith a resistance to all clerical action in politics. To be sure, a tension between clerical and lay authority, varying in intensity and nature, was a part of the political reality of Europe from the conversion of Constantine.[1] But that tension

---

[1] It is obvious that the conversion of the Roman emperor threatened to make the Church a mere department of the imperial administration and thus make the clergy, from the deacon to the pope and bishops, merely civil servants under imperial headship. This is evident in the writings leading up to the *"duo sunt"* of Pope Gelasius (see *HMPT*, vol. 1, pp. 175–193). However, the success of Gelasianism rested in some measure on the weakness of the imperial power in the West. With the coronation of Charlemagne, the imperial problem began a renewed career, later complicated by the rise of national sovereigns. Cf. e.g., *HMPT*, vol. 1, pp. 253–292; vol. 2, pp. 76–91; 160–249; vol. 4: vol. 5, pp. 152–440; H.-X. Arquilliere, *L'Augustinisme Politique*, vol. 2: *L'Église et l'État au Moyen Age* (Paris: 1934); *idem, Saint Grégoire VII*, vol. 4: *ibidem.* Ernest H. Kantorowicz, *Laudes Regiae* (Berkeley and Los Angeles: 1946); Fritz Kern, *Kingship and Law in the Middle Ages*, trans. S.B. Chrimes (Oxford: 1948); J. Rivière, *Le Problème de l'Église et de l'État au temps de Philippe le Bel* (Paris: 1926); Richard Scholz, *Die Publizistik zur Zeit Philipps des Schönen und Bonifaz' VIII,* hft. 6/8, *Kirchenrechtliche Abhandlungen* (Stuttgart: 1903); Gerd Tellenbach, *Church, State and Christian Society at the time of the Investiture Controversy* (Oxford: 1940); *idem,* "Römischer und christlicher Reichsgedanke in der Liturgie des frühen Mittelalters," *Sitzungsberichte der Heidelberger Akad. der Wiss.,* phil.-hist. Klasse, Abh. 1, 1934–35.

was increased to an unendurable extreme by the confrontation of Pope Boniface VIII and King Philip the Fair of France.

The Church never definitely proclaimed as her own an elaborated doctrine of extreme papalism such as that of Giles of Rome, or of James of Viterbo, or of Henry of Cremona. And, indeed, pope and king disagreed about the meaning and import of the pope's words.[2] Nevertheless, popes tended to speak and act in a way that, at the very least, suggested the orthodoxy of such a position. But, there was another element as well. There can be no doubt that, in addition to the relatively narrow and negative basis of Giles' position, a line of great medieval popes made tremendous efforts to institute a very Christendom, a city of God on earth, efforts that were obviously doomed with the death of Boniface VIII. Although it is not my intention nor is this the place to attempt an historical study of those efforts, it is necessary to note here that they were in many ways moved by a vision of what St. Robert Bellarmine was to call a "*respublica Christiana.*" There can be no doubt of the normative lure definitively to order the world of human thought and action in terms of the truth about God and man that, with the advent of Christ, had flooded into the dim world of history and illuminated recesses of the soul that had hitherto been but poorly known.

In any case, the encounter between Boniface and Philip included a series of events that manifested for practical purposes the immense gulf between the papal vision of a *respublica Christiana* and the real condition of men. The Pope's attempt to exercise lordship over the King of France was unable to achieve even the temporary surface success of the days when a pope could bring the Holy Roman Emperor to Canossa as a penitent and leave him standing outside in the snow. In this case, the royal reply was less humble. Philip the Fair denied all of the Pope's pretensions to overlordship and proceeded to send

[2] Carlyle, *HMPT,* vol. 5, pp. 374–393.

his agents to Italy to arrest the Pope and threaten him with death unless he abdicate. Boniface was arrested at Anagni in August 1303. Though he steadfastly refused to step down in the face of every threat and indignity, and although he was freed shortly thereafter by a popular rising, the shattering of his dream world by the crude response of the Catholic King of France broke his health as well. He was dead by October of the same year. By 1305, the King of France had procured the election of a French pope, Clement V, and the papacy removed its residence to Avignon to begin the "Babylonian captivity."

The violence and depth of the King's reaction seems to have been the occasion for that perception of the abyss of chaos that moved Giles of Rome to write a desperate defense of absolute papal power. But the very violence and depth of the royal reaction, although it objectively shattered any illusions about the practicability of a papal policy directed toward the definitive institutionalization of a *respublica Christiana,* at the same time made it extremely difficult, if not practically impossible, for the Church to adopt a more moderate view than that expressed by Giles of Rome, or of James of Viterbo, or of Henry of Cremona. The enunciation of a more moderate position, such as that of John of Paris, for example, would have appeared as a capitulation, the withdrawal of all Church influence from the political sphere. In the face of a monarch who was, in practice, asserting the primacy of the political, the Church could not help but assert the primacy of the spiritual. The Church could no more admit the authority of the French King as final in questions relating to the divine than Socrates could admit a like authority in the Athenian *demos* with respect to the transcendent reality to which philosophy had opened his soul. So the papacy found itself unable to resist the tendencies toward the absolutization of politics in the rising national states except in terms of a doctrine that was the ecclesiastical equivalent of an

60

assertion that only philosophers are legitimate rulers. In short, the papacy was condemned either to pursue a practically impossible objective or to abandon all concern for the sphere of politics, a situation which, naturally, resulted in an alternation between the two policies. But whenever the papacy summoned the energy to exercise influence in the political order, the fact that the attempt necessarily appeared to proceed from a claim to a universal political overlordship necessarily produced a political resistance.[3] The consequence for the Church was the dissipation of her energies and of the prestige of the papacy in an impossible task that, paradoxically, tended to secularize the papacy by drawing it into innumerable debasing and fruitless political intrigues and maneuvers in the very pursuit of what it took to be the demands of its spiritual mission.[4] The consequence for politics was either chaos produced by recurrent and bitter conflict of Church and state, or the victory of the kings and thereby an assist to royal absolutism, neither of them desired by the papacy.

The doctrinal polemic in support of the king was, by comparison with papalist writing, relatively moderate.[5] Nevertheless, in Italy where assertions of the unlimited political power of the pope were all-pervasive practical reality, a more extreme counter-doctrine was developed. In England and France, there were political organs centered on the kings capable of mounting

[3] A resistance that varied, naturally, according to circumstances.

[4] It may be objected here that such an interpretation of the action of the Church and especially of the papacy appears to deny the special care of Providence for the Church and especially the pope (Mt 16:13–20; 28:19–20). However, such an objection seems to suppose that the ways of the Lord are really quite searchable after all. For myself, while I have no doubt of Christ's guarantees to the Church and the pope, neither have I any doubt about the ability of the Divine Providence to procure the divine glory and the good of the Church in spite of, and indeed out of, the foolishness of men, including of the pope. To suppose anything less seems to me to trifle with the immensity of the mystery of Providence.

[5] See Carlyle, *HMPT,* vol. 5, pp. 420–440.

61

successful resistance to papal intervention in their affairs. In Italy, there was chaos and the pope at the center of it. There was still a half-millennium till Italian unification, but the very depth and pressure of papal involvement in Italian politics suggested more extreme solutions than had been thought necessary elsewhere. Every perception of the nature and exigencies of human civic communion demanded the rejection of a doctrine that asserted the omnicompetence to intervene in politics by one whose intervention was casual, unpredictable, uninterested in the natural ends of politics, and who had no special claim to political prudence or justice. Indeed, papal politics had been so long accompanied by political disaster in Italy that the six popes beginning with Clement V found it undesirable to take up residence there. Further, the very extravagance of the papalist claims, under circumstances in which they must be regarded altogether seriously, tended to stimulate a radical reaction. Within a decade of Boniface's death, Dante had written the imperialist tract, *De Monarchia*. Less than twenty-five years after Boniface's death, Marsilius of Padua attacked the whole structure of Catholic ecclesiastical polity in a more revolutionary way than Dante ever imagined. Short of the absolute abolition of the Church or its overt reduction in all respects to a department of the civil administration, Marsilius' work, *Defensor Pacis*,[6] is the most extreme and brilliant counter to the papalist position.

[6] I have used the edition by C.W. Previté-Orton (Cambridge: 1928). I have also compared my translations of passages in the text with that by Alan Gewirth in his *Marsilius of Padua*, 2 vols. (New York: 1951), which is referred to hereafter as "Gewirth." The first volume of his study includes a comprehensive bibliography. Cf. also Felice Battaglia, *Marsilio da Padova* (Firenze: 1928), pp. 263–270. For the dispute as to its authorship, cf. Marian J. Tooley, "The Authorship of the *Defensor Pacis*," *Transactions of the Royal Historical Society*, 4th series, vol. IX, (1926); Gewirth, "John of Jandun and the *Defensor Pacis*," *Speculum*, vol. XXIII (1948). 267–272; Richard Scholz, "Marsilius von Padua und die Genesis des modernen Staatsbewusstseins," *Historische Zeitschrift*, vol. 156 (1937), 93–94. The

Despite its considerable length and the range of subjects it treats, *Defensor Pacis* is narrow in intent. This is made quite clear in the opening chapter. It is not a defense of the good simply, of the good itself. It is rather the defense of a single good that is, nevertheless, a precondition of "the greatest human good." A defense of the "tranquillity or peace of civil regimes," and not the whole range of political matters is the subject of the book.[7] It was not even a general defense of the tranquillity or peace of civil regimes that Marsilius had in mind. Aristotle had accomplished that already. Marsilius was concerned solely with a "singular and quite hidden" cause of strife which "neither Aristotle nor any other philosopher of his time or earlier could have seen."[8] That cause he took to be clerical interference in politics, presented in its most concentrated form in the papal claims to a plenitude of power in ecclesiastical and secular affairs.[9] It was this special cause of disorder and civil upheaval that Marsilius wished to destroy in defense of civil peace. This intent structures the whole work. To inordinate ecclesiastical hopes and claims Marsilius opposed civil peace as the necessary prerequisite of "civil happiness, which in this world seems to be the highest good man can desire and the last end of human acts."[10] Against those who had hoped to escape this world for the next and who had wrought chaos and war, Marsilius set out to defend all who hope for something other than war in

biographical data are reviewed in C. Kenneth Brampton, "Marsiglio of Padua: Part I. Life," *The English Historical Review,* vol. XXXVIII (1923), pp. 1–18; "Marsilius of Padua," *Proceedings of the British Academy,* vol. XXI (1935), pp. 137–183; E. Emerton, *The Defensor Pacis of Marsiglio of Padua* (Cambridge: 1920); Georges de Lagarde, *Marsile de Padoue ou le premier théoricien de l'État laique* (Saint-Paul-Trois-Chateaux: 1934); R. Scholz, "Marsilius von Padua und die Genesis des modernen Staatsbewusstseins," *Historische Zeitschrift,* vol. CLVI (1936), pp. 88–103; Leo Strauss, "Marsilius of Padua," in Strauss and Joseph Cropsey, eds., *History of Political Philosophy* (Chicago: 1963), pp. 227–246.
[7] *Def. Pac.* I. i. 1.   [8] *Def. Pac.* I. i. 3, 7.
[9] *Def. Pac.* I. xix.   [10] *Def. Pac.* I. i. 7.

this world.[11] Therefore, not without a certain malice, he quoted Luke 2:14 to the priests.[12]

The external structure of the work is simple. It is divided into three discourses. The first discourse is based on reason, the second on the Christian faith. The third consists of a brief list of the conclusions drawn in the first two. But, given the different axiological bases on which they rest, the first two discourses differ considerably in content, as Gewirth pointed out:

> The first and second discourses are distinguished from one another in two complementary ways. The first is in terms of the difference between a general and a singular causal analysis. Both discourses are concerned with the causes of civil peace and strife. But the first discourse treats of the "usual" and "general" causes, while the second discourse treats of the "unusual" and "singular" or "special" cause, namely, the acts and pretensions of the papacy deriving from its claim to plenitude of power. Thus the first discourse is concerned with the general structure and functioning of any state as such, while the second discourse examines the "singular" threat to that functioning within Christian states which arises from the papacy's claim to universal hegemony.[13]

Furthermore, the treatment of general political subjects in the first discourse is so structured as to stand as an introduction to the second discourse, rather than with a view to a statement of a general political doctrine. And, as will become plain, a number of considerable difficulties in interpreting the Marsilian doctrine in the first discourse may be clarified only by reference to the narrow objective that Marsilius clearly assigns to the whole work. Consequently, I shall focus attention on the doctrine of the second discourse as the center of the Marsilian Church-state doctrine. And, within that context, I shall begin with what is most easily seen: the radical alteration in the structure of the Church that Marsilius advocates. The conse-

---

[11] The influence of the work seems to have varied. C.W. Previté-Orton indicated some of the *loci* of Marsilian influence in "Marsilius of Padua," *Proceedings of the British Academy,* vol. XXI (1935), pp. 163–169.

[12] *Def. Pac.* I. i. 1.   [13] Gewirth, *Marsilius,* vol. II, p. xxi.

quence that emerges from this new structure is to place a juridically absolute control of the exercise of the powers of holy orders in the hands of the political authorities. Stated otherwise, the priesthood is subtly but effectively reincorporated into the state in Aristotelian fashion.

Looking at externals first, Marsilius places the final control of the temporal goods of the Church in the hands of laymen. The ministers of the gospel ought to be in a status of supreme poverty. That means that they ought not to be able to have any legal ownership (*dominium*) of things or their use or usufruct. Of course, the priests have need of daily bread and clothing, and they may legitimately consume and use such things, though no more than is necessary. But even these things they may not claim by suit at law, even though they may rightfully demand them by divine law if those to whom the gospel is preached are able to provide them. Of course, the priests will also use buildings and land in order to perform their functions. They may even be entrusted with the administration of large benefices, the proceeds of which they are to give to the poor. However, legal ownership according to human law will be theirs in none of these cases, not even of the bread he eats. "The ownership of temporalities that have been appointed for the support of ministers of the gospel belongs to the [human] legislator or to the individual or group who were deputed to that task by the legislator, or by the donors, if it were private persons who gave the above-mentioned temporalities and ordained them from amongst their goods for the aforesaid use."[14] And if the income from ecclesiastical benefices exceed the needs of the ministers of the gospel, the political authorities may take the excess for "reasonable purposes," all of the amounts involved to be determined by the same authority.[15]

[14] *Def. Pac.* II. xi–xiv; and cf. I. xv. 2, 4; II. xi. 2–4; xii. 13–16; xiii. 31, 36, 38, 39; xiv. 1, 6–10; xvii. 16–18; xxi. 11–15; III. ii. 23, 38.
[15] *Def. Pac.* II. xvii. 18; III. ii. 27, 28.

65

Second, control of the clergy is lodged in the hands of the political authorities in another way. Selection of candidates for the priesthood, their assignment to particular ministries, and, when necessary, the power to compel them to exercise those ministries pertain to political authority. Not only the number of clergy, but the persons to be ordained is rightly a subject of human legislation and governmental action.[16] Not only is such a procedure demanded by Scripture, but errors in such matters confront the people with "the danger of eternal death and very many civil troubles." But if a people were not in a position to control such affairs either directly by legislation or indirectly by governmental action on their authority, then they would be unable to avoid evils which they are able to discern along with the means to their removal. And the whole people is better able to judge in such matters than priests or a college of them, because "the whole is greater than any of its parts taken separately."[17] Here Marsilius is confronted with a difficulty.

In the event that both legislature and government consist of believers, the exercise of such control is quite in the keeping with the overall Marsilian view of the Church, as will be made clear later. But in the event that Christians are a minority in a civil community of infidels, what then? He is aware that his argument only fits easily with what he calls "perfect communities of believers."[18] When the power to make and enforce human laws is in the hands of infidels, these infidels will certainly be concerned with the civil commotions that can be caused by bad priests, including the corruption of young women, which Marsilius sees as a product of the secret con-

[16] *Def. Pac.* I. xv. 2, 3, 4, 10; II. viii. 9; xvii. 8–16; xxi. 12–13; III. ii. 12, 21–22.

[17] *Def. Pac.* II. xvii. 9–14.

[18] *Ibid.;* and cf. Gewirth, *Marsilius,* vol. I, pp. 291–297.

versations of bad confessors with easily misled girls.[19] Further-more, the infidels may have a public religion of their own that is imposed on all the citizens by law. All of which Marsilius regards as quite natural.[20] Obviously, Marsilius could not say that under such circumstances men ought to obey the civil law. Rather, he says that there are cases in which the divine law and the civil law conflict, and whenever that is surely the case one ought to obey God rather than man. In such cases, there-fore, the whole body of believers in a particular place will elect their priests and ministers. They will have to do so in secret from the ruler, who will, of course, be inclined to attempt to suppress what he will regard as a subversive sect.[21] This is as far as Marsilius goes. Gewirth points out:

To this limited extent, then, Marsilius provides for the autonomy of religion and the church. He does not, however, raise the question of the relation of such an autonomous "sect" to the entire political community of which it is a part. What if the legislator should conceive that the preaching of Christian doctrines is inimical to its secular interests, that the divided allegiance of Christians is inimical to that unity of political authority which is necessary to the preservation of the state? No explicit answer is provided by Marsilius, but the implications of his central emphases are clear.[22]

As is his paralyzingly cautious custom, Gewirth refuses to articulate the implications and ends the discussion at that point. Less cautious, I shall say that the central implication of Marsilius' argument in this context is this: the defense of peace in such circumstances requires the suppression of Christianity. There may, of course, be Christians who are prepared to resist to the last. But the structure of the Marsilian church is such that it will either be torn apart by internal dissension or cap-

[19] *Def. Pac.* II. xvii. 12.
[20] *Def. Pac.* I. v; x. 3–7; II. x.; III. ii. 30.
[21] *Def. Pac.* II. v. 4, 5, 7; ix. 9; x. 7; xii. 9; xiii. 2; xvii. 15; xxvi. 13; xxx. 4.
[22] Gewirth, *Marsilius,* vol. I, p. 296.

67

tured by moderates who will be prepared to suppress or modify the doctrinal or practical aspects of their religion that are the chief source of friction. This much is implication. But Marsilius himself, in accordance with the absolute practical primacy of civil peace in his arguments, wrote, "We do not wish to say that it is inappropriate to coerce heretics or other infidels, but that the authority for it, if it be licit to do it, belongs solely to the human legislator,"[23] who is concerned with all those matters which, when poorly arranged, threaten harm to the community in this life,[24] especially civil strife, of course.

In order to make this point clear, it is necessary to turn to the more central elements of the Marsilian ecclesiastical structure. Specifically, it will be necessary to turn to the power of excommunication, the relationship of holy orders to ecclesiastical jurisdiction, and the power authoritatively to determine points of dogma, morals, and ritual. I have placed the question of excommunication first, even though it is a specific case of ecclesiastical jurisdiction, because Marsilius solves it with one line of argument that stands quite outside any specific doctrine about Church polity. It then may be treated as also a question of ecclesiastical jurisdiction.

In discussing the power of the priestly keys, Marsilius writes that, in addition to that binding and loosing that is effected in the sacrament of penance, there is another sort of binding and loosing for which the action of the priest is also necessary: excommunication. One who is excommunicated suffers a number of different punishments, some in this life and some in the next. With respect to the future life, the excommunicate suffers such punishment as God deems fitting the sin for which he was excommunicated. In this regard, the judgment of excommunication is nothing more than a clear declaration by a priest

[23] *Def. Pac.* II. v. 7; and cf. II. ix. 7; x. 3–11; xix. 3; xxi; xxv. 7; xxviii. 15; III. ii. 30.
[24] *Def. Pac.* I. xii. 7.

68

or priests to a sinner that he has sinned and that punishment appropriate to his sin will be his in the next world unless he repents. However, the priestly act of excommunication does not itself impose the punishment. It is merely a declaration that God, who is the final judge, will do so. Furthermore, the priest may be mistaken or may judge unjustly, and then God does not follow the sacerdotal judgment.[25]

But the excommunicate also suffers a number of penalties in this present life. These, in turn, seem to be divided into two groups: those that can only be imposed by a priest and those that can only be imposed by laymen. In the first group is the invocation of the divine power to punish the sinner in this life, for example, by the torment of a demon.[26] Also in this group, "perhaps," is the cutting off of the sinner from the "suffrages of the church."[27] In the other group, there are this-worldy consequences of excommunication which, in themselves, are not such that they can only be caused by one in holy orders. To publish an excommunication is publicly to defame the excommunicate. It likewise deprives him of the company of others. "And by this he is even deprived of civil communion and benefit."[28] And "because he is defamed and deprived of civil communion,"

It must be said that although the words and action of the priest are required for the promulgation of such a judgement, yet it does not

25 *Def. Pac.* II. vi. 12.
26 *Def. Pac.* II. vi. 13. cf. II. vi. 11–12.
27 *Def. Pac.* II. vi. 13. Marsilius does not make clear exactly what he means to include under "*Ecclesiae suffragia*," but I have decided to include the prayers, rites, and sacraments of the Church. This is supported by the fact that Marsilius suggests that this is what he means by regularly combining references to excommunication and interdict in which such matters are mentioned. Furthermore, there is no other discussion of the clavigeral power to cut off one from such things. cf. II. xviii. 8; xxi. 9; xxii. 4; xxiii. 3, 4, 9–10. Cf. C. Journet, *L'Église du Verbe Incarné* (Bruges, 1951), vol. II, pp. 844–846.
28 *Def. Pac.* II. vi. 12.

pertain to some one priest alone or to a college of priests alone to give a coercive judgement and precept as to who is to be excommunicated or absolved. But to set up such a judge, that is one to whom it belongs to call and examine, judge, absolve or condemn to public defamation or to being cut off from the company of the faithful, this pertains to the whole body of the faithful in the community in which someone is fittingly judged by such a judgement, or to its superior, or to a general council. However, the examination of the imputed crime, as to whether it be such that one ought to be excommunicated for it or not, ought to be done by such a judge with the help of a college of priests or of a determinate number of the more expert among them according to established laws or customs.[29]

Furthermore, when it is a question of excommunication or interdicting the use of the divine offices, then it should be known that, "if a priest or bishop or a particular college of them were to excommunicate or interdict a prince or province out of ignorance or bad will, then would there occur a great scandal to the peace and quiet of the faithful."[30]

As to whether the priests, without the aid of lay authority, may call down the divine power to send a demon to vex a sinner, it would seem that they could do so secretly. To do so publicly would be a transient, this-worldly act and thus subject to human law. It would also be likely to defame the one to whom the demon were sent and thus come under the third this-worldly consequence of excommunication. In any case, Marsilius does not bother to discuss it in detail.

Thus, of the four major aspects of excommunication-interdict that refer to penalties in this life, three of them may only be imposed by the faithful citizenry and according to human laws. The decisive consideration in each case is that a this-worldly, civil effect is produced. Once again, the argument immediately encounters difficulties the moment there is a question of a religiously divided civil community. And again the

[29] *Ibid.*   [30] *Def. Pac.* II. xxi. 9.

criteria for a solution are the same as those that controlled the previous case.[31]

Turning now to the more central question about ecclesiastical jurisdiction, Marsilius excludes any hierarchical structure derived from divine ordinance rather than from human enactment. Marsilius began by admitting that the theologians were not agreed as to whether a priest had one or more specific "characters" imprinted on his soul by virtue of which he possessed priestly powers. But whether the characters be one or many, there are two powers that constitute the "essential or the inseparable authority" of the priest. These two are the power of consecrating the body and the blood of Christ (the Eucharist) and the "power of binding and loosing men from sin." And it was Marsilius' judgment that, with respect to this inseparable or essential authority, all priests are equal. The Eucharist presents no problem, since all agree that all priests have it equally. The question, therefore, revolves about the power of binding and loosing.[32]

To begin with, the Marsilian power of binding and loosing is not much of a power at all, as Gewirth has clearly pointed out.[33] Christ forgives the contrite sinner directly. The function of the priest is only to "show" to the Church that the sinner has been forgiven. However, Christ seems to have quite arbitrarily, if inflexibly, assigned this function to the priests, since they are as fallible as anyone else in the matter.[34] In short, "In Marsilius' view of the purpose of confession, it is of course difficult to understand why even the intention to confess to a priest

[31] Cf. *supra*, pp. 66–68. There is also involved here a special problem concerning the power of a general council of the Church to issue an excommunication or interdict of a specific prince or province. But this can only be treated properly in a later context when the question of the council is raised in full.

[32] *Def. Pac.* II. vi. 14; xv. 4. Yet, in discourse three, it is only asserted that all *bishops* are of equal authority: III. ii. 17.

[33] Gewirth, *Marsilius*, vol. I, pp. 265–269.

[34] *Ibid.*, p. 268, n. 17., and *Def. Pac.* II. vi. 9.

should be regarded as essential to forgiveness."[35] Nevertheless, the text clearly makes it so.[36] In other words, the defender of peace does not mind retaining the appearances of the Catholic Church as long as the substructure is such or can be made such as to ensure no room for independent, authoritative action by the clergy.

Furthermore, inasmuch as the essential priestly powers as instituted by Christ are the same for all priests, all of them can administer all the sacraments, including the ordination of other priests. Thus, there are no degrees of perfection or participation in the priestly power (in what has traditionally been called the power of orders).[37] All other distinctions among priests are "separable" or "non-essential"[38] and rest on human authority. Such distinctions are the result of the "human institution by which priests are assigned to specific provinces and peoples to teach and instruct them in the Divine Law, and to administer the sacraments and to dispense those temporalities that we have called ecclesiastical benefices."[39]

But, as soon as Marsilius has made it clear that he regards the whole priestly hierarchy from pope to parish curate as of human institution, it is necessary to ask again the question that has already arisen with respect to the election of priests from the body of the lay multitude.[40] One cannot help asking about the place of political authority in the construction of a sacerdotal organization and the filling of the offices thus constructed, because Marsilius regards the priesthood as a political office, since it has grave consequences for the civil peace. Also, the construction of such hierarchy and the filling of its offices is likely to have far graver implications for civil peace than the harm that bad priests can work on impressionable women, the

---

[35] Gewirth, *Marsilius*, vol. I, p. 268.   [36] *Def. Pac.* II. vi. 6.

[37] *Def. Pac.* II. xv.; and cf. Gewirth, *Marsilius*, vol. I, p. 271.

[38] *Def. Pac.* II. xv. 9; xxv. 4.   [39] *Def. Pac.* II. xv. 10.

[40] Cf. *supra*, pp. 66–68.

reason he gave for this-worldly concern for the election of priests.[41] Once again, the Marsilian text leaves the same superficial uncertainty behind which stands a firm solution to a clearly defined, but narrowly defined problem. And it is this very point concerning the humanly instituted, separable authorities of different priests that is, according to Marsilius, the very heart of his work.[42]

The argument begins[43] by affirming that both reason and revelation agree that, inasmuch as Christ did not appoint his apostles to the ministry in such a way that one was ordained to minister to a specific people and not to some others (citing especially Mt 28:19), therefore either human institution (e.g., Gal 2:9) or a special revelation must determine it (e.g., Acts 22:17–18, 21). But in either case, the apostles so assigned received no new priestly perfection.

Next, it is argued that both revelation (citing Acts 6:6; Mt 23:8–11, 20:24–27; Lk 22:24–26) and reason indicate that in the appointment of successors and secondary church officers, the apostles, when together, acted collegially and in strict equality, as indeed they should have according to Christ's admonitions. The arguments from reason being that deliberation of many about such appointments would be less subject to error than if by one. Second, collegial decision would not be likely to produce the scandal and strife that would follow a struggle for primacy.

---

[41] *Def. Pac.* II. xvii. 12. There is, of course, plenty of evidence that Marsilius' judgment as to the political importance of the clergy is not mistaken. Not only in a medieval setting, but in a diversity of modern settings the existence of ecclesiastical organizations independent of the control of the public powers has been of great political moment. One might mention, for example, such diverse contemporary cases of the Catholic hierarchy of Poland under Stefan Cardinal Wyszynski and of the predominantly Baptist, Negro, Protestant ministry in the civil rights movement in the United States.

[42] *Def. Pac.* II. xvii. 1.

[43] All that follows in this connection is, unless otherwise noted, drawn from *Def. Pac.* II. xvii.

73

At this point, his method forced Marsilius to make an important admission. The way in which it arises in the course of the argument and the manner in which it is solved are illuminating for the whole work. An integral part of the Marsilian approach is to insist on the primacy of arguments from the New Testament and to literal readings of the texts wherever possible.[44] This accomplishes a number of things. As Gewirth pointed out, "In refusing to deal with the Old Testament, Marsilius is thus denying the relevance of one of the primary foundations of the papalist position."[45] It also focused all attention on the institutions of the primitive Church as the normative standard for ecclesiastical organization. Thus, Marsilius can freely criticize as divergences from biblical standards what others regarded as necessary developments and precisions of institutions only barely adumbrated in the primitive Church. It further permitted him to contrast the relative fluidity and lack of uniformity of biblical references to ecclesiastical offices to the far more fixed, precise, and uniform usage of the hierarchical structure in the Middle Ages. But, whatever the polemical value of a method that permitted him to deny any normative value to post-biblical ecclesiastical development, in our present context the same method compelled Marsilius to acknowledge that in some instances the biblical account of the usages of the primitive Church did not present a uniform image of apostolic collegiality in the matter of episcopal and other ecclesiastical appointments. In many cases, single apostles appointed bishops over newly converted groups without any reference being made to the apostlic college. Furthermore, and more important here, it does not appear that in such cases the appointment was made by popular election, but by the sole decision of the appointing apostle. Now, that would surely seem to indicate biblical sanction for some authoritative hier-

[44] *Def. Pac.* II. iii. 9; ix. 10; and cf. Gewirth, *Marsilius*, vol. I, pp. 72–77.
[45] *Ibid.*, pp. 72–73.

74

archy quite independent of popular or state sanction. But at precisely this point, Marsilius himself resorts to a developmental view of ecclesiastical organization. And it is a developmental view that rests on rational rather than on revelational bases.

In the primitive Church, the Defender of Peace admits, it was often expedient for a single apostle to place a bishop in charge of a newly converted multitude, rather than permit the multitude to elect its own bishop, "because of the grave deficiency in quantity and quality of the multitude; for in the beginning [of the Church] they were crude in many provinces, especially outside of Judea, and easily seducible." Under such circumstances, the "life and wisdom" of an apostle "was weightier and broader (because he had the Holy Spirit) than those of all such a multitude together." But this is no longer true of the multitude of believers.

The communities of the faithful are now "perfected." Now, no longer crude [and therefore filled with the Holy Ghost?], the faithful communities handle all the ecclesiastical structures, and appointments and removals, for themselves. The text then makes clear at once that by speaking of perfected communities of believers, Marsilius means those in which the believers constitute the effective political power.[46] In such cases, "it is permitted to no priest or bishop singularly or collegially to appoint anyone to take such [holy] orders without the license of the human legislator or the ruler by its authority." This, of course, leaves untouched all the difficulties about the relationship of infidel political authorities to congregations of the faithful that have already been pointed out with respect to the election of priests, which he treats in the same chapter,[47] and which is part of the same problematic since he regards priests and bishops as different only in non-essentials.

But his doctrine is clear, consistent, and fully developed only with respect to the juridical status of ecclesiastical ministers in

[46] Cf. *Def. Pac.* II. xviii. 3–7.   [47] Cf. *supra,* pp. 66–68.

75

those cases in which the political community is wholly or almost wholly composed of believers. In that case, the clergy and its organizational structure are to be firmly under the control of the political authorities. Thus it is clear that, among other things, Marsilius was not concerned with a solution to the problems of religious pluralism. He did not elaborate an argument on those questions, even though some tentative implications might reasonably be drawn out of his doctrine.[48] But his central concern is carefully worked out: how to provide a solution to the politically disastrous consequences of clerical domination in political communities of Christians? And at the core of his problem lay the historic claim of the papacy to be the guarantor of the universal faith. Obviously, as long as that claim could stand it was impossible fully to eliminate clerical domination in politics.[49] Whatever congregational and political controls he might put over the clergy, they would still tend to submit to the highest form of clerical political power, papal dictation, as long as they regarded the pope as the rock on which unity of faith must rest.

Marsilius had already provided the negative part of a solution to the problem of papal political power by virtue of the arguments just discussed. By divine right, the pope was quite the same as the lowest parish priest. Any powers he legitimately held, he held by human ordinance or consent, which could, of course, be revoked.[50] But that was hardly enough. Writing in terms of a medieval problem, Marsilius had to offer some positive and likely suggestions as to what institutions ought to be

[48] Thus it would seem that, wherever there were believers in large numbers and of reasonably developed virtue, the possibility of clerical domination of a politically relevant segment of the population would be ruled out on one or both of two grounds. The believers would legitimately claim the right to elect and control their own clergy, and the political community as a whole would naturally have the authority to intervene as it saw fit in affairs of such public moment. How such dual authorities can or should be harmonized is another question that Marsilius leaves open.

[49] *Def. Pac.* II. xx. 8; xxi. 9, 11–13.   [50] Cf. *Def. Pac.* II. xviii. 3–7.

76

expected to preserve the unity of the Christian faith.[51] A mere assertion that common acceptance of the canonical Scripture is the only thing necessary for unity of faith would hardly have sufficed. Everybody, including Marsilius, agreed that there are important passages of Scripture that need interpretation, either in themselves or because of an apparent conflict with other passages.[52] Thus, some mode of providing a catholic interpretation of such texts had to be offered. The solution that he offered does not appear to be particularly unusual for the Middle Ages. The unity of faith is to be preserved by resort to a general council. It is necessary, therefore, that we show the structure and authority of a general council as conceived by Marsilius.

Ultimately, according to Marsilius, the authority to determine such questions belongs to a "general council of Christians or its weightier part." But, of course, it would not be possible under most circumstances for all Christians to assemble for such a council, so he immediately adds: "or [to] those to whom the authority had been granted by the whole body of faithful Christians." This is followed by a brief and somewhat vague description of the way in which a council in this last sense is to be convoked.

As to membership: the council is to be composed of two classes of members, priests and laymen. They are to be elected from "all the provinces of the world or notable communities" in accordance with the determinations of their political authorities, "whether one or many." The distribution of seats being settled "according to the proportion [of the communities] in quantity and quality of persons."[53]

Voting power: if the priests are unanimous about an article of faith, their decision shall stand. But if they disagree, then "the weightier part of the faithful has to judge which is the sounder part of [the priests]." However, he immediately adds a

---

[51] *Def. Pac.* II. xviii. 8. Cf. Gewirth, *Marsilius,* vol. I, pp. 130–131.
[52] *Ibid.*　　　　　　　　　　[53] *Def. Pac.* II. xx. 2.

proviso to the effect that the priests must have been ordained in accordance with his system of political control of ordinations.[54]

Authority: since the councils hold the power to determine what is the doctrine of faith, theirs it is also to excommunicate or lay under interdict any "prince, province or other civil community."[55] They are also to decree concerning "ecclesiastical ritual or divine worship" with a view to the "peace and tranquillity of the faithful."[56] Furthermore, there are other matters, "outside the Divine Law," that pertain to the "common utility and peace of the faithful." They are to be settled by the council, and that is a special reason for including laymen in its deliberations.[57]

However, the authority of the council to act independently in any of these areas is strictly limited. The members of the council are only to act as "judges according to the first sense of the word," i.e., as experts and not as giving coercive commands.[58] Only the political authorities may "order the observance of its doctrinal decrees" and "punish transgressors in and for the status of this present world."[59] With respect to matters of church ritual, the decrees of the council may not be binding "under any penalty for the status of the present world *or the world to come*" [emphasis added] without the "intervening decree" of political authority. And it may not, without grant of power from political authority, decree concerning "other human acts," whenever such decrees bind "under any ecclesiastical censure, such as interdict or excommunication or other similar penalty major or minor." The foregoing applies all the more when the decrees are to bind under a wholly this-worldly penalty. Lest there be any doubt as to the amplitude of this political control, Marsilius gives a long list of examples from fasting to marital laws.[60]

[54] *Def. Pac.* II. xx. 5.
[56] *Def. Pac.* II. xx. 2.
[58] *Def. Pac.* II. xx. 2 and II. ii. 8.
[60] *Def. Pac.* II. xxi. 8.

[55] *Def. Pac.* II. xxi. 9.
[57] *Def. Pac.* II. xx. 3.
[59] *Def. Pac.* II. xxi. 7.

Thus, it appears that all conciliar decisions other than definitions of articles of faith are absolutely dependent on political validation. What, then, of doctrinal determinations? Marsilius declared that only the political authorities may punish the unorthodox by penalties in "this present world." But he had already made clear that excommunication involves penalties in this world, and therefore may not be imposed by the priests without the affirmative decision of the political authorities.[61] Furthermore, even in the case in which all the priests of the council are unanimous in a doctrinal decision, they cannot impose excommunication on those who refuse to accept their decision, for "no bishop or priests or college of them may licitly excommunicate anyone" without the permission of the political authorities.[62] Last, but not least, the conferring of licenses in the various learned disciplines is a power of the political authorities and not of any priest or group of them.[63]

In sum, the following matters respecting the general council are to be controlled by the political authorities: ordination and appointment and removal of all priests; election of priests and laymen to a council; its convocation; the distribution of its seats; the publication and enforcement of its decrees by any penalty with consequences in this world, including excommunication or interdict. With the Church thus thoroughly controlled from top to bottom by political authorities, Marsilius is then prepared to admit the possible utility of setting up a pope, provided the office be clearly understood as being a human construct under political control, purely executive in authority, and not necessary to the unity of the faith.[64] Indeed, "a universal prince is more able to hold the faithful in unity than a universal bishop."[65] But it is "neither expedient nor true" that there should be a single coercive judge for the whole world, "for it is adequate to main-

---

[61] Cf. *supra,* pp. 68–71.
[62] *Def. Pac.* III. ii. 16.
[65] *Def. Pac.* II. xxviii. 15.

[63] *Def. Pac.* II. xxi. 15; III. ii. 25.
[64] *Def. Pac.* II. xvii.

tain the peace of men that there be numerical unity of the government in each part of the world."[66] And, as for the utility of a single world-ruling prince to maintain the unity of the faith, a necessity for salvation, Marsilius didn't think that could be demonstrated.[67] It is at this point that Marsilius's concern for the unity of the universal faith is revealed as a matter of camouflage for solely political concerns.

Since, at best, Marsilius did not support a universal monarchy except perhaps in special circumstances,[68] the utility of a general council is hardly very great from the point of view of maintaining unity of faith. Under most circumstances, there will exist a number of different political communities whose members are Christians. Therefore, there can be no council without the unanimous consent of those political authorities each of which "lacks a superior."[69] It can not be convoked, nor its seats distributed, nor its members elected. And if all those hurdles be overcome and the council actually assembles, who will be authorized to excommunicate any who obstinately refuse to accept the doctrinal determinations of the council? The political authorities and they only. What if a particular position, condemned by the

[66] *Ibid.* In discussing Marsilius' arguments about universal government in ch. xv of discourse I, Gewirth writes: "So thoroughly intra-state is his conception of the peace and unity for which he argues, that when the question arises as to whether the requirement of a single supreme government does not entail government for the whole world, he can reply that this question 'deserves reasonable study, but is different from our present project.' In his very statement of the question, moreover, he raises numerous objections: such a government would have to extend over widely separated parts of the world and to deal with persons speaking different languages and differing greatly in morals and customs; moreover, nature herself would seem to be against such world government, since she uses wars and epidemics to lessen the population in order that the earth may provide enough sustenance for all" (*Marsilius,* vol. I, p. 127).

[67] *Def. Pac.* II. xxviii. 15.

[68] Cf. Gewirth, *Marsilius,* vol. I, pp. 125–131, 287; Leo Strauss, "Marsilius of Padua," in Strauss and Cropsey, eds. *History of Political Philosophy,* pp. 241–242, hereafter referred to as: Strauss, "Marsilius."

[69] *Def. Pac.* II. xviii. 8; xxi. 1.

council, is upheld by a particular political community, upheld by its delegates to the council and by the political authorities? If the heretics are obstinate, no sentence of excommunication can be pronounced within their borders. To be sure, other communities may choose to cut themselves off from communion with the dissenters,[70] but the latter may naturally put any face on the affair they choose. They may refuse to permit anyone to teach or preach the doctrine of the council, or even to teach or preach that the doctrine maintained at home is at variance with that of the council and therefore with the catholic faith. Of course, the dissenters may not take this course. They may take any one of a great variety of courses. But the point of the Marsilian argument is that every state is, according to his doctrine, always legitimately in a position to preserve its peace from turmoil caused by religious disputes. If the political authorities of a particular sovereign community so choose, they may prevent the publication of the least indication that there is any question as to the catholicity of the religious doctrine taught within that community. Nor does the general council have any means whereby it may legitimately challenge that camouflage of heterodoxy. Actually, that is an overstatement. It would seem that the priests of the council might send down upon the heretics a vexing visitation of devils.[71] Inasmuch as that judgment could also be prevented from being published in the heretical community, Marsilius could scarcely be expected to be overly concerned. And, indeed, he does not even mention it in this context.

In short, Marsilius, as he himself wrote at the opening of his work and repeated at the close,[72] was concerned with only one political problem: the strife caused by clerical interference in

---

[70] Which, as a defamation, might be taken as a cause for war or other reprisals.

[71] Cf. *supra*, p. 70.

[72] *Def. Pac.* I. i; xix; III. i. Cf. Lagarde, *Marsile*, pp. 54–55.

81

of a great variety of things, among them the Reformation and politics. He has been credited with being a medieval forerunner democracy.[73] But the acidity of his assaults on clerical, and especially papal, corruption should not be mistaken for the zeal of a religious reformer. There is no sense in his text of a burning love for Christ and His spouse, the Church, that makes him spend himself to see the Church without spot or wrinkle. The polemical assaults on clerical corruption are rather part of a carefully calculated fabric of political Averroism.[74] Thus, it misses the point to write, as Gewirth does, that "the Protestant outcome of national churches is probably what Marsilius himself would have espoused could he have broken away from the idea of a universal faith determined and enforced by a single universal agency."[75] The preceding analysis shows that he was not unprepared for national churches. But two things must be made clear: first, he could hardly hope to get any hearing at all if he had espoused such a solution in the first half of the fourteenth century. Second, and more important, it was not Marsilius' object to reform the Church on national or imperial lines. It was his object to secure civil peace against the ever-present clerical interference of the Catholic Church. In some circumstances, that object would lead to a universal imperial Church. In other circumstances, it would lead, as we have seen, to national churches. Marsilius, since he is prepared to approve an empire or no empire according to circumstances (like a good Aristotelian), is prepared for either kind of church as a necessary consequence of

[73] Gewirth gives a systematic review of the fantastic variety of things, many of them contradictory, with which Marsilius has, at different times and by different people, been credited (*Marsilius,* vol. I, pp. 3–6). The very variety should give pause, especially since the writer says he is concerned solely with a single, narrow problematic.

[74] Gewirth, again, reviews the main references (*Marsilius,* vol. I, pp. 39–44). Although he has reservations, he concludes that "this Averroist secularism results in a politics which is free from domination by theological ends." Add to Gewirth's references, E. Gilson, *History of Christian Philosophy in the Middle Ages* (New York: 1955), pp. 524–527.

[75] Gerwith, *Marsilius,* vol. I, p. 131.

political control of the clergy. His supposed democratism[76] is as tenuous, a product of reading a narrowly conceived argument as a general theoretical treatment of the problem of the forms of government.[77] What is true is that as a counter to the papalist barbarization of the philosophic argument for monarchy,[78] Marsilius emphasized, and in context correctly, the legitimacy of the non-hierarchic elements in political order *under less than perfect circumstances.* However, in order to avoid further complicating an already complicated treatment, I have avoided the problem in the foregoing analysis by using the term "political authorities" in place of "legislator" and "ruler" or "government," terms which Marsilius sometimes distinguishes (placing the former over the latter and thus giving rise to his "democratism"), and sometimes uses interchangeably.[79]

But all these peculiarities of Marsilian thought cannot be conceived except in the context of a reaction against papalism, and that is why he is profoundly important as a first representative of the depths of the disaster that papalist views helped to produce in the West. He has been described, among other things, as a forerunner of Machiavelli, Hobbes, Locke, Rousseau, and even the totalitarians.[80] It does not seem that his work sig-

[76] Cf. *ibid.,* vol. I, pp. 4–6, 142, 167, 176–177, 181, 189, 195–196, 224–226; also C. H. McIlwain, *The Growth of Political Thought in the West* (New York: 1932), pp. 307–308.

[77] Cf. Leo Strauss' cogent treatment in "Marsilius," pp. 233–240.

[78] The arguments of both Plato and Aristotle for monarchy assume that, at least relative to his fellow citizens, the monarch must be a certain integral representation of the highest good, the good simply. The papalist argument, though referring to a different supreme good, attempts to take this argument, which essentially refers to personal virtue, and apply it to an office. This is quite clearly seen in Giles of Rome, who is well aware of the distinction between personal and official perfection (cf. *supra,* p. 48). This is also what gives the peculiar flavor of political unreality to the bureaucratically abstract arguments of the papalists.

[79] Gewirth, who warily argues for a democratic element in Marsilius' thought, nevertheless admits that there is "a frequent coalescence of legislator and ruler in the second discourse" (*Marsilius,* vol. I, p. 254). Cf. Strauss, "Marsilius," pp. 234–235.

[80] Cf. *supra,* p. 82, n. 73.

nally influenced their thought. Nor are they Aristotelians, as he
is. But all of them are concerned to defend politics against its
disruption by institutionalized Christianity, including its most
dangerous form: the Catholic Church centered on the pope. And
all of them, in one way or another, are prepared to attempt to
write a politics that retreats not only from Christian hope, but
also from the all-illuminating ultimate regimes of both Plato
and Aristotle. The philosopher-king of the Republic and Aristotle's *pambasileus,* who stands to his fellow citizens as a whole
to parts,[81] are both of them incarnations, as it were, or epiph-
anies of the transcendent good, and therefore make conceivable
an order and illumination for the whole range of statistically
more normal regimes for which men are ordinarily fitted. But
Marsilius found himself in a situation in which any such argument for an archetypal kingship would necessarily redound to
the benefit of the pope, whose partisans would make the argument that only the pope would be such a ruler, since, in the
Christian dispensation, the pope, more than any lay king, was
concerned with the highest good, the good simply.[82] On the
level of ways of life and the hierarchy of virtues, the consequence of dealing solely with such a set of circumstances and
with so narrow an object as Marsilius had, is that contemplation
of the transcendent, eternal, absolute good can no longer be
viewed as the ultimate and regulating activity of man. The
Christians, in their new way, the way of the *visio Dei,* of beatific
vision of God in heaven, had insisted on the ultimate primacy of
contemplation as much as, if not more than, the philosophers.
But the papalists had radically institutionalized at least a part of
the primacy of contemplation. Thus, the pope, by rank (i.e.,
regardless of his personal life and virtues), is the chief of con-

---

[81] *Politics* iii. 17. 1288.ª 26–30.

[82] Cf. Strauss, "Marsilius," pp. 236–239. I have applied the argument that
Strauss makes concerning aristocracy to the question of monarchy where, it
seems to me, it applies with greater force.

templative men, and therefore ought to rule all men.[83] And even if the apex of the hierarchy of virtues were to be said to be a virtue concerned with action rather than with contemplation, the papalists would argue that charity holds an absolute primacy in such matters, and that the works of charity are appropriately under the direction of the clergy and especially the pope. The logic of his anti-clericalism therefore leads to an assertion of the primacy, for politics, of human positive law over natural law, and the primacy, for politics, of the "sufficient life" of the mass of men (consisting chiefly of useful goods for physical well-being, although certain moral goods may be desirable but seemingly as ministerial to the former) rather than the good life of virtuous activities that are choice-worthy for their own sake.[84] Thus it is that Marsilius, the professed Aristotelian, "says much less than Aristotle even in his *Politics* about the highest end which is natural to man . . . he lowered his sights."[85] This lowering of sights has been characteristic of political thought since the collapse of the papalist dream.

The collapse of that dream did not immediately produce an open attack on religion in the name of philosophy or anything else. Any such attack would have been simple folly in the face of believing people. Furthermore, the philosophers were aware that the many could not become philosophers, and thus, for them, it was quite important that this-worldly political sanctions be bolstered by internalized religious sanctions to be effected in an after-life.[86] It was possible, however, to attack clericalism in

---

[83] Cf. *supra*, pp. 27–29.

[84] *Def. Pac.* I. x. 4–5; xiii. 8; and I. iv. Cf. *Def. Pac.* I. iii. 4; iv. 2; v. 2–4; xvi. 17, 23; xvii. 8; xix. 13; II. xii. 7–9, and I. i. 7; xii. 5, 8; xiii. 5; Gewirth, *Marsilius,* vol. I, pp. 55, 132–166, and 98–111, 118; Strauss, "Marsilius," pp. 243–245.

[85] Strauss, "Marsilius," p. 244.

[86] *Def. Pac.* I. v. 11–14. Averroes had already worked out this line of thought within the Muslim world in two works: "On the Concord of Religion with Philosophy" and "On the Demonstration of Religious Dogmas."

the name of politics, but to do so involved that lowering of sights noted by Strauss. It meant the abandonment, at least for the time being, of discussion of the primacy of contemplation. It meant the abandonment, at least for the time being, of discussion of the primacy of natural justice. It meant the abandonment, at least for the time being, of discussion of the ultimate normality[87] of rule in terms of a divine justice brought to men by some incarnation of the divine, whether in the form of the philosopher-king or Christ the King.[88] It meant, finally, the death of religion, however much Marsilius may have thought its preservation useful.[89] I say "at least for the time being" because it does not seem at all reasonable to refuse to believe Marsilius when he wrote that Aristotle had solved all the political problems better than anyone else except for this one peculiar problem raised by Christianity, and that he wished to solve only that one because it was particularly pressing and its solution was the

---

Cf. L. Gauthier, *Ibn Rochd (Averroes)* (Paris: 1948), pp. 17–46.; E. Renan, *Averroès et l'Averroisme* (Paris: n.d.), pp. 152–162, 167–172; Gilson, *History of Christian Philosophy in the Middle Ages*, pp. 218–220.

[87] A normality that is, of course, not at all statistical, since the regimes in question are, from a statistical point of view, either particularly unusual or quite unique.

[88] I have kept both the philosopher and the Christian hope for the human community together, since the Marsilian position involves at least a temporary silence about both of them. So it is not necessary here to raise the question as to their compatibility.

[89] It should be apparent that I have not viewed Marsilius as being a believer in the revelation of Christ. Strauss cites the locus of the evidence: *Def. Pac.* II. xix ("Marsilius," p. 243). But he has objectives of his own, and, having raised the question, he then decides to remain silent. The Marsilian text, however, is characterized by a subtly satiric play on the theme of the circular argument. He writes that, according to the Scriptures, the Scriptures must be believed as true. It can also be shown from the same Scriptures that the decisions of a general council on doubtful interpretations of the texts are true. But he then points out that the determination of which books are part of the Bible in the first place can only be ascertained by virtue of a decision of a general council. And this after a wry remark that, "for the sake of brevity," he will omit the proof that the Scriptures must be accepted as true, since this can only be proved from the Scriptures themselves.

sine qua non of a return to any reasonable politics.[90] But two things must be noted. First, whatever Marsilius' personal inclinations about a later return to the broader scope of Aristotle's thought on politics, his own work is singularly narrow and has within it nothing to ensure a return to that broader context after the special problem is solved. Indeed, it tends to make any such return impossible precisely because, in the measure that it is effective at all, it tends to produce an habitual mode of viewing politics in which peace and not virtue is the ultimate standard in the light of which action is to be guided. Second, others will abandon all reservations and argue for a politics that simply omits all reference to a transcendent ultimate standard. Thus, Machiavelli will attempt to restructure politics in terms of the glorious act of forcibly making an enduring polity. Hobbes will do so in terms of self-preservation. Locke in terms of comfortable self-preservation. And then Rousseau will attempt to reintroduce into politics by human guile the unity, freedom, goodness, and absolute truth that had previously been seen as existing firstly and chiefly in a transcendent order and as an object of human contemplation. From this point on, the various totalitarianisms of the modern world begin to devour the human community.

It would, of course, be absurd to attribute the whole of the development to Marsilius. It would even be absurd to attribute a great part of it to him.[91] But that was not my point in writing about him in this connection. It was rather that, even in his case, even in the case of a thinker who makes the reservation that his are extraordinary times needing extraordinary measures, it is not possible to abandon the treatment of the universal political problems until some more favorable era. There may be a price to

---

[90] *Def. Pac.* I. i. 3, 6–7; III. i.

[91] Cf. Gewirth, *Marsilius*, vol. I, pp. 303–304; Previté-Orton, "Marsiglio of Padua. Part II," *The English Historical Review*, (1923), pp. 14–15; idem, "Marsilius of Padua," *Proceedings of the British Academy*, 1935, pp. 162–169.

pay in the way of certain immediate and hoped-for effects by including the permanent questions. The price may even include hemlock or the stake. But, be that as it may, one must wonder how much human deformity this lowering of sights by "a son of Antenor,"[92] or anyone else, introduces into the fate of Padua, her sisters in Italy,[93] and the world.

But not only does the Marsilian solution to papalist extremism lead to its own deformation of the city, it also leads to the death of religion, even in those respects in which it seemed desirable to him to keep it alive. No doubt, popular religion may be given a great variety of forms, especially in its institutional externals (whether the most deeply experienced substrata are easily changed is quite another matter). But the question must necessarily be raised whether a noble lie fabricated by philosophers will be capable of touching and forming the depths of souls so as genuinely to produce that inner conformation to licit standards of action for which, according to Marsilius,[94] unbelieving philosophers have been prepared to tell their religious fables. Indeed, as Marsilius himself described it, these religious constructs were essentially and crudely moral in the sense of eternal reward for the good and eternal punishment for the bad. But such a narrowing of popular religious experience to a stick-and-carrot construct is exactly the rationalist philosopher's misunderstanding of his relationship to his non-philosophic fellows. Because the mass of men do not engage in the *theoria*, philosophic contemplation, he assumes that there is no contempla-

[92] *Def. Pac.* I. i. 6.
[93] *Def. Pac.* I. i. 2. Cf. Warren Winiarski's article, "Niccolo Machiavelli" (in Strauss and Cropsey, eds., *History of Political Philosophy*, pp. 247–276). In spite of a rather preposterous reduction of Christian morality to the absolutized moralism ordinarily associated in this country with certain popular forms of Calvinism (cf. H. Richard Niebuhr, *Christ and Culture*, New York: 1951), his article brings out the magnitude of the implications involved in this lowering of sights in political philosophy and its relation to a reaction against the Church. Albert Camus brought out certain other aspects of the development in *The Rebel*.
[94] *Def. Pac.* I. v. 11.

88

tive element in their spiritual existence. But a religion constructed on that assumption must inevitably prove relatively inefficacious precisely because an important aspect of psychic activity has been ignored. The likelihood is that the constructed religion will be supplemented, overtly or convertly, by remnants of a previous religious structure, or by importations, or perhaps by a total overthrow by some doctrine that includes an important element of initiation into the divine presence. Whether that presence be seen as the source of life (as in fertility rites), or of power (as in magical rites), or of order (as in those concerned with ritual purifications for having fallen from "the way"), or of salvation in a variety of senses, in each case there is, along with other things, a decisive sense of being in the presence of the ground of being, and that very fact is seen as good-in-itself. This seems to be essentially contemplative rather than active in mode, even though, unlike philosophy or the high forms of religious mysticism, it does not achieve a distinct articulation of that element of the total psychic experience.

Greek religious history, to which Marsilius appeals, shows that Greek religion was not a construct of philosophers, although rationalist criticism of the myths did a good deal to transform and sterilize them. Second, the relatively sterile, anthropomorphic civic cults of democratic Athens were hardly able to resist the influx of Oriental mystery religions. However, all of the foregoing[95] may be thought to be irrelevant to Marsilius' case, since he is concerned with a reform of the clergy in Christianity, which already has in it a great element of initiation into the presence of the divine in both a large body of dogmatically determined

[95] For much of the foregoing I have relied heavily on Martin P. Nilsson, *Geschichte der griechischen Religion* (Munich: 1941); *idem, A History of Greek Religion,* 2nd ed. (Oxford: 1949); *idem, Greek Folk Religion* (New York: 1961); H.J. Rose, *Religion in Greece and Rome* (New York: 1959); Mircea Eliade, *Patterns in Comparative Religion* (New York: 1958); *idem, Cosmos and History: The Myth of the Eternal Return* (New York: 1959); Fustel de Coulanges, *The Ancient City* (Garden City: 1956).

revelation and in a set of rituals centering on the eucharistic banquet, which is understood as a foretaste of the heavenly union with the divine in the contemplative, beatific vision. But, be that as it may, the fact is that Marsilius' work shows no concern with such matters.[96]

Therefore, it is necessary to question whether it can be supposed that a non-believing intellectual élite can long maintain the vitality of popular religion and the façade of its belief in it without performing a collective rhetorical feat of enormous proportions. Is it really likely that, not themselves believers, they can regularly penetrate to the depths of the popular religious experience, articulate it vitally, and appear to believe? Such a performance might be accomplished by an occasional rhetorical giant, but can hardly be expected as a permanent trait of philosophic followers of Marsilius. Least of all can it be expected of them, since the master's work itself is devoid of any living religious concern.

However, the Marsilian reaction to the excess of papalist absolutism indicates how deep the wounds of medieval clericalism go. There will, of course, usually be a tension between different offices in any community. But the depths of anti-clericalism in most countries with a Catholic history suggests that the Church has by no means worked out a satisfactory working

[96] He does admit that the power of eucharistic consecration is an essentially priestly power and not, as such, derived from human institution. But this is part of the process by which he distinguished essential from accidental priestly powers, the latter being instituted and controlled by political authority, and, through that avenue, the exercise of the essential powers is also controlled. That is to say, he only adverted to the power of eucharistic consecration in a context in which the object is to secure political control of priestly acts. The same is true in the matter of doctrine. Marsilius piously affirmed the importance of right doctrine but again in a context of securing political control of doctrinal pronouncements lest doctrinal disputes disturb the peace. And, on the assumption that I am correct in thinking that Marsilius was quite prepared to provide for differences in doctrine between political communities (cf. *supra*, pp. 76–81), it is necessary to regard his concern for unity of faith as rhetorical only. In addition, he did not include any serious reference to substantive points of revelation.

polity for the second millennium of her existence. The one extreme of clerical domination in all spheres, brought to a sharp point by the papalists, engenders the other extreme of anti-clericalism in defense of the natural order of existence. But, precisely because it is an extreme reaction, it ends by destroying everything in its wrath. Along with the priesthood, understood as performing a divinely instituted re-presentation of God to man, the anti-clericals expel the whole revelational and contemplative element of religion. And in the heat of anti-clerical passion, they are prepared to mold the city in terms of the battle against the priests, forgetting for the time being, at least, their commitment to a deeper salvation of politics.

On the level of politics, the papalists had, in effect, demanded a choice between nature and grace, and between action and contemplation. A measure of their importance, as well as of the disastrous results of their efforts, is that a considerable portion of their opposition accepted the challenge on precisely those terms. Even Marsilius, who seems to have hoped to salvage something for contemplation, thought it necessary to take the challenge on its own terms, at least as a tactical maneuver valid for the time of battle, the special political situation having been created by Christianity. Successors in the resistance to that situation, beginning with Machiavelli, abandoned contemplation altogether. Thus, the very attempt to destroy the risks of action provoked a defense of pure action, a human creating, that is all risk and ends at the crematory.

But the very fact that Marsilius represents a transitional position in the fight against clerical deformation of politics makes it possible to employ his case to illuminate another consequence of the resistance to clericalism. Like Averroës in a different context, the Latin Averroists were aware that heresy or unbelief, or the suspicion of them, seriously endangered their lives. Their tactic in all cases seems to have been a greater or lesser degree of camouflage, a feigning of belief and orthodoxy. Without deciding

91

the broader issue of the legitimacy of the use of force in defense of a public religious orthodoxy, the case of Marsilius and the Latin Averroists suggests that one inevitable result of such a policy is the production of what has been called a kind of uremic poisoning of the Church. Position and perhaps even life depend on the appearance of orthodoxy. In such a situation, the inescapable result is that many of the unorthodox and of the unbelievers tend to adopt, through a variety of stratagems, the appearance of orthodoxy while continuing to pursue their own objectives.[97] The stratagems are eventually noted by the defenders of orthodoxy, and inquisitorial activity is intensified to combat the secretiveness of the opposition. At least in the case of large scale and powerful opposition, the inquisitorial and repressive measures necessary to cope with it are likely to be so great as to generate a certain oppressive momentum of their own. Furthermore, they tend to produce a degree of fear and circumspection that dries up creative initiatives and thereby prevents the institution of needed and legitimate reforms that might have gone a long way to reducing the magnitude of the resistance. The ordinary consequence of such a descending spiral of conflict is a polarization of forces around a radically oversimplified set of two alternatives, orthodoxy or heresy, or, later, belief or unbelief, a polarization that not infrequently leads to open war with no possibility of limitation or reasonable peace, since absolute values are invoked on both sides.

This is obviously a political or natural psychological analysis of the process at issue. For the moment, I have not attempted to add two necessary aspects. The whole question must also be viewed in the context of the Church's doctrine that faith must be free, that one cannot be forced to adhere to Christ, and that it is both absurd and illicit to attempt to force what, by its

[97] Cf. *supra,* p. 85, n. 86, and Gilson, *History of Christian Philosophy in the Middle Ages,* pp. 387–402; 521–527. On the ecclesiastical reaction, cf. pp. 402–410.

nature, cannot be forced. But even on the level of natural, political analysis, it is not true that the tendencies toward camouflaged heresy or unbelief, inquisitorial excesses, the resultant ossification, and the excessive simplification and polarization of forces are so great as automatically to lead to a condemnation of all uses of force in defense of orthodoxy. It is not true because the analysis is too narrow to justify the conclusion. It is necessary to ask what role is played in human affairs by physical power both in individuals and in communities. It is also necessary to attempt to outline the typical alternatives and their consequences in typical situations in which politically organized repression of manifestations of heresy or unbelief seems to some to be desirable.

Nevertheless, it is necessary to repeat that, whatever may have been the alternatives, the very power and extremism of the papalists inaugurated the series of reactions from which the Church, as can be seen from Vatican II, is still trying to extricate herself.

John of Paris

In Search of Measure

THE heat of battle is seldom the easiest of circumstances for calm reflection. Nonetheless, it may on occasion prove illuminating for certain aspects of persons or things that might otherwise be missed. This seems to have been one of the rationales given for the early medieval custom of trial by battle. But, whatever its defects, it is still popular in our time on the level of intellectual judgments. The optimistic assumption is that the opinion that succeeds in winning a victory by capturing the greatest number of heads is more likely to be true than the alternatives. Or, when that seems too ludicrous, the heads that are to be held relevant for victory and defeat are limited to those of "recognized experts."

John of Paris[1] seems to have been somewhat less sanguine. He lived in the middle of the controversy between the Pope and Philip the Fair of France, and, when he took up his pen to write a tract on the power of king and pope,[2] he was aware of certain

[1] He seems to have borne a number of names, including Jean Quidort, Jean Le Sourd, and Johannes Dormiens in addition to that by which he is usually named: Johannes Parisiensis. A member of the Order of Preachers, he died in 1306.

[2] *Tractatus de potestate regia et papali.* I have used the critical edition prepared by Dom Jean Leclercq, O.S.B., and appended to his *Jean de Paris et l'Ecclésiologie du XIIIe Siècle* (Paris: 1942), pp. 171–260. Hereafter, references to the text will be cited as *Tractatus,* followed by the numbers for chapter, page, and line in this edition. Leclercq dates the *Tractatus* "at the

94

pitfalls. "Now and then it happens that, wishing to avoid some error, one falls into the contrary error." But "between these two errors is the sound doctrine." That is how he begins his work.[3] That suggests enough difficulty to satisfy anyone, but he is aware that battles are seldom the occasions when it is desirable to be caught in the middle. At least as far as the papalists are concerned, there is no middle. Anyone who is not prepared to describe the pope as lord of the whole world in every respect is immediately considered "among the partisans of the prince,"[4] if not among the heretics.[5] But it is one of John's virtues that he takes those risks, because it is his purpose to find that middle ground between contrary errors that is held by faith.[6]

His attempt to find that middle ground is interesting not only for its own subtlety, but because the most important contemporary American Catholic thinker on the church-state question has been influenced by John's work. John Courtney Murray interpreted the doctrine of the *Tractatus* on two occasions. He concluded that John of Paris had found a genuine middle way that is "indeed 'the great Catholic tradition' and, . . . if developed *in eodem sensu*, it may show the way to the solution of the contemporary problem, which has itself developed in the sense taken by the problem in the fourteenth century."[7] Nevertheless, Murray did not attempt a "critical study of John of Paris, that

---

end of 1302 or the first month of 1303" (p. 14). Cf. Martin Grabmann, *Studien zu Johannes Quidort von Paris O. Pr.* (Munich: 1922), p. 12.

[3] *Tractatus* i. 173. 1–2, 7–8.   [4] *Tractatus* i. 174. 14.

[5] *Tractatus* xi. 207. 23–25. Gilson reports (*History of Christian Philosophy in the Middle Ages*, p. 731–732, n. 67) that John was subjected to a theological censure for his work on transubstantiation by a board of censors under the presidency of *Giles of Rome,* issuing in a suspension of his teaching activity (1305), after which he appealed to the pope; he died in 1306, apparently before a decision had been made.

[6] *Tractatus* i. 173. 11.

[7] John Courtney Murray, S.J., "Contemporary Orientations of Catholic Thought on Church and State in the Light of History," *Cross Currents,* no. 5 (Fall, 1951), p. 24. The article originally appeared in *Theological Studies* in June, 1949. Cited hereafter as J.C.M., *Cross Currents.*

estimates his weaknesses." He limited himself to selecting certain aspects of John's work and extending "the virtualities of his thought."[8] However, there is some controversy as to the solidity of John's position.[9] So let us begin at the beginning.

John lays the groundwork of his analysis by recapitulating in his first chapter the conventional, Aristotelian views of the nature and source of kingship. "Kingship is the rule of a perfect multitude ordained by one to the common good."[10] "Perfect" distinguishes it from the paternal rule over a household which is sufficient unto itself neither for a long time nor for the whole of life's objects.[11] Kingship is only one among six kinds of rule over such a multitude, three of which are ordained to the common good: kingdom, aristocracy, and polity, whereas tyranny, oligarchy, and democracy are directed to the good of the ruler. Furthermore, the rule of one, kingship, is "derived from natural law and from the law of nations," and is more useful than rule by many or by a few virtuous men,[12] a judgment that he qualifies later by asserting the superiority of a mixed regime including a king.[13] However, it would be fatuous to attempt to draw out of John's text a systematic evaluation of the forms of government. The problem with which the *Tractatus* is concerned is the relationship of *kingly* power to papal power. Thus, like most arguments about the church-state question, the relevance of the

[8] John Courtney Murray, S.J., "Governmental Repression of Heresy," *Proceedings of the Third Annual Meeting of the Catholic Theological Society of America*, June, 1948, p. 52, n. 24. Cited hereafter as J.C.M., *C.T.S.A. Proceedings.*

[9] Cf. Charles Journet, *L'Église du Verbe Incarné* (n.p.: 1955), vol. 1, p. 312, n. 2.; and Richard Scholz, *Die Publizistik zur Zeit Philipps des Schönen und Bonifaz' VIII*, 6/8 Hft. of *Kirchenrechtliche Abhandlungen*, ed. Dr. Ulrich Stutz, 118 vols. (Stuttgart: 1902–1938), cited hereafter as Scholz, *Die Publizistik*. See also Gilson, *History*, pp. 413–414.

[10] *Tractatus* i. 176. 24–25.

[11] *Tractatus* i. 176. 28–30. He cites book i of the *Politics*.

[12] *Tractatus* i. 176. 38–177. 2, 19–36.

[13] *Tractatus* xix. 236. 1–237. 29.

forms of government to a solution is unfortunately ignored in favor of a more constricted, polemical field of vision within which the subtleties about the diverse circumstances to which diverse regimes are appropriate have no place.[14]

One thing seems clear for John of Paris. The political life of man in general, and therefore the life of a kingdom, springs from natural problems in seeking "food, clothing and defense" as well as "from speech which is to another."[15] In short, political life has its roots in both the animal and rational levels of man's nature. Furthermore, rulership is a necessary part of political existence, for the multitude "is scattered and dispersed in diverse parts unless it is ordered to the common good by someone who has charge of the common good," i.e., the king in this case.[16] And this common good, this complex of life's objects that is pursued by the human multitude, composed as it is of "naturally civil or political and social animal[s],"[17] is all "such good as can be acquired by nature, namely to live according to virtue." Contrasted with this is a supernatural end of man, eternal life.[18]

The political part of the argument is Aristotelian enough, to be sure, and, plainly, John's object is to insist on the fact that the object of politics is fundamentally *moral,* and not simply material, as is suggested by much of the papalist argument.[19] Nevertheless, given the conclusion, it seems on its face to involve

---

[14] Thus the argument for the superiority of the mixed regimes only arises accidentally, as it were, occasioned by a papalist argument concerning the kings of Israel.

[15] *Tractatus* i. 177. 3–4.   [16] *Tractatus* i. 177. 9–10.

[17] *Tractatus* i. 177. 41.   [18] *Tractatus* ii. 178. 15–17.

[19] John returns to this point later, specifically raising the papalist argument that, since spiritual affairs are superior to bodily matters, the pope, having charge of the former, ought to control the king, who is in charge of the latter. He attacks the argument on a number of grounds. The first and most important point is a denial that politics aims at mere life. Its object is genuinely moral: the life according to virtue. He cites Aristotle to the effect that the object of the legislator is to make men good and to lead them to virtue and thus the legislator "has the care of souls." *Tractatus* xi. 203. 29–38 and xvii. 225. 26–34.

a Semi-Pelagian view of the relationship of nature and grace.[20] Nature seems to be self-perfecting without grace, so that grace merely confers on man an additional and higher end (as well as the means to it). The latter may "happen" to perfect nature, but nature is not in need of it. Inasmuch as what is at stake here is the whole relevance to man of the order of grace, of the good news and the influx of the spirit that proceed from the incarnate and risen Christ, any solution of the church-state question in the narrower sense of the juridical relations between ecclesiastical and political officers will be profoundly influenced by the more fundamental question.

Furthermore, it cannot be said that John of Paris was altogether unaware of the issue. A number of things make this quite clear. He includes among the papalist arguments that he lists and refutes the following from St. Augustine's *City of God* (ii. 21): "Without true justice it is impossible that a commonwealth be ruled. But there is no true justice where Christ is not founder and ruler." But the pope is the vicar of Christ, and therefore "has both [the spiritual and temporal] jurisdictions immediately from God."[21] He answers the argument by an interpretation of St. Augustine's views based on the book of excerpts from his works made by Prosper of Aquitaine.[22] I have seen no evidence that John of Paris knew of the Semi-Pelagian controversy, of Prosper's part in it, or of the second synod of Orange that condemned Semi-Pelagianism. In any case, John's paradoxical and perhaps even perverse interpretation of Augustine-via-Prosper is that there *can* indeed be true justice without Christ as founder

[20] Denziger, Bannwart, Umberg, *Enchiridion Symbolorum* (1937), 174–200.

[21] *Tractatus* xi. 204. 25–30.

[22] Migne, *Patrologia Latina*, t. LI. Dom Jean Leclercq decided (at *Tractatus* xviii. 229, n. 3) that, since John of Paris does not specify the passage in Prosper's book of sentences, it must be cap. vii at col. 428. There seems to be no reason to believe that John had only one passage in mind. A considerable number are relevant. The whole work is a summary of St. Augustine's views by his great champion against the Semi-Pelagians of Southern Gaul.

and ruler, although Christians would not act justly if they were not obedient to Christ's vicar in spirituals.[23]

The whole of John's response is singularly ambiguous in contrast to the argument of the papalists, which is thoroughly clear and distinct by virtue of converting the whole matter into a mere question of juridical structures. John's position can be read in a variety of ways. It can be taken as simply an unwitting Semi-Pelagian position. It can even be seen as an outgrowth of

[23] *Tractatus* xviii. 229. 22–35. Murray writes (*Cross Currents*, p. 53, n. 60) that John's argument "need not have a Semi-Pelagian sense (although, as is well known, the Second Council of Orange was curiously not familiar to medieval-writers). John of Paris recognizes the state's need of the Church, even 'that justice may be observed' (229. 34). He asserts too that 'the two swords are obliged to assist each other out of the common charity that unites all the members of the Church' (215. 26)." But Murray's argument is hardly convincing. His second quotation is not related to the problem directly enough to be decisive in itself. His first quotation is taken out of context. The full text of John's argument against the papalist interpretation of St. Augustine runs as follows: "The acquired moral virtues can be perfect without the theological virtues nor are the former perfected by the latter except by a certain accidental perfection, as Augustine intimates in the *Book of Sentences* of Prosper. And therefore, without Christ as founder and ruler, there is true and perfect justice such as a kingdom requires since a kingdom is ordered to life according to acquired moral virtue to which it happens [sometimes? always?] that it is perfected by further virtues [e.g., only acquired intellectual virtues?]. Or, Augustine says that there is not true justice there where Christ is not the foundation, not because it is impossible, but because there was not even acquired justice among those who thought to observe justice by serving demons and idols, against which Augustine says that they did not observe true justice [simply? or only in that respect?]. It can even be said that a commonwealth of Christian people is not ruled rightly unless the founder and ruler be the pope who is the vicar of Christ in spirituals nor would justice be observed otherwise except it [the commonwealth] be obedient to him in spirituals as is just." The least that can be said is that that is a curious Augustine and, whether Augustine or not, it is curiously unclear. It seems that only Christians absolutely require Christ as founder and ruler [*rector*] in order to have true justice. Why? Yet the pagans who served demons and idols did not have it or, in any case, not all of it. Why? By accident? Or is there an existentially necessary bond between Christ and true justice even though there is no formally necessary, or essential, connection? How so? On the grounds of a consequence of original sin? And if that were so, John's text would be inadequate insofar as it opposes an existentially irrelevant formal distinction to an argument based on the existential personal unity of Christ (in spite of formal distinctions) that inaugurates a new creation.

the influence on him of Latin Averroism.[24] In that case, it would be a moral equivalent of the speculative two-truths doctrine, although not, for John, as a cover for unbelief.

The root of the difficulty is that, while John of Paris wishes to work out a flexible and realistic set of juridical Church-state relations, he does not take the trouble to provide an equally flexible and realistic theological substructure. Pressed by the polemically charged circumstances of the moment, he enters the fray on marshy ground, attempting to establish an acceptable order out of the confusion without taking the trouble to divert the disputants to a drier and less confusing battlefield.

As it is, the serious problem of the nature of the Church is never clarified. There is the usual alternation between "the Church" taken as a whole company of believers and "the Church" taken as the ecclesiastical hierarchy with no theoretical explanation of their relationship. This is an inescapable problem inasmuch as, talking chiefly of political communities with a religiously homogeneous membership, he necessarily notices that the same body of men who have an ecclesiastical hierarchy also have a political hierarchy, and that those hierarchies interact. Since he admits the legitimacy[25] of their interaction, it is necessary to know the grounds on which that legitimacy is asserted. Since John, unfortunately like most writers on the subject, limits himself to the more obvious relationships that are of immediate polemical interest, it is necessary to follow his attempts to adjust the overt claims of each party and raise the pertinent theoretical questions as the argument proceeds.

His theme is developed as follows: beyond the good that man can achieve by nature, namely to live according to virtue, "man is ordained to a further, supernatural end, that is, eternal life." Were it possible to achieve this end "by the power of human

<hr />

[24] Cf., e.g., Alois Dempf, *Sacrum Imperium* (Munich and Berlin: 1929), pp. 422–430.

[25] Cf., e.g., *Tractatus* xiii. 214. 1–36.

nature," the direction of men to that end would necessarily belong to the office of the king. This not being possible, there is need for "some one" to lead men to it. And this is Christ, Who is called a king by Jeremiah [Jer 23:5].[26]

But, since Christ was to withdraw His bodily presence from the Church, "it was necessary for him to institute some ministers" of the sacraments. Thus priesthood, unlike kingship, or political rule in general, is from the divine law and not from the natural law. Thus, he defines priesthood as "the spiritual power of a minister of the church conferred by Christ for dispensing the sacraments to the faithful."[27] Thus the root of priestly power is purely spiritual: the dispensation of the sacraments and especially the Eucharist.[28]

John immediately follows this[29] definition with a discussion of the need for a single chief minister in the Church and of the lack of necessity for all *princes* in the world to be under *one* chief. Although he gives a rational justification of papal supremacy,[30] his chief argument is biblical.[31] The ministers of the

---

[26] *Tractatus* ii. 178. 16–28. [27] *Tractatus* ii. 179. 20–21.

[28] Cf. Scholz, *Die Publizistik*, p. 304. Cf. also Journet, *The Church of the Word Incarnate*, vol. 1, pp. 21–25, 30–31, 493–495.

[29] In cap. iii. [30] *Tractatus* 179. 26–180. 9.

[31] He cites Ap 21:3; Osee 1:11; Jn 10:16; and especially the *Pasce oves* text, Jn 21:17, and Lk 22:32: "And thou being once converted, confirm thy brethren." Yet it should be noticed, as Scholz points out (*Die Publizistik*, p. 302), that John of Paris writes (*Tractatus* x. 199. 34–35): "But the power of prelates (Scholz reads: "inferior prelates") is not from God by the mediation of the pope but [from God] immediately, and from the people by election or by consent," citing Mt 10; Lk 10; Jn 20:21–23; Gal 1:1, 11–12, 17–18. Cf. Journet, *The Church of the Word Incarnate*, vol. 1, pp. 403–405. Scholz further argues (*Die Publizistiik*, pp. 302–303) that John of Paris subsequently limited this to the episcopacy in a later writing: *Determinatio de confessionibus fratrum* (cf. Grabmann, *Studien zu Johannes Quidort von Paris O. Pr.*, pp. 19–21). The Gallican possibilities are obvious. Cf. also Leclercq, *Jean de Paris*, pp. 117–131. Scholz writes (*Die Publizistik*, p. 306): "It is significant that John in the *De confessionibus* has again a more strongly hierarchic notion of the primacy [of the pope] than in the tract *De potestate regia*." In the former (a later work), he defends a papal grant of power to the mendicant orders to hear confessions without prior permis-

Church, then, are ordered to one by "divine statute." "However, the faithful laity do not so have it from divine law that they be under one supreme monarch in temporals: but by a natural instinct [*instinctu*], which is from God, they tend to live civilly and in community, and, as a consequence, to elect diverse rulers with a view to living well in common, but in accordance with the diversity of communities." And the laity are impelled to be under one supreme monarch in temporals "neither by natural inclination nor by divine law."[32] He gives four reasons.

The first is that men differ by virtue of their bodies,[33] and "so the secular power has greater diversity according to the diversity of climates and bodily constitutions than does the spiritual power, which varies less in such things."

Second, the spiritual power can easily extend itself to the whole world, "since it is verbal." Not so the "sword of the temporal power . . . since it is manual: for it is easier to extend a word than a hand."

Third, "the temporalities of laymen are not communal . . . but anyone is master of his own things so far as they are acquired by his own industry; therefore, the temporalities of the laity do not stand in need of a common steward, since anyone is the steward of his own things at will." This individualistic remark is followed by the contrast with the Church: "But ecclesiastical goods are joined to the community." The contrast is somewhat softened by the conclusion: "That is to say, it is not so fitting that some one be set over the whole world with respect to the

---

sion from the local secular clergy. (Cf. Grabmann, *Studien zu Johannes Quidort von Paris O. Pr.,* pp. 19–21.) Murray judges that "the Gallican touches were accidental to his system and readily separable from its substance (such, for instance, as his suggestions in regard of the relation between Pope and General Council, and on the deposition of the pope)," in *Cross Currents,* p. 25.

[32] *Tractatus* iii. 180. 25–32.

[33] But not by virtue of their souls "all which are constituted in essentially the same rank because of the unity of the human species."

temporalities of laymen, as it is with respect to the temporalities of clerics."[34]

Fourth, all the faithful must come together in one Catholic faith, without which there is no salvation. The unity of faith requires "that there be one superior in spirituals by whose judgment controversies are ended." Such unity, however, is not necessary in political matters. For the faithful laymen, "there can be diverse modes of living and diverse polities, according to the diversity of climates and languages and conditions of men, and what is virtuous in one nation is not so in another, as even concerning individual persons the Philosopher says, in *Ethics* ii [6. 1106ª24–1106ᵇ9], that something that is little for one may be too much for others."[35]

It will be noted first that his arguments strike at the heart of the direct power theory insofar as it converted a metaphysical understanding of unity directly into an operative political principle, with the result that the pope was the source of political power. But his arguments also act as a possible groundwork for a justification of the French King's independence of the Emperor. This averts what might be called a flank attack on the independence of the French King by making him subject to the Emperor, and thence to the Pope, since the Emperor was generally recognized as having some kind of special relation of subordination to the Pope.[36]

Second, John points out in the next chapter that kingship is prior in time to priesthood. Nevertheless, the priestly power is greater than the royal power, and exceeds it in dignity because of the superiority of the end it pursues. For the end of kingship

---

[34] *Tractatus* iii. 180. 35–181. 14.   [35] *Tractatus* iii. 181. 15–25.

[36] This possibility is also ruled out by John of Paris, since he says in another place that, the pope having requested the exercise, by the emperor, of the secular jurisdiction "because of some necessity of the spiritual good," and "if nevertheless he [the emperor] will not do it or if it does not seem expedient to him, the pope cannot do anything else" (*Tractatus* x. 200. 25–28).

is that the "congregated multitude live according to virtue." But the end of the priestly power is the "enjoyment of God."[37]

But, though the priesthood is greater in dignity and greater simply than kingship, insofar as the things of the spirit are greater than temporal things, nevertheless it is not greater in all things. To say that it is greater in all things would be as ridiculous as to say that, "because a doctor of letters or an instructor ordains everyone in the household to a nobler end, namely to the knowledge of the truth, therefore even the physician, who regards a lower end, namely the health of bodies, should be subject to him with regard to his medicinal preparations."[38] This is so because the secular power does not have its source in the spiritual power, "but both flow immediately from one supreme power, namely God." In short, "the priest is greater than the prince in spirituals, and, conversely, the prince is greater in temporals."[39]

John then approaches the problem in another way. He speaks

[37] *Tractatus* v. 183. 36–184. 2. Thus making it doubly clear that John of Paris recognizes the moral function of government as Murray argues (*Cross Currents*, p. 28), though the examples in cap. i and the arguments in cap. iii largely refer to economic or military considerations. His reply to the twentieth argument fully confirms this view (*Tractatus* xvii. 225. 26–226. 10).

[38] *Tractatus* v. 184. 15–31.

[39] *Tractatus* v. 184. 23–24, 31–32. Among the heathen, the priests are rightly subordinated to the kings, because those priesthoods and their cults are for the sake of temporal goods. Thus the king, who has the care of the whole common temporal good, rules the priests, who have the care of but a part. And even under the old law, "priesthood was less noble than the royal power, because the king was not directed by the priests to any higher good than that of the multitude the care of which was incumbent upon him" (*Tractatus* 184. 38–185. 7). It should be noted, as Scholz points out (*Die Publizistik*, p. 288), that this last section of cap. v (184. 37–185. 22) is an almost literal transcription of the end of cap. 14, bk. i of *De regimine principum* by St. Thomas Aquinas. But John does not reproduce the immediately preceding statement by St. Thomas: to the Roman pontiff "all kings of the Christian people ought to be subject, as to the Lord Jesus Christ himself. For those who are concerned with the subordinate ends of life should be subject to him who is concerned with the supreme end and be directed by his command."

first of external ecclesiastical goods: "The pope is not the possessor [*dominus*] of all ecclesiastical goods generally, just as neither are inferior prelates such with respect to the goods of their societies [*collegii*]." This is so because "ecclesiastical goods, as such, are assigned [*collata sunt*] to communities and not to single persons," and this applies to persons as public persons also. "And thus, no single person has property and dominion in ecclesiastical goods, but only the community [has such]." Nevertheless, "there is some member who is the chief and head of the community, such as the bishop . . . but he has the administration and general stewardship of all the goods of the community." With respect to the whole Church, "the pope is the universal distributor and steward of [ecclesiastical] goods."[40]

This stewardship does not cover the external goods of laymen. Here, the pope is not even steward. But John makes one great reservation: the pope is not steward of the external goods of laymen, "except perhaps in an extreme necessity of the Church, but even in such necessity, he is not the steward, but the revealer of the right [*juris declarator*]." The pope is not steward because the goods of the laity, unlike those of the Church, are not held in common:

. . . but they are acquired by single persons by art, labor, or individual diligence, and single persons, as such, have right, power, and true dominion in them, and of his own things anyone can arrange, dispose, distribute, retain, and alienate at will without injury to another, since he is the owner. And therefore, such goods do not have an order and connection among themselves, nor to one common head whose it is to arrange or distribute them, since anyone is the disposer [*ordinator*] of his own things at will. And thus, neither the prince nor the pope has dominion or stewardship in such things.[41]

[40] *Tractatus* vi. 185. 25–188. 6.
[41] *Tractatus* vii. 189. 13–30. This passage should not be understood as a doctrine of absolute private property, as John makes clear in the following paragraph. Among other things, the prince acts as the measurer "in taking goods from individuals according to a just proportion for the common need or utility."

If there are any who refuse what is called for in such a papal declaration of right that distributes the burdens of meeting a necessity of the Church, then they may be "compelled," but only "by ecclesiastical censure."[42] In other circumstances, where such a necessity of the Church does not exist, the pope can do no more than "give indulgences to the faithful for giving aid" to him from their external goods.[43]

But at this stage of the argument, it is clear that, having begun by affirming the moral content and end of politics, John of Paris has shifted to a central concern with "external goods," and these chiefly material (there are, of course, external goods that are not material, e.g., one's good name[44]), as well as those immaterial external goods that are intimately connected with material goods. The shift is understandable, but unfortunate. John is obviously concerned to limit arbitrary papal taxation. Therefore, he defines papal power in this regard strictly in accordance with a common need. That is to say, the papal power springs from an office, a duty the pope has to perform for the commonweal, rather than from a right he holds for his own aggrandizement. But to effect this end, John emphasizes the individualistic element in human ownership of material goods, and assimilates all temporal goods of laymen to this standard. Politics, by default, as it were, thus seems to be concerned chiefly with the judgment of disputes about material property.[45] The remainder and chief bulk of the work (nineteen of twenty-five chapters) is formally concerned with the question of what sort of power the pope has over the external goods of laymen understood in this relatively narrow context. Thus, no distinction of species is made between a clearly political action, such as depo-

[42] *Tractatus* vii. 189. 30–190. 6. The only necessity he specifically mentions is an "invasion of pagans" (189. 36).

[43] *Tractatus* vii. 189. 14–18.

[44] John even mentions "secular honor" in *Tractatus* xiii. 214. 15.

[45] E.g., *Tractatus* viii. 190. 22–27; xiii. 214. 37–39.

sition of a king, and an economic action, such as usury.[46] The reason for this assimilation of what he starts out by distinguishing appears to lie in his objective. The papalists had asserted the universal lordship and even ownership of everything by the pope. John of Paris is, therefore, concerned to defend the multiplicity of particular lordships, or masteries, or ownerships of particular goods, material or moral, against their evacuation in favor of the papal overlord. So he devises a polemical strategy whereby both sorts of particular mastery may be defended together, since to defend political lordship but permit the pope to take away the lord's landholdings would be patently absurd under the circumstances. Thus, the bulk of his work consists of a set of answers to a list of forty-two arguments for universal papal jurisdiction in external temporal goods, including thrones and kingdoms. However, this procedure, whatever its polemical advantages, has a serious drawback in that it does not focus attention on the ultimate center of the problem: the relationship of the ecclesiastical and political hierarchies in the authoritative judgment and decision about moral action by the political community. This can best be seen by following the overall structure of John's counter-argument.

Before launching into his detailed treatment of papalist arguments, John presents an analysis of priestly power in general in order to discover which, if any, priestly powers are relevant to

---

[46] *Tractatus* xiii. 214. An historical interpretation of the text might argue that this is simply a reflection of the union of economic and political arrangements under a feudal hierarchy. It may very well be true that that is what John had in mind. But it is also true that John is quite capable of thinking in other contexts. His defense of private property takes the form of an individualistic labor theory (*Tractatus* vii. 189. 14–23), which is hardly reflective of feudal economic relations. Secondly, John himself specifically draws attention to the classical distinction between the material and moral objects of a common life and, on that basis, distinguishes between household and village, on one hand, and the city or kingdom, on the other. He refers, of course, to the first book of Aristotle's *Politics*. Therefore, it is clear that John is quite capable of going beyond his feudal environment both on the broadest theoretical level and on the level of specific institutions.

his problem. This analysis must, of course, be strictly theological. Arguments concerning the origin, nature, functions, limits, and end of the temporal power are not in themselves decisive. The spiritual or priestly power is the result of a specific divine act in history, an act that modified, among other things, the relationship of priests to kings.[47] Therefore, arguments about the political do not, taken by themselves, afford adequate solutions. It is necessary to counterbalance them, so to speak, with an analysis of the spiritual power in order to show what modifications, if any, must be made in the conclusions of political philosophy.

So it is not enough for John to reply to the papalists that "there were kings in France before there were Christians,"[48] or that to live in civil society is a thing natural to man. It is necessary, in addition, to discover whether nature is destroyed or superseded by grace, or whether it is, rather, perfected by it, and, if so, how. Therefore, he makes an analysis of the spiritual power that is decisive in his total argument. Murray notes its broad outline:

It begins with the general definition that had been laid down at the outset, that "the priesthood is nothing else but the spiritual power granted to ministers of the Church for the dispensation of the sacraments which contain the grace whereby we are set on the way to eternal life." (*Tractatus* xii. 207. 37–208. 2.) His concern is to show that this power is singly and solely spiritual in character; and he does this by an analysis of it into its five component powers. (*Tractatus* 208. 9–211. 21.) These are the consecration of the sacramental matter by the power of orders; the administration of the sacraments, especially

[47] Cf. *supra*, p. 104, n. 39. Murray e.g., admits the same thing in broader terms: "a part of the *minoratio naturae* effected by the introduction of the supernatural was a diminution of the power that the state would, or might, have had in an economy of pure nature." "For the Freedom and Transcendence of the Church," *American Ecclesiastical Review*, vol. CXXVI (January, 1952), p. 28, n. 1. Cf. also his "On the Structure of the Church-State Problem," *The Catholic Church in World Affairs*, eds. Waldemar Gurian and M.A. Fitzsimons (Notre Dame: 1954), p. 12.

[48] *Tractatus* x. 199. 21–22.

of penance—the absolution from sin in the forum of conscience by the power of the keys; the preaching of the gospel by "the authority of the apostolate"; the imposition of penalties in the external forum by "the judicial power" or coercive power; and the distribution of ecclesiastical offices and faculties by the power of jurisdiction. To these is added a sixth power, that of requiring from the faithful what is necessary for the support of the spiritual minister of the Church.[49]

"Now let us see what power bishops and priests have in temporalities and over princes from the powers committed to them, and it seems that from none of the said powers do they have direct power in temporalities or temporal jurisdiction, except that they can take those things necessary to the sustenance of life."[50]

The first two powers cause no difficulty. Both are "wholly spiritual." Their effects are produced wholly in the spiritual order. So, too, with the third. "Nevertheless, by this power of teaching, [bishops and priests] indirectly have a power in temporalities [*indirecte possunt in temporalibus*], inasmuch as they lead men to penance and the restitution of stolen property, and to the largesse of temporal goods in accordance with the demands of the order of charity."[51] This power is surely no more

---

[49] J.C.M., *Cross Currents,* p. 30.   [50] *Tractatus* xiii. 211. 25–29.

[51] *Tractatus* xiii. 212. 16–18. On this point, Murray remarks (in *Cross Currents,* pp. 31–32 and 54, n. 1); "Note that Quidort does not say that the Church has an 'indirect power,' but that the Church 'indirectly has a power,' which is more correct. It is not to be thought that the Church has two powers, one direct, the other indirect; actually she has only one power, which is purely spiritual, but which indirectly operates temporal effects. Some Catholic theologians reject the term, 'indirect power,' as a misnomer." Speaking of the consequences of such action, he writes: "These are temporal effects, but the power of the Church does not terminate at them directly; they are repercussions in the temporal order of an action which itself remains purely spiritual. Moreover, the action in question is authoritative, in such wise as to establish a connection between the spiritual effect and its temporal repercussion. Consequently, this action is a genuine means of directing the temporal processes, but a means proper to the order in which the Church exists, the spiritual order. The pope, says John of Paris, is 'the general teacher (*informator*) of faith and morals' (*Tractatus* vii. 189.

than what Charles Journet has described as the canonical or spiritual power "directed to the inspiration of the temporal,"[52] and it is a rather remote inspiration at that, since the pope does not instruct the prince "*de regimine*," even though the "earthly power . . . is directed to the blessed life by the spiritual power."[53]

But, be that as it may, "the whole difficulty concerns the fourth power: the power of judgment in the external forum."

John distinguishes two aspects of the power, "keys" as he calls them. The first is the authority of judging and the second is the power of coercing [*auctoritas discernendi seu cognoscendi* and *potestas cohercendi*]. But the Church's authority of judging is limited to "spiritual cases the which are called ecclesiastical," i.e., to cases of faith and morals, including the Church's own law, of course. In these, the prince has no competence. However, the cognizance of the ecclesiastical judge does not extend to temporal matters, except "by reason of delict" [*ratione delicti*]. And not any sort of delict, but only one that "is reduced to a spiritual and ecclesiastical crime." If the delict is temporal, it can only come into the cognizance of the ecclesiastical judge if the question is raised whether the temporal delict is licit or not "by divine law, according to which the ecclesiastical judge judges." But insofar as it is a question whether "human or civil laws" have been violated, then judgment pertains solely to the prince.[54]

As for the Church's direction of the temporal order by the power of coercing, it would seem to extend legitimately only to such cases of offense arising, directly or reductively, under the divine law. This would exclude from its scope papal coer-

---

32). That is all he is; he is not a sort of super-prince, as the hierocrats would have it." He goes on to say that "this teaching cannot be without effects on his princely rule, at the same time that it is no threat to his legitimate power."

[52] *The Church of the Word Incarnate,* vol. 1, p. 261.
[53] *Tractatus* xvii. 226. 1–10.   [54] *Tractatus* xiii. 212. 19–40.

cive power to force on a prince specific and licit courses of action judged by the pope to be necessary, in some way or other, to the salvation of souls.

But even within those limits, the interesting question concerns the means at the pope's disposal to exercise that power. John's answer to this question is the center of his whole solution to the relative powers of ecclesiastical and political authorities.

Ecclesiastical power in the public judgment of sin is, according to John,[55] directly spiritual only. This is so not only in terms of its end, but also in terms of the means at its disposal to compel compliance. The function of that power is "to lead men back to God and draw them away from sin and to correct them." To do that, the ecclesiastical judge has only the means given him by God, and those are: denial of the sacraments and denial of the company of the faithful to the recalcitrant sinner, and similar penalties.[56] John continues: indirectly and *per accidens,* the pope can procure the most important temporal political penalty of all. "If a prince were heretical and incorrigible and in contempt of ecclesiastical censure," the pope could excommunicate all who obeyed such a prince. Then the people would proceed to depose the prince. Thus, the prince would be deprived "of secular honor and deposed by the people" directly, but by the pope indirectly and *per accidens.*

There are difficulties in such a position and we shall turn to them presently, but John immediately follows it with a balancing procedure. The prince has a similar weapon. The prince can excommunicate and depose the pope indirectly and *per accidens!*[57] For if the pope were "criminal and were to

[55] The whole of the argument that follows is in *Tractatus* xiii. 214–216.

[56] He notes that ecclesiastical judges sometimes impose fines or corporal punishment. But he argues that they can only be imposed conditionally, i.e., if the sinner will accept them. If he will not, then only spiritual penalties can be imposed.

[57] Murray, who recapitulates John's argument here, omits all mention of this bit of the text (*Cross Currents,* p. 33).

scandalize the Church and were incorrigible" even after the prince had warned him, either directly or through the cardinals, then the emperor could impose material and bodily penalties on one and all to prevent them from obeying and following the incumbent as pope. The people then would depose the pope and elect a new one.[58]

So far, this double power of deposition refers to ecclesiastical crimes, e.g., heresy on the part of the king and giving scandal on the part of the pope.[59] In both cases, "the people" are the intermediaries. But John then raises the equally important question of crimes against the law of the state. If "the king were to sin in secular matters, cognizance of which does not pertain to the ecclesiastical judge, then the pope would not be the one to correct him at first, but rather the barons and peers of the realm; and if they could not or dared not, they could call for aid from the Church; then the pope, called by the

[58] There is a special question concerning the use of *"princeps"* and *"imperator"* in the text. Sometimes, as here, he uses both in the same sentence as if they were interchangeable. But he makes it clear that only the emperor has a universal jurisdiction. And he elsewhere speaks of the imperial authority as if it were not in existence *de facto*. And he devotes considerable skill to proving that it is not naturally desirable to have one (cf., e.g., *Tractatus* iii; xiii. 214. 24–26; 39–40). This cannot be attributed to mere sloppiness on John's part. Like Marsilius, John has practical reasons that make an imperial authority both desirable and undesirable. To admit the imperial authority is to subordinate the King of France to the Emperor, and then the whole question centers around that, ultimately spurious, point of the donation of Constantine. Therefore John, like King Philip the Fair, denies it (cf. Carlyle, *HMPT,* vol. 5, p. 375). But, in attempting to construct a countervailing power in the political authority to check the Pope, the Emperor seemed a far more likely candidate than anyone else, because he alone among sesular rulers has "universal jurisdiction" as does the pope. In any case, I do not think that John's full position on imperial authority, if he had one, can be satisfactorily established from the text, because it is only peripherally concerned with the question. Thus, any attempt at a reconstruction could hardly rank as more than a somewhat exotic amusement.

[59] Other examples given of papal spiritual delict are "conferring benefices symoniacally, scattering the churches, depriving ecclesiastical persons and chapters of their rights, or pronouncing or teaching wickedly about those things that pertain to faith or good morals" (*Tractatus* xiii. 215. 17–20).

peers to support the law, could warn him and proceed against him in the way already mentioned." And if the pope break the civil law, the emperor has the primary power to correct him "by warning and secular punishment."[60]

John consistently follows this interpretation in a great variety of cases involving imperial action against the pope and papal action against kings and emperors. The way in which he envisions its concrete application can be seen in his treatment of the famous deposition of Childeric.[61] The papalists claimed that Pope Zachary had deposed Childeric, the last of the Merovingians, and put in his place as king, Pepin, the ancestor of Charlemagne. They took this as a precedent for papal power over thrones in general and the French throne in particular. But John argues that that is a great distortion of the reality. According to him, the facts of the case are that Childeric was a wholly incompetent king whose realm was actually governed by Pepin, who was called mayor of the palace. The barons of the realm wished to transfer the royal dignity to him who actually bore the burden of ruling, but were hesitant about the rightness of such an action. Hence, they asked the Pope to advise them about their doubts in the matter. The Pope thereupon advised them that this was a licit course of action. John urges all this as a matter of history, supported by the *Glossa ordinaria* on the *Decretals* and by Martin's *Chronicle*. But then he points out that the peers could have done all that without any reference to the Pope, since that is quite within their proper powers,

[60] It seems that, when the pope breaks the civil law, the emperor may punish the pope directly and at once. But, when the pope is guilty of some ecclesiastical crime, it seems that there is a distribution of responsibilities similar to the case in which the king or emperor breaks the civil law. In such a case, the cardinals, "who stand in place of the whole clergy," should attempt to correct the pope first. Only if they fail should they call upon the emperor's aid. And it seems that the emperor should only act when summoned by the cardinals (cf. *Tractatus* xiii. 214. 20–21 and 215. 17–24).

[61] *Tractatus* xi. 202. 17–18, 28–30; xiv. 218. 34–220. 28; xv. 222. 32–223. 6.

which, as he had already established, are not derived from the pope.[62]

As for the further argument that the Pope in this case absolved all the Frenchmen who bore arms from their oath to the King, John gives a whole battery of replies. Aware of the scarcity of full historical data on the affair, he prefaces his remarks by saying that whatever the Pope may in fact have done proves nothing about what he may do legitimately. He then undertakes a double reply. The first is historical and the second theoretical. He says that the Pope's action in this case had the character of a declaration of right to the effect that an oath did not bind in such a case, rather than the character of an absolution from the oath. In any event, it seems to have been done with the consent of the King, who was perhaps aware of his ineptitude as king and who wanted to enter a monastery. Naturally, the possibility of dispute about so ancient a case is almost unlimited. So John reconsiders the matter theoretically.

A vassal, he says, is doubly bound to his lord: by reason of the *quid pro quo* involved in the feudal relationship, and by reason of his oath. With respect to these, the pope can free

[62] Actually, the nature of the case seems to have been quite different. Childeric held his kingdom by a title rooted in pre-Christian Germanic view of sacred kingship. He held a religiously understood "blood-right" to his throne that showed itself in his long hair, a manifestation of his special and mysterious connection with the divine source of rule and order. Therefore, before daring to tamper with this ancient folk-belief, the barons, now Christians, appealed to the chief priest of the new religion for assurance about their proposal to violate the rules of the old religion which the Pope, of course, regarded as mere superstition. It is indicative of their feeling that they didn't simply cut off the royal-sacred long hair of the last of the Merovingian dynasty. John of Paris points out that Childeric received the tonsure and entered a monastery (*Tractatus* xiv. 219. 12–13), i.e., the barons not only got the Pope's approval first, but they got a monk to do the deed of shearing the king of his hair and thereby of his kingdom. Neither John of Paris nor the papalists seem to have understood this part of the case to which they both appealed. For a treatment of the problem in a broader context, cf. Fritz Kern, *Kingship and Law in the Middle Ages*, trans. S.B. Chrimes (Oxford: 1948), pp. 1–68.

114

the vassal from the divine bond of the oath for a reasonable and evident cause, and, secondly, the pope can declare that in such and such a case a vassal is not bound to follow his lord —if, for example, his lord is a heretic—but ought to free himself from his obligation by returning his fief. That is to say, quite aside from the presence or absence of the religious obligation of the oath, the vassal is naturally bound to follow his lord as long as he continues to hold that which the lord gave him in return for his service. Plainly, the argument is not altogether congruent with the earlier treatment, and John separates the two parts, putting this part of it in a different chapter, even though both refer to the same case. In his first treatment, the vassals expelled the lord from his lordship, which is quite another matter from resigning their fief. There is also a switch in reference to the cause of action from incompetence to heresy. Speaking of the pope's power earlier, he had said that the pope could induce the people (as organized for action by the magnates of the realm) to depose an obstinately heretical king. Now he seems to suggest rather that they have to return their fiefs to him in order to be free of his rule. But if they were genuinely to return them to him, he could grant them to others, which, in this case, would mean that the whole people would have to leave the kingdom and be replaced by others. This is simply preposterous. What, then, can John mean by this curious shifting back and forth?

In his search for a middle way, John of Paris seems obscurely to apprehend a theoretical problematic that he is unable to articulate in the context of the practical problem of the relationship of ecclesiastical and political officers. He does not perceive a way of formulating the relationship of nature and grace so as to structure a solution to his practical objective. The best he can do, therefore, is to attempt to bring to the concrete juridical elements of the case a set of recommendations springing from an affectively grounded but theoretically blind prac-

115

tical wisdom. Inasmuch as he cannot discover an adequate theoretic measure that he can illumine and communicate discursively, he resorts to a substitute: in place of the universal, theoretical measure, he settles for the measured as a surrogate. That is to say, he attempts to secure measure through an immediate balancing of the diverse claims of the ecclesiastical and political organizations of human life. For this reason, his position is at once both suggestive and inadequate.

His basic solution is to provide for the mutual checking of one set of offices by another. The object of this is to provide a remedy for abuse of authority in either hierarchy, political or ecclesiastical. This seems to be justified for him by the fact that both sets of offices are within the Church, "Church" [Ecclesia] being understood as the assembly of believers. Kings and emperors, on the one hand, and popes, on the other, rightly interfere in one another's affairs because they are all members of the Church, and are, therefore, bound to one another by a bond of charity which includes a mandate to help depose the other when he abuses his power.[63]

To the obvious question why there are two hierarchies, political and ecclesiastical, within the same assembly of believers, John gives a double response. The same people have a double end: the life of natural human perfection and eternal life. To

---

[63] *Tractatus* xiii. 215. 23–26; xxiv–xxv. And when it is not a question of charity, it may be a matter of legitimate self-defense. John gives an example. The papalists said that the pope could free a bishop from the command of his prince if the prince wishes the bishop to remain at home when the pope calls him to the curia. But John replies that, as long as the bishop holds a fief from the prince, the prince may licitly compel him to stay. And, quite aside from the question of fiefs, if the prince discovers that the pope has called the bishop in order to engage in treasonous machinations against the prince, then the prince can repel this danger to the commonwealth in the way appropriate to his sword, i.e., by force. And if he on whom the care of the commonwealth rests could not do so, "he would bear the sword without reason" (*Tractatus* 238. 1–239. 24). This is a plain defense of King Philip's arrest of the Bishop of Pamiers in spite of the insistence of Boniface VIII that he be freed to come to Rome. See Carlyle, *HMPT*, vol. 5, p. 384.

each end there corresponds a set of governing institutions, which come to a point respectively in the pope and the king, or emperor if there be one. Further, each is to be distinguished from the other by the nature of the ultimate instruments each may legimately use in procuring obedience to the imperatives he serves. Thus, the pope's sword consists in ecclesiastical censure, i.e., it is wholly spiritual. The sword of a king or emperor is literally a sword. It is, as John of Paris puts it, "manual."[64]

But it immediately becomes clear that both pope and prince pursue both ends because they are, at one and the same time, men and believers. It furthermore appears that their jurisdictions overlap, for the pope, as pope, is concerned with sin and virtue according to the divine law, according to revelation, but that includes many matters also subject to natural and human law. Thus, to use an example that John raises, usury is against nature, and therefore is sometimes a subject of human legislation. But it pertains to the pope to proscribe it as sin against the divine law. Thus, the question arises: what if pope and king disagree on such a common matter? John seems to wish, on occasion, that no such question could arise. The easiest way to prevent it from arising is to insist that each exercises jurisdiction over a quite separate and distinct subject matter. Indeed, John sometimes writes as if this were the case, and this is in conformity with his seeming Semi-Pelagianism.[65] But he does not follow up such a line. He knows that genuine disputes can and will arise. Perhaps it is true that the pope does not instruct the prince *de regimine,* but it must also be true that it is the office of the pope to tell the prince which of his actions will win him salvation and which damnation. And thus John finds it quite reasonable for the French barons to call in the pope to clarify their consciences when action against the king is

---

[64] *Tractatus* iii. 181. 5.
[65] *Tractatus* xvii. 226. 1–3, but cf. xiii. 212. 28–40.

proposed. May not the king, in like manner, call in the pope to clarify his conscience when contemplating action against rebellious barons? And if king or barons set themselves to perform some great sin against justice, must the pope be silent? May he not condemn it, if he is to perform the duties of his office? Must he remain silent until he is legally called in by some party to the dispute? That would only be sensible if both parties were free to invoke the papal protection. But an opponent can be silenced, intimidated, arrested, as was the Bishop of Pamiers.

In short, there will be disputes, even violent ones. John is quite aware of it and he has armed both parties. He is also afraid that, being armed, they will use their weapons too quickly, too immoderately, too imprudently. Thus, the next question in his dialectic of balancing offices and powers is: how to moderate the powers that he has distributed to the ecclesiastical and political hierarchies? His solution is to provide both of them with a constitutional structure that tends to exclude extremism. The political hierarchy ought to be that of a mixed regime, for this is the best way to moderate a political system. There ought to be a king to preside over all, some sort of senate of the best men as an element of aristocracy, and an element of democracy in that the rulers are elected from and by all the people. But also, "such would certainly be the best regime for the Church, if under one pope others were elected from and by each region, so that in the regime of the Church each would have his share in some way."[66] But even if this were the case, there might still be great disputes. Although it might seem that the people would exercise an identical influence on both hierarchies chosen from and by them, this would not necessarily be the case unless there were an empire co-extensive with the Church. But John objects to a universal empire, and, if there be no empire, then Church and state rest

[66] *Tractatus* xix. 236. 21–237. 14.

on distinct and different electorates.[67] Thus, he considers the possibility that the Pope might declare that all are heretics who deny that the King of France is subject to him in temporals.

Should something of that sort happen, all should try to find some sane meaning to his words. If he insists on an untraditional and harmful sense, then it should be borne patiently as far as can be without grave danger to justice and truth. And all should have prayerful recourse to God, Who holds the pope's heart in His hand just as He does the king's. But if there be danger to the commonwealth in such a procedure, if the pope abuses his power and frightens or otherwise moves the people to evil opinions and to rebellion, if the pope refuses to desist, then the Church ought to be moved against the pope by the king. The king can repel papal abuse by his own sword, although he should act with moderation. In such resistance, the king does not act against the pope as pope, but rather the king acts against his enemy and the enemy of the commonwealth. And to do this is not to act against the Church, but for it.[68]

[67] It should be pointed out that John of Paris, unlike Marsilius of Padua, does not regard ecclesiastical jurisdiction as a mere matter of human, political contrivance. This is clear from his analysis of sacerdotal power in chapter xii and xiii. With respect to the election of the pope, he specifically notes that the papal office and authority are from God alone and it is only man's function to elect this or that man to the office (*Tractatus* xxv. 255. 3–20). A Semi-Pelagian sense might also be attributed to his argument in this connection.

[68] *Tractatus* xxii. 250. 7–251. 7. Despite all this, Murray chooses to regard John of Paris as a defender of the popular origin of sovereignty and, more curious still, to make the following remarks: "There is his clear realization that *sacerdotium* and *regnum* are not merely two powers, two functions, within a unitary society; rather, each has place within a distinct *society*. John of Paris does not think of the Church in terms of that total religio-political entity which was so frequently covered by the term in the medieval writers and later even in Bellarmine. Rather, he posits two distinct unities, each created by its own principles and in its own order. And he keeps the unity of the Church in an order transcendent to that in which the political unity of the *regnum* exists" (*Cross Currents*, p. 34). It is true, as Murray then says, that for John of Paris there is a distinction of ends for the two and therefore a certain normal autonomy of each. But this springs from the Semi-Pelagian character of his treatment of the hierarchy

In short, John of Paris attempts to provide a set of constitutional arrangements that will be most likely to avert a tyrannical abuse of authority in either Church or state. Under reasonably fortunate circumstances, this should avert those profoundly dangerous hostile confrontations between Church and state with which the Middle Ages abound. However, when such a confrontation occurs, John will have done his best to provide each with a powerful set of weapons neither of which, although different, are sure of victory in advance. There is, no doubt, a great deal of practical wisdom and a rather cool-eyed assessment of the events of his time behind his recommendations, but a number of fundamental difficulties remain.

To begin with, John of Paris doesn't even attempt to show that Aristotle's arguments in favor of a mixed regime in the state apply to the regime of the Church. It does not even seem to occur to him that, however valuable such knowledge of human structures may be, it is absurd to apply it to the Church without first clarifying the limits within which human prudence as distinguished from divine ordinance may determine the structure of the Church. Murray to the contrary notwithstanding,[69] John of Paris sometimes treats the Church as if its struc-

---

of ends. Nevertheless, if the pope scandalize the Church or if he teach heresy, it is the political ruler who, at the head of his armies if necessary, deposes the pope and secures the election of a new one (*Tractatus* xiii. 215. 17–216. 4).

[69] *Cross Currents,* p. 35 and especially n. 101, in which he admits that John of Paris does what he [Murray] has said John of Paris does not do. He says that John refuses to pattern political rule directly on the divinely established universal monarchy of the Church. And he attributes this to John's understanding that Church and state are two distinct societies with different principles appropriate to both. Then, in the note, he admits that John attempts to pattern the Church on the reason-established mixed regime of the best state. He excuses this as a consequence of a "misunderstanding of the text of his master, St. Thomas (*Summa Theol.,* I-II, q. 105, a. 1)." It is difficult to see how Murray regards it as a "misunderstanding of the text." John adopts St. Thomas' argument almost verbatim, applies it to the polity, as does St. Thomas, and then also applies it to the Church, about which St. Thomas says nothing whatever in that place.

ture and action could be quite satisfactorily established in quite the same way that that is done for the state. Thus, he sometimes considers the problem of ecclesiastical structure and action in the following purely rational fashion: the ecclesiastical ministry has an end, the salvation of souls, by bringing them to the grace of Christ and away from sin; but to exercise such functions, as can be seen, it needs a certain structure and powers; therefore, it must have such a structure and powers in order to avoid absurdity.[70]

If this were all that John said about the matter, one would have to call his doctrine Pelagian. It is, of course, not all that he says on it,[71] but the reason why his doctrine has that flavor is illuminating. The whole of the argument concerning the hierarchy of ends, whether cast in a papalist or a moderate form, is fundamentally philosophical. It rests on a set of observations about the physical universe, in which there is said to be a hierarchic causal relationship between the sun and the moon, for example;[72] and it rests on a set of observations about the moral universe, in which it is seen that there are superior and inferior arts such that one rules another, as the physician does the pharmacist.[73] But the philosophically derived analogies inevitably produce a radical distortion when they are referred to the Church. In the case of the physical universe, the hierarchy begins at god seen as the first cause of a system of natures that also has god as its end, but only in the sense that its extreme and perfected operation constitutes a glorious manifestation or aura of the creative puissance of the self-caused one. In the case of the philosophically perceived moral universe, it too begins at god seen as first cause of a system of intelligences.

[70] Cf., e.g., *Tractatus* x. 199. 7–31.

[71] Cf., e.g., *Tractatus* ii. There his orthodoxy is clear.

[72] Cf. Giles of Rome, *D.E.P.* iii. 10. 196–197, and John of Paris *Tractatus* xi. 203. 29–38; xvii. 225. 26–226. 10.

[73] Cf. *Tractatus* xi. 204. 4–12; xvii. 226. 35–227. 41., and Giles of Rome, *D.E.P.* ii. 10. 90–92.

And they also have god for their end, but, again, only in the sense of their constituting what might be imagined as a series of diminishingly bright reflections of the divine self-knowledge. Furthermore, although the final object of the created system of intelligences is "the god of the philosophers," god is perceived as cause; that is to say, god is perceived through things, as related to things. And, finally, god is apprehended by human thought without any further self-revelation on god's part other than what is implied in creation itself. This reveals the degree to which it is useless to refer to the Church analogies derived from the order of the stars or of the arts.

The work of the priesthood is not to perfect the order of nature (physical, moral, or intellectual), even though it may have important consequences for that perfection. John of Paris realizes this at many parts of his argument. Thus, in replying to the thirty-second papalist argument which was based on the notion of a hierarchy of ends structuring a hierarchy of arts: "it is not true that the pope is master and lord [dominus] of spiritual things, for he is wholly a servant [minister]."[74] This is the necessary key to the whole question of sacerdotal function vis-à-vis that of the statesman. The priest must always be seen first as an instrument of the divine self-revelation in the Christian sense. The philosopher is the representative of man who becomes a divine microcosm in grasping that divine self-revelation that is the created universe. But the priest is not first of all a representative of the human species grasping god. He is first of all a representative of God Who leads man out of time, out of creation, into eternity, by virtue of revealing to man His own inner life, first through a glass darkly, and then face to face. If this is the first moment of the priestly function, then the use of human organizational hierarchies or cosmic hierarchies as analogues of the priest's relationship to the polity will be radically false. There is a sense in which one can say

[74] Tractatus xix. 234. 10–12. He cites 1 Cor 4:1.

that a people has been saved from some great defeat or disaster by a great leader in their midst. But one cannot say, in the same sense, that the people of God are saved by the pope or the clergy, however necessary their ministrations.

The priest, of course, also ritually represents the reception of the divine self-revelation by the people of God, and in this way acts as representative and minister of the people, but this is not the primary root of his dignity. Furthermore, as minister of God and as minister of the people, he acts sacramentally or ritually. But, having said that, a host of questions arise that John of Paris and medieval theology do not adequately answer.

Are the power of orders and the power of jurisdiction separate powers, or are they merely different aspects of the same power? John of Paris sometimes speaks of a fivefold and sometimes of a twofold priestly power, but it seems that all depend on the power of dispensing the sacraments.[75] Put otherwise, is the priestly power wholly spiritual in the sense that its work, even when preaching the gospel and judging between sin and virtue, is utterly sacramental? In that case, jurisdictional power would be seen as simply serving that sacramental, mystical, and ritual power.[76] If that were so, then jurisdictional power would belong only to priests, and this seems to be what John of Paris assumes, since he does not speak of it as being in the hands of laymen.

But, having said that, a far deeper problem comes into view, one that John of Paris does not seem to see. Laymen, too, have a priestly character by virtue of baptism and confirmation. By analogy with the hierarchic priesthood, the Christian layman also makes Christ present in the world: in his own person, by becoming an *alter Christus* whereby his very action as a na-

---

[75] Cf. *Tractatus* xii. 207. 37–210. 40; xxv. 258. 11–259. 32.
[76] This is what John suggests at *Tractatus* xii. 207. 37–208. 10. Cf. Journet, *The Church of the Word Incarnate*, vol. 1, pp. 121–192, where a different line is developed.

tural man is transformed into an epiphany of the divine in-ruption into history. Since lay activity in this sense is not neces-sarily individual, since it may take a social character as well, there would appear to be a power of jurisdiction, a governing power, appropriate to and peculiar to its social dimensions. This would appear to be a power of jurisdiction distinct from that proper to the hierarchic priesthood whereby the dispensation of the sacraments is governed. Such a jurisdiction would naturally be quite different from that proper to the hierarchic priesthood. Whereas the hierarchic priest possesses the fullness of his priestly power quite irrespective of his personal sanctity or lack of it, the degree to which the laymen re-presents Christ in his own person is dependent on his personal sanctity in a far more profound way, even though it, too, is dependent on a sacramental character: of baptism and confirmation. And it is precisely because of this deeply personal character of the priestly acts in question, because of the decisive importance of dispositions of soul and of freely given personal graces, that jurisdiction over this priestly work is different from that over the hierarchic one.

Throughout the Middle Ages, there was a sense of the sacred function of the king deriving from a number of sources. But the tendency of the Church was to assimilate kingship to some form of minor orders. Thus the anointment and corona-tion of kings came to be a veritable ordination ceremony of some sort. And, to insure papal supremacy, the pope was crowned too, triply.[77] John of Paris, attempting to reaffirm

[77] Cf. Kern, *Kingship and Law in the Middle Ages,* pp. 1–68 and Joseph C. Fenton, "The Relation of the Christian State to the Catholic Church According to the *Pontificale Romanum," American Ecclesiastical Review* (September, 1950), 214–218. I have here deliberately omitted any attempt to distinguish between Christ as priest, as king, as prophet, as savior. Such distinctions involve a subtlety far beyond what is necessary for a comment on the views of John of Paris on the function of the layman. Cf. Journet, *The Church of the Word Incarnate,* vol. 1, pp. 124–141; Yves M.-J. Congar, *Jalons pour une théologie du laïcat* (Paris: 1953).

the political independence of the king with respect to papal jurisdiction, completely ignores the problem of the royal anointment and coronation at the hands of an archbishop. And it apparently never occurs to him to attempt to structure his argument in terms of the royal and priestly character [1 Pt 2:5, 9; Ap 5:10] of the layman. Even though John does not equate the Church with the clerical hierarchy, the lay members of the Church seem to have lost all semblance of participation in the offices of Christ, at least as far as any articulate reference to such participation is concerned. This is what gives the peculiarly Semi-Pelagian tone to his work. The layman, and thus the man of politics, seems to be wholly a natural man *as far as any office he holds is concerned.* To be sure, he comes to the rescue of the Church with the might of the sword, because he still is bound to it by a bond of charity,[78] but it is altogether unclear as to what capacity he holds when he does so. But, for the most part, he appears in John of Paris to be one concerned to defend his natural rights against the communion of saints. And John of Paris appears as his advocate. Having lost a sense of the royal priesthood of all the faithful, John of Paris, in searching for order and measure in the relationship of pope and king, seems to have become a defender of nature against grace. That, of course, was not at all his intention. He had hoped to find a middle way for Christians between papal-caesarism and caesaro-papism. In fact, he seems to have succeeded only in delineating a certain separation of ordinary spheres of interest: nature for the king, grace for the pope. This separation, however, might be broken by more or less frequent and, to John, quite legitimate intrusions by one into the sphere of the other. But either the intrusions are *sine titulo,* or the separation of spheres is unrealistic.

If John of Paris were alone in this dilemma, he would, perhaps, be interesting only as a curiosity. But the root difficulty in

[78] *Tractatus* xiii. 215. 20–29.

his position, the absence of a theology of the layman, is common to the Middle Ages. It undermines all attempts at an adequate Church-state doctrine. It issues in the Reformation reaction against the hierarchic priesthood in the name of the priesthood of all believers.[79] In Catholic countries, it issued in a virulent anti-clericalism. Seeming to be deprived of a fitting share in Christ's mission in the world, the Catholic kings tended toward a profoundly cynical view of the Church. The means of mutual intervention, that John hoped to balance against each other, became in the hands of the King of France instruments to control the French hierarchy[80] and the tools of a running battle with the Pope. In the absence of a better theological groundwork, John's middle position tended to be seen as little else but a defense of the royal and secular interests against the papalists. Naturally, the room left for a middle position somewhat more in favor of the pope would be filled. Cardinal Bellarmine was to fill it best.

[79] Which leads naturally to the national church and the religious supremacy of the king wherever monarchic institutions existed. The Reformation emphasis on the priesthood of all believers naturally tended to put the supreme priestly jurisdiction in the hands of that believer (or those believers) who ruled the community of believers. For this reason, fights about ecclesiastical polity necessarily became fights about secular polity and vice versa.

[80] If the emperor can depose the pope, by force if necessary, the king can do as much to the bishops in his kingdom. And if he can depose them for faults, may the king not ensure that those whom the king judges to have the requisite virtues are consecrated in the first place?

St. Robert Bellarmine

Mastering Wolves and Rams

THE emergence and consolidation of a national state in France had been the source of the conflict between the Pope and the French King that occasioned the search for a genuine middle position by John of Paris. That conflict, which came to a head in the confrontation between Boniface VIII and Philip the Fair, had been ended for a while by the babylonian captivity of the papacy at Avignon. But the underlying problem had by no means been solved. The breakup of Christianity and Christendom in the Reformation was accompanied by attacks not only on the papacy at its roots, but by the full institutionalization of the trend toward national church under political control. A part of the work of the Counter-reformation was, therefore, devoted to meeting the charges of the reformers about papal tyranny, as well as meeting the challenge of political control of the Church posed by the princes. In the midst of the burning controversies of the sixteenth and early seventeenth centuries was St. Robert Bellarmine, a cardinal of the Roman Church and, fittingly enough for a titan of the Counter-reformation, a Jesuit.

Like John of Paris, St. Robert thought it necessary to find a middle way. The papalists, and the princes and the reformers, were, all of them, extremists. The task he set himself was to find the catholic truth amid all sectarian extremes. "It is not a matter of opinion, but of certitude among Catholics that there is in the pope a power in temporals: even though there is no lack of

controversies as to what kind and what manner of power it is."[1]
Against those who denied papal power in the affairs of this
world, Bellarmine set out to show the unvarying judgment of the
tradition to the contrary. Against those who would make the
pope the lord of the whole world, Bellarmine set out to clarify
the controversies between Catholics.

He begins by distinguishing between three fundamental positions. "The first is: the supreme pontiff, by divine law [*jure
divino*] has a supreme plenitude of power [*plenissimam potes-
tatem*] in the whole world, in ecclesiastical matters as well as in
political matters."[2] This is the central point of the theory of the
direct power. At the other extreme, "all of the heretics of this
time and especially Calvin" teach two propositions:

First, the pontiff, as such and by divine law [*jure divino*] has no temporal power, and cannot, in any way, command secular princes, no less
deprive them of their kingdoms and sovereignity, even if they otherwise deserve to be so deprived. Secondly, . . . it is not permissible for
the pontiff and other bishops to hold temporal dominion which they
now have in certain cities and provinces, whether dominion of that
sort may have been given to them or whether they may have usurped
it; for the divine law prohibits the spiritual sword and the temporal
sword being committed to one man at the same time.[3]

There is, however, a third position between these two, one
that is common to Catholic theologians.[4] "The pontiff, as such,

---

[1] *De Potestate Summi Pontificis in Temporalibus Adversus Gulielmum
Barclaium* iii. 15 (cited hereafter as *Adversus Barclaium*), in *Opera
Omnia*, ed. Justinus Fèvre (Paris: 1870–1874), vol. XII. The page number
in this edition is always the last number cited.

[2] With this, he opens the first chapter of book five ("*De Protestate
Pontificis Temporali*") of the first volume ("*De Summo Pontifice*")
of his *Disputationes de Controversiis Christianae Religionis*, originally
published in 4 vols. at Ingalstadt, 1586–1593. *Opera Omnia*, vol. II.
This fifth book of vol. I of the *Controversiis* will be cited hereafter as "*De
Potestate*," followed by the chapter number and the page number in the
Opera Omnia.

[3] "*De Potestate*" i. 145.

[4] Among whom he cites John of Paris and his *Tractatus de potestate
regia et papali*, as Murray notes, *Cross Currents*, p. 15.

does not have any direct and immediate temporal power, but only spiritual power; yet by reason of the spiritual power, he has at least indirectly a certain power, and that the highest [*eamque summam*][5] in temporal affairs."[6]

Bellarmine's refutation of the erroneous extremes is, in the words of Murray, "basically . . . a dogmatic refutation by appeal to tradition—the acts and teaching of the Church, the Scriptures, the Fathers and Doctors."[7]

Bellarmine refutes the direct-power theorists first. To do so, he sets out to prove three things: "first that the pope is not the lord of the whole world; secondly, that he is not the lord of the whole Christian world; thirdly, that he is not the lord of any province or town and has no merely temporal jurisdiction by divine law."[8]

To show that the pope is not lord of the whole world, Bellarmine, taking the obvious example, writes, "The pope is not lord of those countries [*earum provinciarum*] that infidels occupy." In support of which he cites John 21:7, noting that Christ commissioned Peter to feed only His sheep and that infidels are not such; and he cites 1 Corinthians 5:12: "What have I to do to judge them that are without?" But he is not content to leave it at two biblical references. He invokes the whole dualist tradition that accepted the validity of rational political philosophy.[9] "Infidel princes are true and supreme rulers of their own realms; for dominion is not founded on grace or faith, but in free will and reason; nor does it descend from divine law, but from the law of nations." Nor is there anything in this view contrary to

[5] Murray, quoting from the *Opera Omnia* published at Naples in 1856, has "*eamque supremam*" in "St. Robert Bellarmine on the Indirect Power," *Theological Studies*, vol. IX (December, 1948), p. 496, cited hereafter as "Bellarmine."

[6] "*De Potestate*" i. 145.   [7] "Bellarmine," pp. 495–496.

[8] "*De Potestate*" ii. 146.

[9] F.-X. Arnold, *Die Staatslehre des Kardinals Bellarmine* (Munich: 1934), p. 87.

129

Scripture, for "God approves the royal authorities of the nations [*regna gentilium*] in both Testaments."[10]

But not only is the pope not the lord of the whole world, he is also not the lord of the whole Christian world. "Christ did not withdraw nor does he withdraw kingdoms from those who had them; for Christ did not come to destroy those things that were good, but to perfect them; therefore, when a king becomes a Christian, he does not lose the earthly kingdom that he obtained lawfully, but he acquires a new right to an eternal kingdom: otherwise, the favor of Christ would injure kings, and grace would destroy nature." Further, "if the pope is the supreme lord of the whole Christian world, then individual bishops are temporal princes in the cities under their episcopacy (inasmuch as what the pope is in the Church universal, the bishop is in a particular Church) . . . and this is plainly not so."[11]

In fact, the pope has directly and by divine law [*jure divino*] temporal dominion nowhere on earth. "Christ, as man, while He lived on earth, neither accepted nor wished merely temporal

[10] "*De Potestate*" ii. 146. He cites Dn 2:37; Mt 22:21; Rom 13:7. On the famous passage at Mt 22:21, he says: "Note: 'Return [*Reddite*],' not: grant [*donate*] those things that are Caesar's, that is to say, those things that are owed to him by right [*jure*]." Cf. *De Controversiis* ii. 3 ("*De Laicis sive Saecularibus*"). 5. In *Op. Om.*, vol. III and cited hereafter as "*De Laicis*." There he writes: "Political rule [*principatus*] is so natural and necessary to the human race that it cannot be withdrawn without destroying nature itself. For the nature of man is such that he is a social animal." Man, he says, is born unskilled and lacking all necessities, and has enemies in the wild beasts and in robbers. And, even if he could surmount these, "yet he would always remain ignorant and destitute of wisdom and of justice and of many other virtues, although, indeed, we are born for this: to especially develop the mind and will. For the sciences and arts were developed over a long time by many men, and without a teacher they cannot be learned; it is impossible, moreover, to exercise justice in society since it is the virtue determining equity among many" (p. 9). And all of this shows the need for a ruler. "If human nature needs social life, certainly it also needs a rule [*regimen*] and a ruler [*rectorem*]; for it is impossible for a multitude to long hold together unless there be one who holds it together and who has the care of the common good." Cf. also "*De Laicis*" 6 and 7.
[11] "*De Potestate*" 3. 147.

dominion over a single country or city; however, the supreme pontiff is the vicar of Christ and represents Christ to us as He was while He lived here among men; and thus the supreme pontiff as vicar of Christ, and precisely insofar as he is supreme pontiff, has merely temporal jurisdiction over no country or city."[12]

This is the core of Bellarmine's rejection of the direct-power theory of the hierocrats (Bellarmine sometimes refers to them simply as "canonists" and distinguishes them from "theologians").[13]

Against the theory of the direct power of the pope in temporal affairs, Bellarmine asserts the "opinion of the theologians,"[14] and, in developing it, he at the same time refutes "all of the heretics of this time and especially Calvin" who teach that "the pontiff, as such and by divine law, has no temporal power" and that "it is not permissible for the pontiff and other bishops to hold temporal dominion."[15] "We assert," he writes, "that the pontiff, as pontiff, although he has not any merely temporal power, nevertheless has, in their relation to the spiritual good, a supreme power of disposing of the temporal things of all Christians; which very many explain by the resemblance to the art of bridle-making and the equestrian art." Bellarmine rejects the simile on the ground that political power is not solely ministerial to ecclesiastical power.[16] But he finds another similitude to be far more apt. "Just as there is in man spirit and flesh, so there

---

[12] "De Potestate" 4. 148.   [13] E.g., Adversus Barclaium v. 26.
[14] "De Potestate" 6. 155.   [15] Cf. supra, p. 128.
[16] "De Potestate" 6. 155. "But this similitude is not wholly appropriate; for, in these arts [the political and ecclesiastical], the inferior does not exist solely for the sake of the superior, so that, the superior being removed, the inferior is also abolished straightway: for if there be no equestrian art, surely the art of making bridles is superfluous. But the political power is not solely for the sake of the ecclesiastical; for even if there were no ecclesiastical power, there would still be political power, as is plain among infidels, where there is true temporal and political power, yet without ordination to any true ecclesiastical and spiritual power."

are in the Church those two powers."[17] And the end of the political power is temporal peace, and of the ecclesiastical power eternal salvation. "Sometimes they are found separate, as at the time of the Apostles, and sometimes they are found conjoined as now; however, when they are conjoined they make one body, and thus they ought to be connected, and the inferior subordinated to the superior."[18] Thus it seems that Bellarmine, having got himself out of the difficulties of the bridle-making-equestrian simile by simply discarding it, gets himself into new difficulties with a different one as well worn as the first.[19] He does not press his similitude to the length of saying that the pope is the ordinary ruler or regulator of temporal affairs.[20] Yet the similitude

[17] "*De Potestate*" 6. 155. He continues: "The flesh has sense and appetite, to which correspond acts and proportionate objects, and the immediate end of all these is health and good constitution of body; the spirit has intellect and will, and acts and proportionate objects, and for an end the soundness and perfection of the soul; flesh without spirit is found in brutes, spirit without flesh is found in angels. Whence it appears that neither is precisely for the sake of the other. Yet flesh is found joined to spirit in man, where, since they make one person, they necessarily have subordination and connection."

[18] "*De Potestate*" 6. 156. Cf. *Adversus Barclaium* xiii. 51-54.

[19] It would seem that Bellarmine's own criticism of the harness-maker-equestrian art similitude also applies to his own similitude: e.g., the superior (i.e., the spirit) being removed, the inferior (i.e., the flesh) is also abolished straightway (i.e., becomes corpse). He counters this by noting that flesh and spirit exist separately in brutes and angels respectively. All of which is but a proof of the inadequacy of similitudes and it should be noted that Bellarmine himself only tries to work it out at length in ch. 6 in which he explains the opinion of theologians but not in ch. 7 where he offers proofs.

[20] "*De Potestate*" 6. 156: "And so the spiritual power does not mix itself with temporal business, but permits everything to proceed as it did before they were conjoined, as long as temporal affairs do not hinder the spiritual end, or are not necessary to achieve it. If, however, something of this kind happens, the spiritual power can and ought to coerce the temporal power by all methods and ways that seem to it to be necessary." And thus: "With respect to persons, the pope as pope cannot ordinarily depose temporal princes, even for a just cause, in the manner in which he deposes bishops, that is just as an ordinary judge; however he can change kingdoms and remove [a kingdom] from one [king] and confer it on another as he is the highest spiritual leader, if it be necessary for the salvation of souls, as we shall prove. With respect to laws, the pope

appears to lead him to conceive of the two powers as being within and forming one body which is the Mystical Body, the Church. At the time of the Apostles, when the political power was not in the hands of Christians, it seems that the spiritual power could not coerce the political power: *de facto,* obviously, but *de jure?* That is not so simple. In any immediate sense, one would have to answer: no.[21] But, since all are called to faith in Christ and membership in His Church, the situation in apostolic times was an imperfect one, as it is in any land outside of Christendom, which Bellarmine sometimes seems simply to identify with the Church [*Ecclesia*]. Thus it seems that the most that could be said in Bellarmine's terms would be that the spiritual power was only potentially able, *de jure,* to coerce temporal powers outside of or before the existence of Christendom.[22] But this is not the case now, he says. Now they both form one body,[23] and both powers are in it, and the spiritual power may rightly coerce the temporal to act in a certain way or not to act in a certain way when the end of the spiritual power, i.e., the salvation of souls, requires it.[24]

Nevertheless, "it does not pertain to him [the pope] to contrive necessities at will, or under the color of necessity to gratify cupidity,"[25] although "judgment as to the existence of the occa-

---

as pope cannot ordinarily make civil laws or confirm or annul the laws of princes, because he is not himself political prince of the Church; however, he can do all these things, if some civil law be necessary for the salvation of souls and yet kings will not make it, or if another law be noxious to the salvation of souls and yet kings will not repeal it."

[21] Cf. the remarks on countries held by infidels, *supra,* pp. 129–130.

[22] But cf. *infra,* pp. 135–136; *"De Potestate"* 7; and the references cited by Murray in "Bellarmine," p. 525, n. 78.

[23] A *"respublica Christiana,"* see, e.g., *"De Potestate"* 7. 156.

[24] Murray, in "Bellarmine," p. 497, lists a number of other formulations by Bellarmine regarding the occasion on which the pope can exercise this power: one created "by a serious reason, especially a concern of faith;" "the salvation of souls, the welfare of religion, the preservation of the Church;" or "a necessity of the Church."

[25] *Adversus Barclaium* xii. 49.

sion and its gravity rests, of course, with the pope."[26] Bellarmine supports this position with five reasons[27] and twelve examples.[28]

The first reason is "the celebrated *argumentum unitatis*."[29] "When both powers are part of the same Christian commonwealth [*respublica Christiana*], the civil power is subject to the spiritual power." And this is true of the civil power "not only as Christian, but even as political." "For the temporal end is subordinate to the spiritual end, as is plain, because temporal felicity is not the ultimate end absolutely, and thus ought to be referred to eternal felicity; . . . powers [*facultates*] are subordinate so far as the ends are subordinate." Further, "kings and pontiffs, clergy and laity do not make two commonwealths [*respublicas*], but one, that is, one Church, for we are all one body, Rom 12[:5] and 1 Cor 12[:13]." This is decisive for Bellarmine, because the one body demands such a subordination that "if temporal administration impedes the spiritual good, everyone holds that a temporal prince is bound to change the mode of administration, even to the detriment of the temporal good."[30] This is not a question of a work of charity on the part of the temporal power, but of a bounden duty resulting from the subordination of parts to the whole.[31] For Bellarmine notes, "according to the order of charity, one commonwealth is not bound to suffer detri-

---

[26] J.C.M., "Bellarmine," p. 497, citing *Adversus Barclaium* xii.
[27] "*De Potestate*" 7.　　　　　　　　[28] "*De Potestate*" 8.
[29] J.C.M., "Bellarmine," p. 515.
[30] "*De Potestate*" 7. 156–157. Cf. *Adversus Barclaium* v; xiv.
[31] John of Paris, in *Tractatus* xix. 235. 31–34, argued that, if heretics are compelled to return to the Church by princes, such is done "by the favor of princes." And "the emperor ought to exercise the secular jurisdiction, for the sake of a necessity of the spiritual good, when the pope suggests it. However, if he [the emperor] is unwilling or if it does not seem expedient to him, the pope can not do anything else" (x. 200. 25–27). Murray remarks (*Cross Currents*, p. 54, n. 69): "For the rest, his thought on the mutual aid of the Church and State is summed up in the traditional idea that a providential reason for the distinction of the two powers is the 'fostering of mutual love and charity' among the members of the Church by 'ministration to reciprocal need,' since 'the prince needs the priest in spiritual things, and conversely' (x 196. 18–22)."

ment so that a nobler commonwealth may not suffer a similar detriment; and one private person who is bound to give all his goods for the conservation of his own commonwealth, is not, however, bound to do likewise for the sake of some other commonwealth however much more noble."

Bellarmine's second reason is that "the ecclesiastical commonwealth ought to be perfect and sufficient unto itself in relation to its end; . . . but the power of using and disposing of temporal things is necessary to the spiritual end, . . . therefore [the Church] has this power." And this power includes the ability "to command" the temporal commonwealth, "to compel the changing of administration," and "to depose princes and set up others." And this is all the more so since the temporal commonwealth is but a part of the great Christian commonwealth, and subject to the higher part in that great Christian commonwealth.

His third reason is that it is "dangerous and harmful" to elect a non-Christian king or not to depose such a one, for he may undertake to lead his subjects into his heresy or infidelity. "But to judge whether a king is inducing to heresy or not pertains to the pontiff, to whom is given the care of religion; therefore, it is for the pontiff to judge that a king ought to be deposed or not deposed." And the only reason that the Christians did not depose "Nero, Diocletian, Julian the Apostate, and Valens the Arian and the like" was simply "because they lacked temporal power" to do so.

His fourth argument is as follows:

When kings and princes come to the Church in order to become Christians, they are received under the express or tacit agreement that they subject their sceptres to Christ and promise to preserve and defend the faith of Christ even under pain of losing their kingdoms; therefore, when they become heretics or are a hindrance to religion, they can be judged by the Church and even deposed from the principate.[32]

[32] *"De Potestate"* 7. 157–159. When this occurs, the one body is formed in such a manner that the spirit (the ecclesiastical power) is joined to the flesh (the temporal power), so that the Church can exercise her full

His fifth reason bases itself on John 21:17: ". . . Feed my sheep." Bellarmine says that this gave the supreme shepherd "every power that is necessary for the shepherd to protect the flock." And there are three such powers. The first is over "wolves" (heretics), whom, if they be kings, he can excommunicate and deprive of their positions. The second is over "rams" (evil kings and princes), whom he can "expose and reduce to the order of sheep." The third is over "sheep" (the faithful), whom he can "command and force" to do their duty according to their state in life, which for kings is "to serve God by defending the Church and punishing heretics and schismatics." And the pope forces them to do so, when they are recalcitrant, "by excommunication and other convenient methods."[33]

As for the twelve examples, I shall follow the classification of Murray, who casts them into two groups. One "group of seven are all examples of papal action in the founding and rule of Western Christendom."[34] The other is a group of five, two of which are from the Old Testament.[35] To these latter two, Murray remarks that "today we are chary of conclusions as to

authority. Thus, in the case of pagan emperors who persecuted the Christians, it would only seem to have been necessary for a king or prince, of sufficient power, to enter the Church in order that the pope could demand that he come to the aid of the Church against the offending emperor even though the emperor had not so subjected himself to the Church. And the same extends even to the lands of infidels: the Christian king can be called upon to secure, against the will of infidel kings, the entry of Christian missionaries, "for he [the pope] has the right of sending preachers of the Gospel through the whole world" "*De Potestate*" 2. 146. Giles of Rome did not go much further.

[33] "*De Potestate*" 7. 159. On the fifth argument as a whole one might comment by quoting a remark of John of Paris: "It is plain that an argument is of no efficacy insofar as it rests upon allegory" (*Tractatus* xix. 235. 17–18). It should be noted, as Murray remarks in "Bellarmine," p. 499, that "Bellarmine was thinking of a power genuinely to depose a king, and not simply declare him deposed." He cites *Adversus Barclaium* xxxvi.

[34] "Bellarmine," p. 519.

[35] The exile, by priestly sentence, of King Ozias (II Par [Chr] 26:16–23) and the slaying of Queen Athalia by order of Joiada the high priest (II Par [Chr] 23:14–15).

the organization of a Christian society drawn from the happenings in the Jewish theocracy." "The third example is the famous incident of [St.] Ambrose [of Milan] and [Emperor] Theodosius; here we have the temporal power brought under moral judgment by the Church and visited with a spiritual penalty."[36]

As for the fourth, its implications are a good deal less than clear.[37] The last in this group "is the excommunication of Leo the Isaurian by Gregory II; here a spiritual penalty appears as having temporal consequences, the loss of the revenues of Italy."[38] But what Bellarmine interprets as a papal assertion of the right to take away imperial taxes, and even to take away a part, i.e., Italy, of the Emperor's dominions, seems to be more a refusal by Gregory to act as a viceroy and tax collector for the iconoclastic Emperor who styled himself "priest and king."[39] In short, Murray's judgment appears wholly sound: "None of these examples [in the group of five] supports Bellarmine's theory in its full amplitude,"[40] which extends to direct deposition of kings, transferrence of kingdoms, making and repealing laws. But the group of seven is not as easily disposed of. They are:

[36] "Bellarmine," pp. 518–519.

[37] Bellarmine quotes (in "De Potestate" 7. 159) an extract from one of three charters granted to a hospital, a church attached to a monastery, and a nunnery respectively: "If anyone, whether king, priest, judge, or any secular person" violate this charter, "let him be deprived of his station." The text in Johannes B. Lo Grasso, S.J., Ecclesia et Status, de mutuis officiis et juribus fontes selecti (Rome: 1939), p. 125, n. 5, has "let him be deprived of the dignity of his power and station [honoris]," and threatens excommunication and penalty before the divine judgment. The charters concern, among other things, the manner of electing the abbot or abbess and include an injunction against simony on the part of any king, bishop or other person in the process. Granted on the request of Queen Mother Brunichildis of the Franks in 602, there is more than a little doubt as to what papal power Gregory intended to assert in the quoted passage. Cf. F. Homes Dudden, Gregory the Great (London, New York: 1905), vol. II, pp. 84–85.

[38] J.C.M., "Bellarmine," p. 519.

[39] Cf. Walter Ullmann, The Growth of Papal Government in the Middle Ages (London: 1955), pp. 44–49.

[40] "Bellarmine," p. 519.

The deposition of Childeric [Childeric III, Merovingian king of the Franks] by Zacharias [in 751],[41] the transfer of the Empire to the Germans by Gregory V, and four of the string of depositions in the Middle Ages: that of Henry IV by Gregory VII, of Otho IV by Innocent III, of Frederick II by Innocent IV, and of Louis of Bavaria by Clement VI. These are the real foundations of Bellarmine's case; and among them the actions of Gregory VII, Innocent III, and Innocent IV are leading. . . . In substance, then, Bellarmine derives his theory, in what is special to it, from the most resounding acts of the mediaeval papacy in its most imperial-minded representatives.[42]

There are, of course, a variety of ways in which acts of this sort have been interpreted. On the face of it, it seems that, in at least some cases, the popes in question did, in fact, depose kings and emperors whatever the *de jure* situation may have been. It seems that they thought that they were doing just that and doing it *de jure*. But even granted that they did it by right, the question is: by what right? Murray contends that this empowerment was not a permanent and absolute possession of the Church by divine right, but "was dependent upon a particular set of historical circumstances, on a special relation in which the Papacy of the time stood to the temporal order of the time."[43] The contingent, historical cimcumstances that gave rise to this empowerment[44] were defects in the temporal order itself, political defects in short. "The circumstances of those centuries [roughly 750 to 1350] were exceptional; at their outset, the Papacy stood 'between a dying system and one waiting to be born,' as the only living social and cultural force left after the complete collapse of a lay civilization; it acquired political status by de-

---

[41] Cf. *supra*, pp. 113–115.   [42] J.C.M. "Bellarmine," p. 519.

[43] *Ibid.*, p. 526. He writes, in the same place, that "in the zeal of controversial argument, then, it would seem that Bellarmine confused the absolute and permanent with the relative and contingent."

[44] Murray grants that deposition was the "climactic datum" of the "sources Bellarmine had to use" (p. 520). This is a reasonable judgment inasmuch as the decisive practical political question, especially in a monarchy, is: "Who shall rule?"

fault and maintained it by necessity—not that of the Church but of civilization itself."[45] Indeed, Murray remarks that one might better speak of "the temporal disorder of the time" than of the temporal order of the time. "In the Middle Ages the one effective institution for the control and direction of society was the monarchy: 'At no other period were active policy and progress in government so dependent on the personality of the king as in the early Middle Ages, with their lack of a bureaucracy and their poverty of initiative on the part of the Estates.' "[46] This is the imperfection, "and in this sense a disorder in society —the disorder proper to immaturity." Thus, certain papal rights over the political order were "possessed in consequence of a lack of development in the institutionalization of the political order." And this leads to the conclusion that they were "possesed *in hypothesi,* because, I take it, the rights that the Church possesses *in thesi* suppose not only her own perfection as a society but the perfection, too, of the State—the development of its institutions in accord with the dynamisms of reason, justice, and political prudence."[47]

More precisely, the political defect involved was "that there were no effectively organized political institutions that could contrive to keep the monarch subject to law, or do away with him if he became a tyrant." Murray grants that "there were under Germanic law institutionalizations of the 'right of resistance,' but they were largely ineffective, and even when effective led rather to further disorder." There was needed against tyranny "a preventive technique, not merely a repressive one." The development of the theory and practice of constitutional monarchy —I think one might say of a form of mixed regime—provided,

---

[45] "Bellarmine," p. 519. Cf. Joseph Lecler, S.J., *The Two Sovereignties,* trans. Hugh Montgomery (London: 1952), pp. 54–59.
[46] He quotes F. Kern, *Kingship and Law in the Middle Ages,* p. 81.
[47] "Bellarmine," pp. 526–527.

according to Murray, the "requisite institution."[48] In the meantime, the papacy filled the breach. Murray does not attempt to establish the existence of the aforementioned situation with any detailed historical analysis. But the interesting question still is: granting the existence of the situation and the fact of papal action, by what title, if any, did the popes act? It is necessary to raise this question because it is plain that the Church and the pope do not exist for the sake of remedying political defects. And "is the right by which they did it a permanent right of the Church, possessed independently of circumstances?"

Before advancing his answers to those questions, Murray suggests that the popes Bellarmine mentions may not have actually deposed anyone.[49] There is a "view" of medieval constitutional law according to which the bad ruler forfeits his authority by the very fact of his evil deeds or of his incompetence. He dethrones himself in the eyes of God and is then simply a man, without authority, using force, and, as such, he may no longer demand obedience from his subjects, who cease to be subjects and may resist his unrightful force. The resisters do not so much depose him as they discover and declare that he has deposed himself. There were no civil organs that were regularly constituted for such a purpose. But the established judicial authority of the Church was available and recognized as competent to judge concerning moral duties of rulers as well as of the ruled. The Church's verdict could be employed in constitutional law as the public declaration of the fact that the king had deposed himself in the eyes of God. The virtue of this procedure being that it avoided the twin dangers of the poorly institutionalized Germanic right of resistance, namely a tendency toward anarchy on the one hand, and a tendency toward ineffectuality on the

[48] *Ibid.*, pp. 527–528.

[49] He bases his argument on an extract from Kern, *Kingship and Law in the Middle Ages,* pp. 101–102.

140

other hand, in the measure that no one was commonly recognized as competent to declare the fact.

In this view of medieval constitutional law, Murray argues, the spiritual judgment of the pope in such a case is merely declaratory of an accomplished fact and is not itself "constitutive of political effects; the political effects were declared, or at most entailed in virtue of public law." So, while the words, of Gregory VII and Innocent IV, for example, "might seem to indicate, though not with full clarity," that these popes "thought that they were actually deposing" emperors and kings, their words may well be understood, as they themselves must have understood them, in the light of prevailing notions of constitutional law."[50] The papal judgment was therefore a spiritual judgment, a judgment concerning sin; that political effects were thereby declared, "or at most entailed in virtue of public law," was the result of historical contingencies, and thus there is no permanent and essential empowerment of the Church to make spiritual judgments having such political effects attached, as it were, to them.

Thus Bellarmine, in Murray's view, makes two mistakes. He assumes that the pope can issue a judgment that, in itself, is constitutive of deposition. Second, he confuses a contingent historical situation for a permanent exigence of the natures of the spiritual and temporal.

Yet such an interpretation of Bellarmine's examples is quite inadequate for making a case against Bellarmine's conclusions. In the first place, it is probably impossible to make a definitive interpretation of each of the historical acts Bellarmine cites. Thus Murray only advances his argument as a "view" on Kern's authority.

But, secondly and of greater importance, even were the view confirmed, that would dispose of the examples, but not of the theoretical problem. As John of Paris had already pointed out,

[50] "Bellarmine," pp. 520–522.

what the popes may or may not have done *de facto* is not necessarily a sure indication of everything they may do by divine right.[51] And Bellarmine goes a lot further than his examples. He does not merely claim a papal power to depose kings and annul laws. These assertions might be interpreted as failures to distinguish, as does Murray, a declarative and constitutive action, failures either from ignorance or only apparent failures deriving from a permissible simplification in view of the specific adversaries with whom Bellarmine was engaged in controversy. But Bellarmine also asserts that the pope can set up a new king[52] or make a law[53] when such is necessary for the spiritual good that the Church pursues, namely the salvation of souls. Such acts (whether Bellarmine has any historical examples of them is beside the point) plainly go beyond any merely declaratory judgment to the effect that a particular king, in virtue of his being unjust, has dethroned himself, and that the constitutional right of resistance to such a one may, in conscience, be licitly exercised and a new king set up. They go beyond any merely declaratory judgment that a given law, in virtue of its being unjust, is no genuine law at all and need not be obeyed. Bellarmine asserts that the Church can depose kings and make them, annul laws and make them, even to the detriment of the temporal good.[54] That is to say, he is clearly not attributing this power to the pope on the basis of civil constitutional law designed temporarily to supplement a primitive set of political institutions. Whatever the nature of the civil constitution, Bellarmine asserts all of the papal powers over the political on the basis of the hierarchy of the ends involved. In this, he is fundamentally at one with Giles of Rome. There is a necessary subordination consequent on such

[51] Cf. *supra*, p. 114.
[52] "*De Potestate*" 6. 156; 7. 157; *Adversus Barclaium* xii. 49.
[53] "*De Potestate*" 6. 156; and cf. J.C.M., "Bellarmine," p. 498.
[54] "*De Potestate*" 7. 157.

a hierarchy. That subordination is great enough so that the Church, and thus the pope, has a plenitude of power to do whatever may be necessary to achieve the good that she pursues.

Bellarmine is perfectly willing to grant that the pope may not "at his pleasure falsely devise necessities,"[55] and that, therefore, he has no power to depose, for example, when there are adequate temporal institutions that can and will depose an unjust king. But Bellarmine has in view those cases in which the temporal authorities either cannot or will not act and in which the good of the Church, the salvation of souls, is imperiled.[56] Bellarmine could admit that in none of his examples did the pope go further than by a declaratory judgment to clarify the consciences of a people who were, in principle, already empowered to resist the one who had deposed himself by his injustice. What of that? Bellarmine interprets the papal assertions of the fullness of their apostolic authority as a declaration that they can do more than that whenever more is required to defend the salvation of souls. And, further, it is only within the competence of the Church, and ultimately of the pope, to judge when more is required.

It is clear, then, that Bellarmine attributes the powers in question to the pope on the basis of his apostolic authority, that is, on divine right, as illuminated by the argument concerning the hierarchy of ends. Therefore, in order to criticize the heart of Bellarmine's position, it is necessary to exclude extraneous considerations of temporal powers that might be in the hands of the pope or of another cleric on some grounds other than the divinely granted sacerdotal powers.

Bellarmine's universe of discourse is fundamentally different from Murray's in certain important respects. Murray writes, naturally, in terms of a distinction between two societies: Church

---

[55] *Adversus Barclaium* xii. 49. [56] *Ibid.,* v. 27.

and state. This is an ordinary modern way of seeing the matter. And thus one may argue, as Murray and others do, that in the Middle Ages the temporal society, the state, was grossly under-developed. But one is still referring to a distinct society. However, Bellarmine and the medieval tradition he defends do not write of two societies, but of *two powers in a single society:* the Christian commonwealth called the Church. Bellarmine does not simply make casual remarks of this sort. He is aware of the alternative and explicitly rejects it. "Kings and pontiffs, clergy and laity do not make two commonwealths [*respublicas*], but one, that is, one Church, for we are all one body, Rom 12[:5] and 1 Cor 12[:13]; but in all bodies, the members are connected and dependent one on the other."[57] Similarly, he says that when princes become Christians, they do so on condition that they promise to defend the faith on pain of losing their offices. Therefore, if they turn out to be wolves (i.e., heretics), then the pope, as chief shepherd of Christ's flock, keeps them away from the flock by every means possible. And if they turn into rams who, raging, hurt the flock with their horns (i.e., sell bishoprics, plunder churches, and the like), then the pastor of the Church will lock them up or put them back to the status of sheep. As long as they are good sheep, each will serve God in accordance with the nature of his office. For kings, that involves defending the Church and punishing heretics and schismatics. And, of course, it is the task of the shepherd to compel each one to do what he ought, and by force if necessary.[58]

[57] "*De Potestate*" 7. 157. This is repeated in a variety of ways throughout chapter 7. And it was already indicated in chapter 6 where the spirit-flesh analogy was employed. But "spirit" [*spiritus*] for Bellarmine is understood not in a Pauline sense, but in a scholastic sense as "soul" [*anima*] with intellect and will. Similarly "flesh" [*caro*] is used as "body" [*corpus*] with sense and appetite. Cf. "*De Laicis*" 18. 34–35, where only "body" and "soul" are referred to.

[58] "*De Potestate*" 7. 159.

In other words, Bellarmine views the existence of a state distinct from the Church as abnormal, and appropriate only to those times or places in which Christians are but a small part of the body politic, in which Christianity does not constitute the shared structure of belief in terms of which the society acts.[59] The normative situation for him is one in which a distinct political society disappears. All that remains is the Church, the great *respublica Christiana*. There are a variety of offices within it, to be sure, and two great divisions of them: the spiritual, which looks to the salvation of souls, and the temporal, which looks to the maintenance of a peaceful order among men in this life. But their existence within a single body social is taken as the norm. And, since the spiritual power pursues a higher end of that same organism, the temporal power must serve that spiritual power, even to its own detriment when necessary.

In other words, the central question of the whole criticism of Bellarmine by Murray is whether such a *respublica Christiana* is a permanent norm toward which Christians, insofar as possible, ought to tend. Murray denies its normative character, charging Bellarmine with a "confusion of the absolute with the relative." "He failed to see how close a relationship there was between the powers assumed by the medieval Church and the structural and political weaknesses of the contemporary political order."[60]

But St. Robert, for his part, is not bound to any particular set of historical examples. He assumes that the community of Christians may also constitute a body politic. He does not see them living two lives, one natural and one supernatural. They live one life that is neither simply natural nor simply supernatural. They live the life of men who were fallen into sin and have now been saved. And in the order of salvation within which they now live and move, there are tragic cases in which natural goods come in conflict with salvation because of the sinfulness of men. Then

[59] *Adversus Barclaium* vi–ix.   [60] "Bellarmine," p. 533.

the Christian ought to choose salvation. On the level of the public life and organization of Christians, that means that their political organs ought to be subject to their ecclesiastical organs, so that if the hand cause scandal it may be cut off and cast away even though it be sorely painful to do it. Heresy in such a society involves a fundamental rupture of the common bond in terms of which the life of the members is lived together. Heresy on the part of the king is the worst possible direct threat to the moral unity, and thus the existence, of that community of Christians.[61] Any prudent constitutional lawyer would, therefore, provide that heresy carries with it automatic loss of throne. While the specific techniques for procuring the deposition are a practically important matter, yet they are but a technical detail altogether overshadowed by the fact that the pope makes the decisive judgment about heresy which necessarily is accompanied by deposition. And thus it makes sense to Bellarmine to speak of the pope deposing the king.

It is plain that Bellarmine regards such a state of affairs as not only possible, but desirable. Any other alternative leaves one with a radical break between the public political life of the citizen and the public religious activity of the same man. If it is possible to choose between such a schizophrenic state of affairs on the one hand, and an interpenetration of the two spheres on the other, Bellarmine will clearly take the latter. Unfortunate circumstances may make it impossible to permit the gospel to penetrate and shape the public actions and rituals of the state, but those are circumstances to be avoided where possible.[62]

In short, Murray's historical critique of Bellarmine's examples is not altogether to the point. The trouble with Bellarmine's position is revealed within the terms of the theoretical argument

[61] For a quite different point of view leading to a similar conclusion, cf. Sebastian de Grazia, *The Political Community: A Study of Anomie* (Chicago: 1948), pp. 73–76, 189–190.

[62] *Adversus Barclaium* vi–ix.

that he himself advances. The fact of the matter is that Bellarmine's work is not at all as systematic as it appears to be. Or, rather, it is polemically systematic, but not theoretically systematic. He attempts to take on all the Protestants and the papalists, too. So he takes up the polemical cudgels against Lutherans, Calvinists, Anabaptists, Hussites, Waldensians, Melanchthon, Wycliffe, and Erasmus, among others, as well as against the papalists. The consequence is that his work is more of a collection of specific arguments against extreme positions rather than a systematic statement in depth of a single position. This is one reason why his work is interesting. It tends to present an unrefined sum of moderate Catholic positions on the disputed questions without seriously attempting a fundamental work of unification. The result is that all the unexamined contradictions in that common body of positions remain unresolved and even unseen. His position is fundamentally inadequate on a number of major points: the argument concerning the hierarchy of ends and the relationship of nature to grace, the problem of pluralism, and the question as to what the Christian can hope for in this world.

With respect to the hierarchy of ends, Bellarmine asserts that the supernatural salvation of man to which the pope ministers is absolutely higher than any other human objective. And he compares the clerical hierarchy to the soul, and the political power to the body that executes the commands of the soul.[63] At the same time, he admits that not only is politics natural to man, but its object is not merely material (i.e., appropriate to a beast, which is what he explicitly suggests when he uses the body-soul analogy).[64] Its object is essentially moral.[65] Consequently, the relationship cannot possibly be as simple as that suggested by the body serving the spirit (which is itself something of an oversimplification). The question necessarily arises: is the natural

---

[63] Cf. *supra,* pp. 131–133 and 144, n. 57.   [64] *"De Potestate"* 6. 155.
[65] Cf. *supra,* pp. 130–131, and especially 130, n. 10.

147

moral good of politics such that it, like the body, ought to be sacrificed to the supernatural good of the Church should there be some conflict? A modern case might be of this sort: one of the fundamental moral goods pursued by a political society is the harmonious living together of men in justice and friendship. But that does not simply occur of its own accord. It requires that the young be trained to it. And that means, at least, that some significant part of the educative structure of the society must accustom them to that. What, then, if they are religiously diverse? May the Catholics insist on a separate school system? And likewise each of the other groups? Bellarmine does not even raise the fundamental problem, even though he senses it when he writes that "when a king becomes a Christian, he does not lose the earthly kingdom that he attained lawfully . . . otherwise the favor of Christ would injure kings, and grace would destroy nature."[66] Nevertheless, every king with any political sense would clearly see that Bellarmine's pope can depose and appoint kings as well as annul and make laws for civil society. And, if that is so, then a king who becomes a Christian loses his kingdom and receives in exchange a papal satrapy. He will not be moved by the argument that the pope may only use his powers when absolutely necessary for the salvation of souls. He sees that the pope alone is the judge of such necessities, and he sees that there have been bad and stupid popes. And if it be said that Christ will judge the pope and the king and that therefore the king can appeal to Christ, then the king will reply that however Christ may judge between them at their death is of no use to him now with respect to a this-worldly kingdom. But it was just such a kingdom that Bellarmine promised would not be harmed. John of Paris at least authorized the King to defend his realm by force of arms against a bad Pope. Bellarmine, for all his assurances about the naturalness of politics, provides no politically valuable way of insuring the practical realization of his promises.

[66] "*De Potestate*" 3. 147.

Any king with some experience of human affairs could not help but notice that baptism in a Church such as Bellarmine articulates would actually involve political castration.

If that is the case, then Bellarmine's grace destroys nature and its goods. But the question was to save it. If the king in fact loses his kingdom for a papal satrapy, that means that the human political order is abolished in favor of a hierocracy.[67] But the question was to conform it to Christ. To a wise king, it is irrelevant that Bellarmine agrees that the roots of his kingship are to be found in the very nature of man. Whatever theologians may think, a king knows that politics is concerned with action, and with theory only insofar as it is relevant to action. But the king knows that human nature is irrelevant if the pope names and deposes "kings," repeals and imposes "laws." Human nature is irrelevant because the pope, who would rule all, makes no claim to the powers of his office on natural grounds. The hierarchy of the Church does not claim to spring from the needs and thrusts, the vitalities, initiatives, and hopes of man, but from the saving grace of a divine initiative. And it is such that its mysterious re-presentation of the saving words and works of Christ is divinely guaranteed even in spite of the vices that may infect its members. The object of that hierarchy is not to perform the human acts that construct a just human order in the concrete. Nor can the ecclesiastical hierarchy claim to be able to produce such an order as a by-product, as it were, of its universal dominance. The political disorder that characterized the states unfortunate enough to live under direct papal rule is too notorious to permit anyone to make such a claim without a smile. The king

[67] It is a fundamental misunderstanding to regard a universal papal monarchy as a theocracy. The popes do not and cannot claim to be God. From the point of view of Christian theology, "theocracy" can only be conceived of in an eschatological framework, i.e., as the regime issuing from the second coming of Christ when His kingship shall be manifest in "power and glory" (cf. Mt 24:21–31; Mk 13:19–27; Lk 21:25–27). That is the reason why I have titled this book *Peter and Caesar*.

with an instinct for the politically relevant asks whether the papacy lays claim to a divine guarantee that it will be a more perfect seat of political prudence than the throne. As long as the papacy makes no such claim, as it does not, the king will leave any further contests to history. The king asks whether the guarantees to Peter and the other apostles include the natural human virtues that distinguish the king from a tyrant. If the answer were yes, he would have to conclude, if he knew something of the history of the papacy in Bellarmine's age alone, that the claims of the Church were lies.

The king also points out that the human, historical community he rules is a peculiar mixture of good and evil. The communities of man can never be characterized as simply good. There is always an admixture of evil, though it may be of greater or lesser extent. And among the evils are always some elements of doubt, despair, unbelief, apostasy, hate, heresy, blasphemy. It is interesting to note that in a community of saints a heretic would not be king. But that is not an adequate observation of the human condition on which to base constitutional law. Bellarmine knows that, but fails to deal with it. He nowhere argues that the Incarnation instituted the final reign of Christ the King on earth. Indeed, he plainly asserts, against the Hussites for example, that the chief title of a ruler to his office is not the grace of God, or divine justice or charity, but nature. And the present condition of that nature is that wicked men sometimes rule, and the darkness in human affairs remains such that there are cases in which they have a valid title to rule.[68] And, indeed, Bellarmine really doesn't expect too much from the run of Christian citizens or from their princes.[69] All he really seems

---

[68] "De Laicis" 8.

[69] There are, to be sure, occasional saintly ones, and St. Robert wrote a pious exhortation to the king of Poland (*On the Office of Christian Princes*) wherein he describes the virtues such a prince ought to have which he then proceeds to illustrate by means of brief accounts of the

to expect of them regularly is that they defend the Church from plunderers, foreign or domestic, and defend the purity of the Christian message by punishing heretics. Beyond that, he doesn't seem to expect too much, unless it be that they refrain from selling bishoprics and plundering churches themselves.[70] Thus, he plainly does not envisage the *respublica Christiana* as some sort of utopia in which Christ the King, represented by the pope, rules over a community in which only the "saints" or the "righteous" would participate, all others being excluded. Bellarmine is no Fifth Monarchy man in a cardinal's robes. While the incarnational strain in his thinking leads him to the conclusion that spiritual and temporal powers are both within the one society, and while he grants the pope the power to depose kings and set up new ones, abrogate laws and institute new ones, nevertheless the eschatological element of the Catholic tradition drives him to make such papal intervention an unusual exception that is to take place, apparently, only an occasion of outrageous provocation on the part of a ruler who begins to rage like a ram or who actually turns into a ravening wolf.

But this tension between the incarnational and eschatological strains in Christian thought is not defined by Bellarmine. He does not clarify the points of contact. The practical difficulties are not squarely faced. What, after all, is a king supposed to do when faced with a pope who "falsely devises necessities"? Nowhere is there evidence in Bellarmine's treatment of the subject that this time between the Incarnation and the Second Coming is characterized by a pluralism in every society, the pluralism of good and evil in their diverse appearances. And, if that is the case, then one must seriously wonder whether the appropriateness of political sanctions against heresy can be chiefly determined

---

lives and virtues of figures from the Old Testament, and from Christian history such as St. Louis of France, St. Edward of England, and St. Stephen of Hungary. Cf. *Opera Omnia,* vol. VIII, pp. 87–235.

[70] *"De Potestate"* 8.

by discovering whether the Church has the power to bring it off or not.[71] In short, one is led to suppose that Bellarmine, having twelve legions of angels at his disposal, would have known better than Christ how to take advantage of that fact.[72]

[71] *Adversus Barclaium* vi–viii.
[72] Mt 26:53, and cf. Jn 18:36–38; 19:9–11.

The Canonists

A Statistical Escape from History

THE Catholic Church has had, no doubt, her full share of troubles with the modern world. Not least among them by any measure has been the difficulty of finding some reasonably stable bases for creating at least a minimally satisfactory *modus vivendi* between Peter and Caesar. Of course, a great variety of practical arrangements have been hammered out either by the Romanist method of the concordat or by the Germanic method of customary adaptation. But the relationship has always been precarious, whether Caesar was Catholic or not. The persistence of the Bellarminian conglomeration of opinion on the matter in ecclesiastical circles has inescapably led to a permanent suspicion of Roman objectives. In predominantly Catholic countries, that suspicion expressed itself and still expresses itself in a deeply rooted anti-clericalism on political matters (as well as in other matters where a similar pattern tends to be found). In predominantly Protestant countries, the suspicion of and distaste for the political implications of "Romanism" have been and remain a part of the general rejection of Roman ecclesiology.

In the United States, the method of customary adaptation has led to considerable practical success, but a success accompanied by polemical heat and a division between Catholics on the doctrinal roots of their adaptation. The American case is especially interesting for a number of reasons. Not only is the American

153

polity profoundly pluralist in its religious structure, consisting of three great groupings: Protestant Christians, Catholic Christians, and secular humanists.[1] A number of modern nations can be so characterized, e.g., Canada and Germany. But the American pluralism has also been accompanied by a more remarkable degree of physical, economic, and social intermixing in an atmosphere of relatively great civic amity.[2] With respect to the religious animosity that existed against Catholics in the past, it is clear that a good deal of it proceeded out of a nativist rejection of anything foreign. That this phase of Catholic relationships to the American body politic is past was confirmed by the election of John F. Kennedy to the presidency. These developments have made American Catholics peculiarly sensitive to certain aspects of the Church-state question. Since they have clearly become a part of what might be called the American Establishment, it has become necessary for them to question the adequacy of the common stock of opinions on Church-state relations that Bellarmine summarized, in effect, for post-Reformation Catholicism. It has been necessary for them to begin to wonder if that common

[1] I trust that the reader will tolerate this obvious simplification. It, of course, ignores Jews, Muslims, deists, and others. And, not only that, any detailed statement would have to take account of the fact that mere head-counting is not enough. Different questions produce different intensities of response in the different groupings. Furthermore, individuals sometimes fall in one category on one question and in another on a different question. Thus, the reason why I have been content with a simplification here should already be clear.

[2] This is patently not true for Canada. The German case is more complex. World War II and its aftermath have produced a far deeper set of Protestant-Catholic relationships there than in the United States. But, until recently, the polity was split between a believers' party (the Christian Democratic Union/Christian Social Union) and an unbelievers' party (the Social Democratic Party of Germany). This, of course, was hardly the sole basis of their distinction but, in our context, it is of the greatest importance. The "Americanization" of German politics seems, however, to have induced the S.P.D. to shed its atheistic version of socialism to permit an appeal to a broader spectrum of the electorate. See the Basic Program of the S.P.D. adopted in 1959.

154

stock of opinions was altogether relevant to the realities revealed to them by their experience.

The United States has always been a religiously pluralistic society. The colonial and early federal periods saw a variety of forms of religious establishment and of religious toleration. They ranged during the Colonial period from the strict Puritan orthodoxy of the early Massachusetts Bay Colony to the relatively broad provisions of the Maryland Toleration Act of 1649, and to the even broader, if not always fully realized, toleration under the Pennsylvania Charter of Privileges of 1701. Thus, it is not surprising that church-state relations have a long history of debate and of different attempts at solution in this country. But the adoption of the First Amendment to the Constitution in 1791 and the abandonment of establishment in the several states (Massachusetts in 1833 being the last to do so) set the pattern of the American practical solution before the arrival of the great waves of immigration that began to roll over the country in the 1840s. The great number of Catholics among the Irish, Germans, Italians, and Poles who arrived prior to the progressive restrictions on immigration between 1917 and 1924 injected a new and politically important religious factor into American politics.[3] Naturally, such a question is seldom the center of a political controversy in isolation from all other political questions. The anti-Catholic elements of both Know-

---

[3] Even Maryland, founded by the Second Lord Baltimore as, among other things, a refuge for his Catholic co-religionists, seems never to have had a Catholic majority, and the Church of England had become the established church there by the end of the seventeenth century. The development of American church-state relationships can be followed in Anson Phelps Stokes, *Church and State in the United States*, 3 vols. (New York: 1950). The most important documents are available in Ben. Perley Poore, compiler, *The Federal and State Constitutions, Colonial Charters and Other Organic Laws of the United States*, 2 vols. (Washington, D.C.: 1877) and Peter G. Mode, ed., *Source Book and Bibliographical Guide for American Church History* (Menasha, Wis.: 1921). See also Albert Clayton Ross, "Legislation Respecting Religious Limitations Upon Civil and Political Rights in the American Colonies" (unpublished master's dissertation, Department of History, University of Chicago, 1923).

Nothingism in the nineteenth century and the Ku Klux Klan in the twentieth was clearly but a part of a far deeper political unrest. Similarly, the "Catholic issue" in the presidential campaigns of Alfred E. Smith and of John F. Kennedy was but a part of a broad spectrum of political concerns. Nevertheless, it is equally plain that, in those contexts, the Catholicism of some Americans has been a matter of burning political importance.

It is quite understandable that Catholics should be viewed with some suspicion in a country whose history has received a predominantly Protestant impress. And this cannot be viewed simply as the ordinary in-group suspicion of strangers. There is, no doubt, a good deal of that. But it should not be forgotten that Protestants are what they are in part because they protested against a variety of things in the Catholic Church in which their forebears were once members. To allay the suspicions and hostilities between them, it is not enough to encourage mutual knowledge and toleration. Since their division is defined by the profound protest of some Christians against some of the practices and beliefs of other Christians, the roots of hostility and suspicion can only be overcome by a genuine ecumenical reconciliation.

In the meantime, Protestants and other non-Catholic Americans have noted the fact of a large and growing Catholic minority (even a majority in some areas). And they cannot help but notice its political relevance in a variety of ways that will become clear in the course of this chapter. In fact, the United States, in terms of religious groupings, is composed of a number of minorities, and the Catholics may well be the largest of them. There are Protestants affiliated with churches whose histories include legal establishment and whose theologies do not exclude it *a priori*. There are Protestants who are in the free church tradition whose histories do not include legal establishment and whose theologies tend to exclude it *a priori*. Among the unchurched, there are a great number of believers who do not express their belief in formal church membership or frequent church attendance. There are unbelievers, some of whom are active secularists hoping and working for the elimination of "superstition" and the inauguration of a fully secular society. And there are, finally, the memberships of smaller religious groups, the most important of which are the Jews, who are likewise divided among themselves.[4]

Perhaps the most easily visible aspect of the Catholic minority's difference from the bulk of the rest of the population is its separate school system with an integral program of religious instruction and formation. Even aside from the periodic political skirmishes about the appropriation of public tax revenues to support that school system directly or indirectly, it inescapably arouses the suspicions of many other Americans. It continually suggests to them the Catholic thrust toward the integration of public life and religious life. The Catholic school system, therefore, constitutes for them a massive expression of what they take to be the authentic tendency of Catholic doctrine: the complete integration of human life around a religious center. This poses a serious threat to them inasmuch as they regard as a natural constitutional expression of that tendency a withdrawal or diminution of the First Amendment guarantees against laws "respecting an establishment of religion, or prohibiting the free exercise thereof."

[4] What is politically relevant here is not simply some sort of formal group membership, but depth of commitment to specific arrangements for church-state relationships, as well as depth of commitment to the group in the event that the group, as such, should take a stand. Thus conventional religious statistics would be virtually useless in this connection even if they were put on a uniform basis. Indeed, it is difficult to suppose that accurate and politically relevant statistics could be obtained. The issue is never simply "establishment" or simply "free exercise," but also a question of a specific arrangement from among the practically infinite variety of possibilities and it arises in a specific historical and political context from among the practically infinite variety of possibilities. Since, in addition, the minimum time span that is of interest here must be in the neighborhood of a century, it is obvious that opinion survey research is absolutely unable to exhaust the important possibilities. Therefore, I have been singularly hesitant to assign any specific weight to one group or another.

157

Naturally, such action is not an immediately impending threat. In a democratic republic with a federal structure such as the American, political action of that sort would not only depend on great numbers, but also on their proper distribution among the states. A few simple calculations reveal that amendment of the Constitution by Catholics is not immediately in the offing. But however true that might be, the uneasiness generated by this perception of Catholic doctrine goes a lot deeper, and rightly so. The nub of the question to non-Catholics is this: there are more than forty million of our fellow citizens who seem to us to have fundamental grounds for holding serious reservations about one of the central provisions of the constitutional structure of our common life.

There are official Catholic statements favoring the American constitutional arrangements.[5] Yet there remains some doubt whether they are only relevant to circumstances in which Catholics are something less than an overwhelming majority. Further, there is a statement of Pope Leo XIII, specifically referring to the United States, that seems to support the views that the American arrangement is only appropriate to present circumstances of great religious plurality.[6] In this connection, an often

[5] For the most authoritative statements of this kind, recourse should be had to the official statements and national pastoral letters of the American hierarchy. Significant passages favoring the American arrangement may be found in the pastoral letters and official joint statements issued by the American archbishops and bishops in 1829, 1837, 1866, 1884, 1919, 1926, 1934, and 1937. These documents are collected in Rev. Peter Guilday, ed., *The National Pastorals of the American Hierarchy: 1792–1919* (Washington, D.C.: National Catholic Welfare Conference, 1923) pp. 36–37 (1829), pp. 81–86 (1837), pp. 205–07 (1866), pp. 234–36 (1884), p. 325 (1919). Cited hereafter as *National Pastorals*. And in Very Rev. Raphael Huber, S.T.D., O.F.M., Conv., ed., *Our Bishops Speak: 1919–1951* (Milwaukee: 1952), pp. 72–77 (1926), pp. 208–209 (1934), p. 220 (1937). A reference to the American arrangement as an adaptation to particular conditions less than the "ideal" may be found in a 1948 statement, *ibid.,* pp. 149–53.

[6] ". . . thanks are due to the equity of the laws which obtain in America and to the customs of the well-ordered Republic. For the Church amongst you, unopposed by the Constitution and government of your nation, fet-

158

cited chapter of a textbook[7] (that would otherwise be consigned to the deserved oblivion generally the fate of the genre) inevitably comes to mind. While it cannot be maintained that *Catholic Principles of Politics* is a work of any genuine theoretical importance, it seems to have been fairly widely used in American Catholic schools. It would require the repeal or revision of the religious clauses of the First Amendment in the event that Catholics were to become an overwhelming majority in the United States.

But the question is even more far-reaching than that. There is a deep suspicion that the thrust of Catholic thought ultimately undermines far more than the religious provisions of the First Amendment. From a host of diverse evidence, the non-Catholic American is suspicious that Catholicism is ultimately at home only in an authoritarian regime of the monarchic or dictatorial type. In contemporary history, Franco's Spain and Salazar's Portugal are never far out of mind. While American Catholics have generally tended pugnaciously to reject this broader suspicion, the pressure of the questioning has forced them to examine the narrower question at some length.

The most brilliant among the Americans who have attempted to clarify Catholic doctrine in such a way that the suspicions of their fellow citizens would become groundless is John Courtney

---

tered by no hostile legislation, protected against violence by the common laws and the impartiality of the tribunals, is free to live and act without hindrance. Yet, although this is true, it would be very erroneous to draw the conclusion that in America is to be sought the type of the most desirable status of the Church, or that it would be universally lawful or expedient for State and Church to be, as in America, dissevered and divorced . . . but she would bring forth more abundant fruits if, in addition to liberty, she enjoyed the favor of the laws and the patronage of the public authority." This English translation may be found under the heading: "Catholicity in the United States: Encyclical Letter *Longinque Oceani*, January 6, 1895" in John J. Wynne, ed., *The Great Encyclical Letters of Pope Leo XIII* (New York: 1903), pp. 323–324.

[7] John A. Ryan and Francis J. Boland, C.S.C., *Catholic Principles of Politics* (New York: 1943), pp. 308–342.

159

Murray of the Society of Jesus. His work led to a series of rejoinders that aimed to reaffirm the positions that had occasioned the suspicions while making as many soothing, practical qualifications and concessions as it seemed possible to make without sacrifice of what were taken as traditional Catholic principles. Although they were written in response to Murray's doctrinal initiative, I have chosen to treat these works first, since they have the character of a restatement and explication of a commonly held opinion against which Murray set out to do battle. The principal voices in defense of the then current view were Joseph C. Fenton, Francis J. Connell, C.SS.R., and George W. Shea, all of them publishing in *The American Ecclesiastical Review*. I have decided to call them canonists in keeping with an old tradition whereby the defenders of this and similar positions were called canonists, and the defenders of more moderate and less legalistic positions were called theologians.[8]

Let it be clear at the outset that no party to the controversy suggested that the present American constitutional arrangement in religious matters can be assailed, given the fact of great religious diversity in the United States. They were aware that, even were there available the necessary number and distribution of favorably disposed Catholic voters, any serious attempt to modify the constitutional arrangement would disastrously rend the body politic. It would poison and inflict deep wounds on our common life to an extent that would seriously threaten, if not destroy, that body politic and the common good it seeks to realize. And they are agreed that such an evil is wholly out of proportion to any real advantages that could conceivably flow from a new constitutional arrangement that—let us suggest an extreme change—would establish the Catholic religion as the religion of the state and would restrict *public* worship and propaganda by non-Catholics. But this is about the limit of agree-

[8] Cf. Bellarmine, *"De Potestate"* i, and Carlyle, *HMPT*, vol. 5.

ment. From this point on, there was scarcely any agreement between the canonists and Murray.

The canonists expounded the doctrine most commonly found in the "manuals of fundamental dogmatic theology and of public ecclesiastical law" that are used as seminary textbooks in the Catholic Church.[9] The argument runs as follows.

All societies have a natural and objective duty publicly to worship God, to pay "the debt of acknowledgment actually due Him because of His supreme goodness and because of our absolute and entire dependence upon Him."[10] But "God wills that the debt of religion (owed by all individuals and social groups) should be payed to Him in a definite and supernatural way." And "the one acceptable and authorized social worship of God is to be found summed up in the Eucharistic sacrifice of the Catholic Church."[11] Thus, the duty of public worship is a duty to perform acts of Catholic religion, i.e., the religion of the state must be the Catholic religion.[12]

But such social acts of worship cannot be performed by a

[9] Joseph C. Fenton, "Toleration and the Church-State Controversy," *The American Ecclesiastical Review*, vol. CXXX (May, 1954), pp. 335, 343. (*The American Ecclesiastical Review* is cited hereafter as *AER*.) George W. Shea gives a great list of these manuals in the footnotes to his article, "Catholic Doctrine and 'The Religion of the State,'" *AER*, vol. CXXIII (September, 1950), pp. 161–174.

[10] Fenton, "Principles Underlying Traditional Church-State Doctrine," *AER*, vol. CXXVI (June, 1952), p. 455. Cf., eg., Fenton, "The Catholic Church and Freedom of Religion," *AER*, vol. CXV (October, 1946), p. 300; "The Relation of the Christian State to the Catholic Church According to the *Pontificale Romanum*," *AER*, vol. CXXIII (September, 1950), p. 218; "The Status of a Controversy," *AER*, vol. CXXIV (June, 1951), p. 455; "Toleration and the Church-State Controversy," *AER*, vol. CXXX (May, 1954), p. 339; also Shea, "Catholic Doctrine and 'The Religion of the State,'" *AER*, vol. CXXIII (September, 1950), p. 166.

[11] Fenton, *AER*, vol. CXXVI (June, 1952), p. 457; Shea, *AER*, vol. CXXIII (September, 1950), p. 167.

[12] E.g., Fenton, *AER*, vol. CXXX (May, 1954), p. 399; Shea, *AER*, vol. CXXIII (September, 1950), pp. 167, 170–173; Shea, "Catholic Orientations on Church and State," *AER*, vol. CXXV (December, 1951), pp. 405–416; Shea, "Spain and Religious Freedom," *AER*, vol. CXXVII (September, 1952), pp. 164–166.

state in which membership "is sharply divided in religious be-lief."[13] This condition prevents the "objective" duty from becom-ing a "subjective" duty.[14] But this is never "*simpliciter* a good thing."[15] Under such circumstances, it may be good for the state to show equal favor to all religions, establishing none as its own, in order that "the law and government" may carry out their objective, which is "to aid us in our essential civil task of living together peacefully and of bringing about our own corporate and individual welfare."[16] Such, indeed, is the situation of the United States, and its Constitution realizes a good and necessary compromise in view of that situation.[17] The decisive factor in the whole discussion is whether the membership of a state is united in the Catholic religion. If there were no dissenters whatsoever, plainly there would be no further problem for Fenton and Shea and Connell. However, they are not so unrealistic as to suppose that dissenters will not, sooner or later, appear. They make no serious attempt to specify what proportion of dissenters there must be in a given state to render the state incapable of rightly offering social acts of worship to God according to the rites of the true religion. Such precise determination is left to prudence in each case. However, it is clear that they do insist that, for such

[13] Fenton, *AER,* vol. CXXVI (June, 1952), p. 456. Cf., eg., Fenton, *AER,* vol. CXV (October, 1946), pp. 300–301; *AER,* vol. CXXIV (June, 1951), p. 452; Shea, *AER,* vol. CXXXVII (September, 1952), pp. 166–167; Francis J. Connell, C.SS.R., "Reply to Father Murray," *AER,* vol. CXXVI (January, 1952), pp. 57–58.

[14] Fenton, *AER,* vol. CXXIV (June, 1951), p. 452. Cf., e.g., Shea, *AER,* vol. CXXIII (September, 1950), p. 167.

[15] Fenton, *AER,* vol. CXXVI (June, 1952), p. 457. Cf., e.g., Connell, *AER,* vol. CXXVI (January, 1952), p. 58.

[16] Fenton, *AER,* vol. CXXVI (June, 1952), p. 460.

[17] E.g., Fenton, *AER,* vol. CXV (October, 1946), pp. 295, 297; *AER,* vol. CXXVI (June, 1952), pp. 459–460; Shea, *AER,* vol. CXXXVII (September, 1952), pp. 166–168; Connell, "Catholic Legislators," *AER,* vol. CX (May, 1944), p. 339; Connell "The Catholic Public School Teacher," *AER,* vol. CXIII (August, 1945), p. 101; Connell, "The Theory of the 'Lay State,' " *AER,* vol. CXXV (July, 1951), p. 9.

acts of worship to take place, Catholics must be "for all intents and purposes its entire membership."[18]

The canonists have taken as their fundamental problem the question of the religion of the state (in terms of the U.S. Constitution, the establishment clause), rather than the question of free exercise of religion, to use American constitutional terminology. The question of free exercise is only answered in principle after they have ascertained the status of the arrangement called the religion of the state. Having decided that there is an objective duty for states to profess the Catholic religion as the religion of the state, and that such an arrangement is the best simply, they then declare that

One must *then* [italics added] face up to the problem of what ought to be the state's attitude toward, and dealing with, the heterodox: the

[18] Fenton, *AER,* vol. CXV (October, 1946), pp. 300–301. Yet earlier in the same article he seems to set as his criterion that "all Americans" become Catholics, the size of the majority of Catholics over non-Catholics in Eire not being enough, pp. 293–294. Shea distinguishes between the size of the majority in Eire and that in Spain (one-tenth of Eire's population being estimated to be non-Catholic whereas non-Catholics in Spain are estimated—all according to figures quoted by Shea—to be less than one thousandth of the population) and says that the Irish situation in this regard justifies a legitimate compromise, but the Spanish majority is adequate to achieve the best arrangement. Shea in his "Catholic Orientations on Church and State," *AER,* vol. CXXV (December, 1951), pp. 413–414, accepts a more comprehensive criterion than mere numbers: the "citizens profess the Catholic faith, and . . . [the state's] entire activity has as its norm the moral values proper to the Catholic faith and Catholic philosophy." This criterion he extracts from Oswald von Nell-Breuning, S.J., *Beitrage zu einem Wörterbuch der Politik* (Freiburg-im-Br.: 1947), vol. II, pp. 20–21. Connell speaks of a nation "essentially Catholic," in "Discussion of "Governmental Repression of Heresy,'" The Catholic Theological Society of America, *Proceedings of the Third Annual Meeting* (Chicago: 1948), p. 100. He also speaks of a "predominantly Catholic people" in "Christ the King of Civil Rulers," *AER,* vol. CXIX (October, 1948), p. 246, although he says that in terms of "practical policy," he "cannot see any probability of a change of circumstances in future (even the gaining of an overwhelming majority of the votes by Catholics) that would justify a change in our national policy of equal rights for all creed." *AER,* vol. CXXVI (January, 1952), p. 55. Yet it should be noted that this is a practical judgment and, further, does not refer directly to official social worship according to the rites of the Catholic Church.

problem of what "logical and juridical consequences," as regards sects, should flow from the situation of Catholicism as "the religion of the state." Before a further word is said on this subject, let it be noted at once that no Catholic holds or may hold that the state would be called upon to impose the Catholic faith on dissident citizens. Reverence for the individual conscience forbids this, and the very nature of religion and of the act of faith. If these be not voluntary, they are nought. Further, it is agreed to by all that the members of sects must be permitted the private external exercise of their religion.[19]

With this reservation in mind, then, "what ought to be the state's attitude toward, and dealing with, the heterodox?" The government of such a state "would have the right to forbid anti-Catholic machinations within its own borders."[20]

Would the Catholic state be under moral obligation (*per se*—as was stated at the very outset, our whole discussion has been moving at the level of principles) to restrict sects in such matters as the *public* [italics added] profession and exercise of their false religion in their propaganda, the spread of their heretical doctrines?

It is no secret that the defenders of the "old thesis" [of which Shea is one] answer in the affirmative.[21]

"In a Catholic or predominantly Catholic country, the Catholic Church should enjoy a preferred status and the special protection of the state."[22]

Connell indicates the end of such action:

It is fully within their [civil rulers'] right to restrict and to prevent public functions and activities of false religions which are likely to be detrimental to the spiritual welfare of the Catholic citizens or insulting to the true religion of Christ.[23]

[19] *AER*, vol. CXXIII (September, 1950), p. 168. In support of the first sentence, Shea quotes Pope Leo XIII and St. Augustine, gives two citations from Pope Pius XII, and cites canon 752, 1 and canon 1351 of the Code of Canon Law, all in note 24 on page 168. Fenton and Connell are also careful to insist on the same reservation.

[20] Fenton, *AER*, vol. CXV (October, 1946), p. 288.

[21] Shea, *AER*, vol. CXXIII (September, 1950), p. 168. Cf., e.g., *ibid.*, 174.

[22] Shea, *AER*, vol. CXXVII (September, 1952), p. 166.

[23] Connell, *AER*, vol. CXIX (October, 1948), p. 250.

He clarifies this a bit more in another place:

> I do not assert that the state has the right to repress religious error merely because it is error; but I believe the State has the right of repression and limitation (although often it is not expedient to use it) when error is doing harm to the spiritual interests of the Catholic citizens. For the spiritual welfare of the citizens (which in the present order is supernatural) pertains to their temporal wellbeing.[24]

The foregoing is the core of the position held by the American canonists. They raised subordinate questions such as the problems of marriage impediments, the Pauline privilege, and ecclesiastical immunities,[25] but they are all dependent on this core. And it, in turn, structured a view of the religious clauses of the First Amendment.

Although present conditions in the United States make adherence to the religious arrangements of the Constitution the best and wisest policy, indeed a policy required by principle, yet if one views the Constitution in terms of what is best simply, in terms of the objectively right, all but one of the religious provisions would have to be scrapped. And the one that remains would, if it were to remain at all, have to be modified to read as follows: Congress shall make no law prohibiting the free *private* exercise of religion. To be sure, contingent circumstances may make this best, or "thetic," relation of church and state inexpedient or simply unrealizable. But, with one exception,[26] the only circumstances specifically treated as having such consequences are questions concerning the proportion of Catholics in a given population. The population may be that of a specific state or of a group of states some of which are unable to realize the thetic ar-

[24] Connell, "Discussion of 'Governmental Repression of Heresy,'" *op. cit.*, p. 100. Cf. also Connell, *AER*, vol. CXXV (July, 1951), p. 17.

[25] See Connell's article, "The Theory of the 'Lay State,'" *AER*, vol. CXXV, pp. 7–18. See also Murray's comment in "For the Freedom and Transcendence of the Church," *AER*, vol. CXXVI (January, 1952), p. 39, n. 12, and Connell's "Reply to Father Murray," *ibid.*, pp. 49–59.

[26] Cf. *supra*, p. 163, n. 18.

rangement. The latter problem appears at first as a question of international relations and international law. But it is fundamentally a question of population, since it seems to hinge on questions of migration, particularly as raised by an international union such as the European Common Market.[27]

But the best or thetic relation of church and state is not rendered inexpedient or impossible of realization by the contingent circumstance that a given state is more or less democratic. The whole question as to the relevance of political forms, of any kind, to the thetic relation of church and state, although raised by Murray, is simply ignored in some cases, and the relevance denied, without discussion, in other cases.[28]

In short, support of the religious provisions of the United States' Constitution rests, for Murray's opponents, on the contingent and lamentable fact of widespread religious diversity. Given a situation in which such is not the case—however remote from the foreseeable future—they suggest no other basis on which support might rest.[29]

I have spoken so far only of the religious clauses of the Constitution. The thetic arrangements suggested by Fenton *et al.* would also plainly require a revision of the First Amendment provisions reading: "Congress shall make no law . . . abridging

[27] The problems raised, for states in which the Catholic religion is the religion of the state, by this type of international project were discussed by Pope Pius XII in the Allocution *Ci riesce* delivered to the Union of Italian Catholic Jurists. (The text, in an English translation provided by the Vatican Press Office, is reprinted in *AER*, vol. CXXX [February, 1954], pp. 129–138.) Cf. Fenton, "The Teachings of the *Ci riesce,*" *ibid.*, pp. 114–123, and Fenton, "Toleration and the Church-State Controversy," *AER*, vol. CXXX (May, 1954), p. 338.

[28] E.g., Shea, *AER*, vol. CXXIII (September, 1950), p. 166; Connell, *AER*, vol. CXXVI (January, 1952), pp. 55–57.

[29] It should be noted that the multiplicity of sects is of no small consequence, in a purely practical way, in ensuring support for an arrangement such as that under the Constitution. James Madison and Edmund Randolph of Virginia, to mention only two, were aware of this and even favored such multiplicity for this reason. Cf. Stokes, *Church and State*, vol. 1, pp. 532–533. Cf. Murray, *Thought*, vol. XXIX (Summer, 1954), p. 192.

166

the freedom of speech, or of the press." Since they do not explicitly advert to this problem, it is difficult to say precisely what revisions would have to be made. Perhaps a general statement of the minimum requirements of the thesis could be phrased thusly: the state must have efficacious authority to prevent the publication (whether by speech or other means) of views on faith and morals contrary to the doctrine of the Catholic Church. The precise form of such preventive action would, presumably, be determined in the light of circumstances.

It is this very silence on so obviously crucial a political question that proclaims the peculiar character of the solution the canonists have urged. In the time-honored way of lawyers they have attempted to isolate a narrow, discrete, legal issue to be decided, and, within that little world, to erect an inescapable and inexorable line of legal reasoning. The natural law as amended by the divine law of revelation imposes an obligation on man to repay in a particular way the debt incurred by man in accepting life and grace from the Creator and Savior. The debt is incurred not only by individuals, but by societies also, since man not only accepts individual existence and individually relevant grace, but also social existence and socially relevant grace. Thus, whenever individuals and societies are able to pay the debt in the specified way, they must do so. Furthermore, the debtors are under obligation to take whatever steps are reasonably likely to assist in ensuring that they will not fall into a condition in which payments can no longer be made. They are, in effect, enjoined to take such precautionary measures to avoid a foreseeable development that would preclude payment of the debt. Evidently, the precautionary measures include a broad limitation on the rights of citizens to public expression in any form that would tend to spread non-Catholic doctrine or practice.

Whatever the theological merits of the argument, a matter that will be held in abeyance for the moment, it is evident that it suffers from an egregious political illiteracy. The canonists do

167

not suggest that they are writing about a single form of political regime, for example, a sacred kingship. It appears that they mean the argument to be valid either for all regimes or at least for all legitimate ones. And there is no evidence that they regard what is popularly known as American democracy[30] as anything less than a legitimate regime. But it is equally plain that they have taken no serious thought about the perfectly obvious question as to whether the systematic suppression of public manifestations of heterdoxy by public agencies is compatible with the guarantees of free expression that are evidently integral to the regimes of modern nation-states that include an important element of democracy in their constitutional structures. Clearly, any democratic element in the constitution of the nation-state becomes inoperative if freedom of public expression and discussion is denied. Furthermore, there are structural reasons why governmental limitations on freedom of expression and discussion are more dangerous to the democratic elements of a nation-state's constitution than in a city-state or town-meeting democracy. The dangers are great enough and obvious enough that any proposal that envisages a systematic suppression of a substantively large area of opinion that may be politically relevant must at least confront the problem if it means to be taken seriously. Governmental action in this area on the scale of the nation-state necessarily involves a large apparatus for surveillance, censorship,

[30] A scientifically inexact usage. It is quite clear to all observers that no large nation state is a simple democracy in which the citizens directly rule. While there is no universal agreement on an adequate scientific typology of regimes, working consensus could probably be obtained for representative republic or democratic representative republic. This would also refer to the political realities of a regime such as the British, in which there are ceremonial elements of the constitution of an hereditary character that only subtly and indirectly moderate the "efficient parts" of the regime. Cf., e.g., F.A. Hermens, *The Representative Republic* (Notre Dame: 1958); Austin Ranney and Willmoore Kendall, *Democracy and the American Party System* (New York: 1956); Herbert J. Spiro, *Government by Constitution* (New York: 1959).

168

apprehension of violators, etc.[31] The compatibility of such an inquisitorial apparatus with the simultaneous maintenance of free expression and discussion in other areas of political relevance is, to put it mildly, at least a serious and unavoidable question. It will later be discussed at some length. For the present, it is enough to point out that the American canonists simply fail to see it. The failure is so obvious that Murray is led to ask sarcastically: "Did the Catholic 'thesis' go out with the Bourbons?" Is the only possible "posture for the universal Church" that of nostalgically looking "back over our shoulder at the diminishing figure of Isabella II?"[32]

But this failure to comprehend the institutional dimension of the problem raised by the canonists' argument for establishment and its consequences as the Catholic ideal is only one aspect of a broader failure. It seems wholly to escape their notice that the peculiar genius of democratic institutions is some sort of liberal spirit. There are all sorts of arguments as to its ultimate springs. It may be attributed to the inherent inclination toward license rather than discipline characteristic of the *demos* or the masses in contrast to aristocracies or élites.[33] Or it may be attributed to a peculiar ideological matrix involving a special set of epistemological principles and psychic experiences that undergird a "democratic faith" that includes a heavy emphasis on the "rights of man" or of the citizen as distinguished from an emphasis on "the right" for man or natural law.[34] But whether it rests on one or

[31] It will not do to object that no such apparatus is envisaged. If it is not envisaged, then the legislative arrangements directed at suppressing the spread of heresy cannot escape being inefficacious objects of ridicule by those who mock them in practice as well as by humorously inclined bystanders and fundamental opponents of the regime.

[32] J.C.M., "The Problem of State Religion," *Theological Studies,* XII (June, 1951), p. 174, n. 18.

[33] Cf. e.g., Plato, *Republic* viii. 557–558; Aristotle, *Politics* vi. 2; José Ortega y Gasset, *The Revolt of the Masses* (New York: 1932), especially chs. 7 and 13.

[34] Cf., e.g., Robert A. Dahl, *A Preface to Democratic Theory* (Chicago: 1956); Hans Kelsen, *General Theory of Law and State* (Cambridge, Mass.:

both bases, it seems, at the very least, likely that democratic institutions are informed by a spirit that rejects the restrictiveness inherent in the canonists' thetic regime. If, then, they had argued that the Catholic Church prefers some other regime or regimes to democracy, one would be able to enter the dispute. Or, if they had argued that the liberal genius of democracy does not extend to this particular matter, then again one would be able to examine the question with them and enter the dispute.

But the only considerations they consider relevant are, with one exception, questions of head counts and migrations. The one clear exception is the statement by Shea that the thetic arrangement requires that, in addition to a numerically Catholic population, the "entire activity" of the society have "as its norm the moral values proper to the Catholic faith and Catholic philosophy." Yet it never seems to occur to him to ask whether it is possible that a society formed by democratic institutions and spirit could be of such a character. This is not the place to attempt an answer. But it is necessary to point out that the question is fairly obvious and yet went quite unnoticed. In consequence, the argument is absurdly jejune. Whatever else one might think about them, Burke and de Maistre are at least interesting. The American canonists are simply boring. They either lack the perspicacity or the courage to be conservative with Burke, or reactionary with de Maistre, or even to engage the devil in a desperate rearguard action with Giles of Rome. Rather, one is inclined to suspect that in all other respects they would, if called on, reaffirm, with all the insistent and even Nativist patriotism of the Irish-American assimilation, the slogans of the liberal American orthodoxy in one or another of its forms.[35]

1945); Jacques Maritain, *Truth and Human Fellowship* (Princeton: 1957); K. R. Popper, *The Open Society and Its Enemies* (Princeton: 1950); Herbert J. Storing, ed., *Essays on the Scientific Study of Politics* (New York: 1962); Leo Strauss, *Natural Right and History* (Chicago: 1953); Thomas Landon Thorson, *The Logic of Democracy* (New York: 1962).

[35] Cf. Louis Harz, *The Liberal Tradition in America* (New York: 1955).

Nevertheless, it is necessary to point to one further major problem in the canonists' position, this one theological in character. It is necessary to do so because the problem is central to any serious consideration of the Church-state issue. At the heart of the canonists' position is a hope, a hope for a particular kind of society. The substance of their "thesis" is a holy people: peaceful, just, meticulous in the performance of their religious obligations, and, especially, obedient to ecclesiastical authority. The beginning and the end of their action would be divine worship, and, in between, the works of justice and charity toward fellow men under the authoritative supervision of pope, bishops, and clergy. In that society, there will neither be heresy nor great public scandal. The principal public occasions of sin will have been suppressed. With a sober, God-fearing, and well-drilled obedience, all will praise the Lord in one voice and willingly do the tasks to which they have been called by pope, bishops, and priests, following their commands with a ready heart.

Naturally, one is inclined to suppose that a façade of such pious and tranquil order would have been imposed by means of the ever-present surveillance, iron discipline, informers, and all-embracing drill-work common in the more dreary convent boarding schools or seminaries in the Jansenist style. For purposes of adapting to the sometimes tougher adults of the world of politics, a good dash of brutality might have to be added at the fringes. It is, of course, relevant to argue that the ecclesiasti-

---

As far as I know, they have not endorsed the opinion that the Declaration of Independence was a product of Bellarminian thought and perhaps even of Thomist thought (cf. John C. Rager, *Democracy and Bellarmine* [Shelbyville, Ind.: 1926], originally done as a thesis for the theological faculty of the Catholic University of America, and Edward Murphy, *St. Thomas' Political Thought* [Washington, D. C. 1921]). Naturally, the European allies of the American canonists were not subject to such schizoid pressures. For example, a reactionary such as Alfredo Cardinal Ottaviani, who entered the fray against Murray ("Church and State," *AER,* vol. CXXVIII [May, 1953], pp. 321–334), would scarcely be inclined to assimilate either Jefferson or modern democracy to the mainstream of a curialist version of orthodoxy.

171

cal informer and the *auto-da-fé* are likely accompaniments of the "thesis," and that one might question the "thetic" character of a doctrine that interpreted the gospels in such a way that this was their fulfillment on earth. Nevertheless, such an argument is always open to the objection that such consequences are not envisaged, and even that, rather than accept such consequences, the thetic society should abandon its thetic character if no other way seems open for its defense.

But there is a deeper question at stake. The question is whether the Christian has a right to hope and work for a consummation in the world of a society free of visible or public disbelief, heresy, and scandal. The question is whether the canonists have not set up as the substance of a genuinely Christian politics a secularized version of Revelation 7:9–17. The question is whether, without even being aware of the magnitude of the problem, as was Giles of Rome, the canonists really believe that it is possible to pull up all the weeds without pulling up also the wheat (Mt 13:24–30; 36–43). And if they think so, do they suppose that they ought to put their judgment before that of their Master? The question is whether it is heretical to suppose that in this provisional order of things between the first and the second comings of Christ, the Church on earth can ignore the fact that she is essentially missionary and that her missionary character refers to the darkness, vice, and unbelief of Christendom as well as of darkest Africa. The question is whether the canonists' thesis is not fundamentally heretical by omitting to recognize certain essential elements of the human condition between the Resurrection and the Second Coming. The question, in short, is whether a summary of statistics on the number of baptized persons in the population is the basis on which the mystic history of salvation can be penetrated, or whether the invocation of such statistical information is rather a way of escaping that history and its implications.

John Courtney Murray

Historicism as an Antidote

THE American canonists put together a strange composition of rationalistic political theory and a political practice to which theory is irrelevant.[1] Having constructed a thesis about the best state of affairs in Church-state relations, they admit that it is irrelevant to the existing situation and almost all conceivable ones. Although they condemn the religious clauses of the First Amendment in principle (and, with them, the other clauses by implication), they are nevertheless prepared in practice to grant to their non-Catholic fellow citizens a guarantee that will support the First Amendment, a guarantee they are prepared to extend to their children's children and beyond. Admittedly, the precise basis on which these assurances are extended is not a little unclear, not to speak of the question how such a guarantee could be enforced. One has only to read any of Paul Blanshard's works[2] to note that all the soothing guarantees hardly prevent the use of the "thesis" as a permanent storehouse of ammunition against Catholicism in America.

Perceiving the rather ludicrous embarrassment of his coreligionists, John Courtney Murray set out to discover whether the Catholic faith committed them to such principles. And, if

[1] Cf. Reinhold Niebuhr, *The Children of Light and the Children of Darkness* (New York: 1945), pp. 127–128.

[2] E.g., *American Freedom and Catholic Power* (Boston: 1949).

not, what better principles could replace them? Is the object of political community such that it cannot legitimately take action in the sphere of religion? Under all circumstances or only under some circumstances? Is the character of the mature political society inherently pluralist in matters of religion?

But, at heart, the problem that Murray faced was always two-sided. He remarked of a book he was reviewing that it only asked: how religion shall be made free in society? However, such a problematic is too simple inasmuch as it does not include the more important question: how shall society be made religious?[3] But he thinks that no pair of formulas can adequately state the Catholic position. That position involves a fundamental tension. Not only do we love God in the truth that He has given us, but we also love man in his conscience, the most divine thing in him. That is to say, we are opposed to falseness not only about the truths of faith, but in the living lie of a man who is forced to profess an orthodoxy which he rejects at the depths of his soul.[4] It is this tension which ought to be preserved on the level of public existence, rather than either denying the truth with a view to guaranteeing the freedom of consciences from external, human pressures, or attempting to force consciences in the name of the truth of the gospels.

To work out the implications of those two perceptions for all the diverse, yet connected, areas of public sociality is obviously a task of some magnitude. And Murray knows the magnitude of the problem. The question of the governmental repression of heresy cannot be raised first and solved by itself. Nor is it the center of the problem. It is "only a peripheral part" of the problem, even though it may be of great practical importance. The broad problem is that of the relationship between the Church in

[3] Review of *Religious Liberty* by M. Searle Bates, in *Theological Studies*, VII (March, 1946), p. 154. Hereafter, *Theological Studies* is abbreviated as *TS*.

[4] J.C.M., "Freedom of Religion: I. The Ethical Problem," *TS*, VI (June, 1945), pp. 230–232.

174

the totality of her membership and mission and the whole, multifaceted thing that is human society. Within that fundamental problematic there is a narrower question: what are the appropriate relationships between ecclesiastical and civil authority? Only within that narrower problem can the question arise whether the civil authorities ought to suppress public manifestations of religious heresy.[5]

Unfortunately, Murray did not find himself in a position to conduct such a thoroughgoing study. In a great many particulars, the broader framework within which the more obvious, popular questions are raised did not receive an articulation adequate to the demands of the relevant questions. But the pressures of the theological milieu within which he spoke and wrote were such that he was repeatedly compelled to direct his attention to rather narrow controversies that were concerned with issues that, by his own definition, were peripheral. In the midst of the fray, however, his almost constant purpose, even when faced with an opponent with a "genius for the peripheral,"[6] was to lead the discussion back to its center. It is a measure of the pressures he felt from those harboring genii of the peripheral that after publishing a dozen major articles on the subject, he found it wise to devote a series of five long essays to showing that the line of argument he was attempting to open up was not contrary to the writings of Pope Leo XIII. The last of the series never appeared, and Professor Murray ceased publishing anything directly on the questions he had begun raising. Inasmuch as Alfredo Cardinal Ottaviani, Secretary of the Holy Office, had taken the trouble to publish in 1953 an article attacking Murray's position,[7] it was generally rumored that he had been

[5] J.C.M., "Governmental Repression of Heresy," *Proceedings of the Third Annual Meeting of the Catholic Theological Society of America* (Chicago: 1948), pp. 27, 31.

[6] J.C.M., "For the Freedom and Transcendence of the Church," *AER,* vol. CXXVI (January, 1952), p. 39, n. 12.

[7] "Church and State: Some Present Problems in the Light of the Teaching of Pope Pius XII," *AER,* vol. CXXVIII (May, 1953), pp. 321–334.

silenced by ecclesiastical authority when, in the following year, he fell silent.[8] Therefore, it is best, by way of clearing the underbrush, as it were, to treat first his fundamentally defensive polemic designed to show that the canonists' "thesis" was not *de fide,* not identical with papal teaching, and that his own line of argument was not *prima facie* heretical.

At the very core of the controversy, the canonists could recall that Pope Leo had said of the Church in the United States that "she would bring forth more abundant fruits if, in addition to liberty, she enjoyed the favor of the laws and the patronage of the public authority."[9] Of course, there was no need to point to that text alone; Leo XIII had written a long list of relevant encyclical letters that regularly used language that confirmed the canonists' opinions.[10]

Murray acknowledges that Pope Leo did indeed denounce the separation of Church and state, that he did indeed defend legislation granting a special status to the Church, that he did indeed argue for a special patronage by the civil power of the Catholic truth as against contradictory opinions. But, he argues, Leo XIII wrote within a particular historico-political context and his writing is relevant to that situation. It is a peculiar situation. It is not

---

[8] Naturally, it seems preposterous to report rumors in such matters. However, the squalid state of affairs that prevails in the handling of them by ecclesiastical authorities, especially when the vow of obedience is involved, is such that nothing else but rumor exists to account for the sudden silences that have afflicted other theologians as well as Murray. When I wrote him to ask about the fate of the fifth and promised essay on Leo XIII, he very briefly replied that it had not been published and that "I shall not bore you" with the reasons. Since there seemed to be no point in increasing his evident discomfort, I have not pressed him. Therefore, the reader is free to accept or reject at his pleasure the rumor I have reported.

[9] Encyclical *Longinque Oceani, Acta Sanctae Sedis,* vol. XXVII (1894–1895), p. 390. Connell quotes it triumphantly in "Reply to Father Murray," *AER,* vol. CXXVI (January, 1952), pp. 56–57.

[10] Principally, *Inscrutabili* (1878), *Diuturnum* (1881), *Humanum Genus* (1884), *Immortale Dei* (1885), *Libertas* (1888), *Sapientiae Christianae* (1890), *Graves de Communi* (1901).

ours. Very briefly put, the nature of that situation is as follows.[11]

The regal absolutism of the European continent had in fact been accompanied by a radically immature mass of subjects, ignorant of the historic bases of their civilization, the human patrimonies derived from the experiences of classical antiquity and the Christian West. With the overthrow of the *ancien régime,* the ignorant masses were confronted with what Talmon has called totalitarian democracy.[12] The aggressive Jacobinism of Pope Leo's opponents involved the post-revolutionary republics in the official patronage of a "new truth" that was to be substituted for the "old truth" of the absolute kings. The Jacobins were committed to a program of indoctrinating with the religion of humanity the ignorant masses left behind by the *ancien régime.* The religious substance of Jacobin democracy was the assertion that man stood under no law and no judge other than one made by himself. Separation of Church and state and the "modern liberties" were in fact simply aspects of a general assault on divine religion in the name of the religion of man concerted in a systematic and penetrating two-pronged attack. Negatively, it encompassed the suppression of all public manifestations of shared confession of faith in God; positively, it centered on the exclusive control by the state of the educational system, a control that not only involved the negative element of excluding religious instruction and practice from the schools, but that also

[11] The following paragraphs are a drastic summary of Murray's exegesis of Pope Leo XIII's Church-state writings that are the principal concern of four articles: "Leo XIII on Church and State: The General Structure of the Controversy," *TS,* vol. XIV (March, 1953), pp. 1–30; "Leo XIII: Separation of Church and State," *TS,* vol. XIV (June, 1953), pp. 145–214; "Leo XIII: Two Concepts of Government," *TS,* vol. XIV (December, 1953), pp. 551–567; "Leo XIII: Two Concepts of Government: II. Government and the Order of Culture," *TS,* vol. XV (March, 1954), pp. 1–33. Cf. also "The Church and Totalitarian Democracy," *TS,* vol. XIII (December, 1952), pp. 525–563.

[12] J.L. Talmon, *The Rise of Totalitarian Democracy* (Boston: 1952). This work formed one of the principal bases of Murray's "The Chuch and Totalitarian Democracy," *TS,* XIII (December, 1952), pp. 525–563.

sponsored a positive indoctrination in the worship of humanity accompanied by the systematic unmasking of the idiocies of Christian superstition.

The kings by divine right had at least admitted that they were subject to the edicts of the divine will, and, therefore, that they were subject to the divine judgment, even if they denied that anyone might use the divinely established standards to judge them here on earth. Thus, despite the inherent abuses of the union of throne and altar under the absolutist kings, the pope could not help but prefer some such union, whether of throne and altar or of republic and altar, if the alternative was a systematically anti-religious and, indeed, blasphemous assault on the faith of the ignorant masses by a state that claimed to represent the unlimited authority of a god-like humanity. This limitation of the alternatives that presented themselves at the moment structured the pope's writing, which was fundamentally pastoral in nature rather than theoretical. That is to say, although it necessarily rested on and appealed to generally valid principles, it brings them to light only insofar as they are relevant to the practical political problems of his flock on the continent. Therefore, when other circumstances prevail, it is necessary to bring to light other aspects of the applicable body of general principles which Pope Leo wholly or partly ignored. This is precisely what Murray thinks is necessary a half-century later, especially for the quite different circumstances of Anglo-Saxon politics, particularly the American variety.

In order to speak of the American arrangements in these matters, it is necessary to adopt new accents and emphases, because the American institutions have quite different roots. "The American political tradition, whose parentage was English rather than Continental, has remained substantially untouched by the two radical vices which ruined the medieval heritage on the Continent—absolutism and the sacralization of politics." In fact, "the American constitutional system, as a structure, still reveals the essential lines of a Christian structure of politics." And at the heart of that faithfulness to the Christian structure of politics "is the firmness with which the United States Constitution asserts the distinction between society and state and the principle of a government of limited powers."[13]

Thus, before touching on Anglo-American constitutionalism, it is necessary to turn to Murray's treatment of the medieval organization of politics. His attitude toward the medieval arrangements of ecclesiastico-political matters is curiously ambiguous. On the one hand, the medieval organization of politics, for all its faults, is supposed to reflect the genuine Christian structure of civic life in the measure that it was neither regalist nor papalist. It laid the groundwork for modern constitutionalism by providing for a distribution of competencies and duties and hence for limited government, limited by law and by the people in its scope of action. At its core lay the Gelasian dualism of two authorities, the sacred and the royal. It is this very dualism, institutionalized and defended in the Middle Ages, that is also, with modification obviously, at the heart of the American polity. It is ineluctably opposed to every form of totalitarian monism.[14]

At the same time, the medieval polity seems to him to have been radically defective. The medieval state was, at it were, in a stage of adolescence.[15] The progressive decline and collapse of the Roman Empire left a political vacuum. The available institutions, leaders, and operative political principles were simply inadequate for the creation of even an approximation of a rational political order. The Church was the only institution

[13] J.C.M., "Leo XIII," *TS*, vol. XIV (June, 1953), p. 151.
[14] Cf. especially "The Church and Totalitarian Democracy," *TS*, vol. XIII (December, 1952), pp. 525–563; "Leo XIII," *TS*, vol. XIV (June, 1953), pp. 145–214. He says the same thing in an abbreviated form, without the references to Pope Leo and Cardinal Ottaviani that seem to have caused him so much trouble before, in his *We Hold These Truths*, which is subtitled "Catholic Reflections on the American Proposition," pp. 198–211.
[15] J.C.M., *C.T.S.A. Proceedings*, 1948, p. 63.

179

capable of attempting to remedy the defect. The use of the papal power of deposition as a weapon to prevent medieval kingship from degenerating into tyranny has already been discussed.[16] But at a far deeper level, Murray points out, there was a reliance of the medieval state on the Church.

Unable to work out a satisfactory temporal basis for political unity for a variety of historical reasons, the medieval regimes rested on religious unity instead. Adherence to the faith became one of the constitutive elements of citizenship, and thus the faith and law of the Church became the foundations of public law. This is the heart of what Murray refers to as the medieval *union coutumière* of Church and state, the essence of which was not the mere arbitrary fiat of an absolutist king who employed religious politics in the face of "the indifferentism of the cultured classes and the apostasy of the working-class. On the contrary, the medieval, customary union rested on popular consent." Nevertheless, that very state of affairs is a sure sign of the political immaturity of medieval polity. The "Papacy stood 'between a dying system and one waiting to be born,' as the only living social and cultural force left after the complete collapse of a lay civilization; it acquired political status by default and maintained it by necessity—not that of the Church but of civilization itself."[17]

Unfortunately, the fragmentary way in which medieval problems are treated leaves some of the most interesting questions unanswered. For example: how much, if anything, does the modern constitutionalism that Murray praises owe to the peculiarly religious substance of that *union coutumière,* and how much is it an elaboration (to cover large numbers of people

[16] Cf. *supra,* pp. 137–141.

[17] Murray does not attempt any systematic study of the medieval kingdom; his notion of it can only be gleaned from fragments dropped along the way, as it were. See particularly *C.T.S.A. Proceedings,* 1948, pp. 40–41, 62–63, 64, 72, 86–87; *Cross Currents,* pp. 23, 48; "Bellarmine," p. 519; "On Religious Freedom," *TS,* vol. X (September, 1949), p. 431.

settled over large areas) of the typical constitutional structures of the Germanic warrior bands that swept into the Western part of the Roman Empire? Structures whose essential features lie also at the Greek and Roman roots of our civilization?[18] In short, what is it, precisely, in the "medieval heritage" that is still present in the "American Constitutional system, as a structure," and that "still reveals the essential lines of a Christian structure of politics"? There is no point in pursuing the question here, since Murray did not attempt a systematic answer.

The medieval, customary politico-religious unity rested on a broad consensus that adherence to the Catholic faith and communion with the pope constituted the basis for membership in a Christendom, the temporal expression of which was the Holy Roman Empire. The temporal ineffectiveness of the Empire gave way to the national kingdoms that rested on more genuinely political grounds. The failure of the papacy to grasp this fact then led to the disputes between the popes and the kings. On the continent, for a variety of reasons, the development took the direction of royal absolutism and a state religion under the headship, for all practical purposes, of the king. The leading personages in the society took an increasingly cynical attitude toward the political uses of religion. The lower strata of the commons were increasingly depressed and atomized to become mere subject masses. As for the emerging mass of workers, their direction was apostasy. This is the context, argues Murray, in which the notion of a legally imposed religion of the state was developed, powerfully aided, of course, by the manifestation of the breakdown of Christendom by the Reformation that brought forth the principle *cujus regio, ejus religio*. This argument is not developed as a whole in any one place, but by bits and pieces; in

[18] Cf., e.g., Tacitus, *De Germania* 7–16; F. Kern, *Kingship and Law in the Middle Ages,* trans. S. B. Chrimes (Oxford: 1948), pp. 181–205. For antique references, cf. *supra,* p. 16, n. 2.

longer or shorter form it appears repeatedly in his work, especially in the articles on Leo XIII.[19]

The historical vista exposed by Murray consists of four basic eras, with a church-state structure peculiar to each. The danger in antiquity was caesaro-papism, in the Middle Ages the danger was papal-caesarism. He judges that the Middle Ages avoided that danger and was on the way toward limited, constitutional government when the appearance of royal absolutism signaled the death of the goose that was about to lay the golden egg. However, in the "Anglo-Saxon" countries, the fatal apparition was too brief to accomplish its work. On the continent, all the perversion and corruptions that Pope Leo had to deal with flowed from the decaying societies, but the "Anglo-Saxon" goose brought forth an egg that, although "colored to some extent by eighteenth-century ideology," consisted of the genuine gold of democracy.[20]

This is the noble, Platonic tale that Murray tells with a view to taming the excesses of both Catholics and non-Catholics so that they can live together. In short, the "historical approach"[21] of Murray turns out to be a fragmentary but intuitively brilliant attempt to restructure and unify the myths that have given identity to the main streams of modern, Western man. His tale shows the canonists that their "thesis" about "religion of the state" is in fact an aberration from the central Catholic tradition manifested in the West. The tale shows the democratists to be outside the very tradition that has brought forth democracy. Insofar as they assert that "ultimate value resides in the forms of the democratic

[19] And cf., e.g., *C.T.S.A. Proceedings*, 1948, *passim*, and especially pp. 40–41; *Cross Currents*, pp. 16–17, 48.

[20] Cf., e.g., *C.T.S.A. Proceedings*, 1948, pp. 39–42; 52–62; *Cross Currents*, pp. 16–17; 20–23; *We Hold These Truths* (New York: 1961), p. 202. It seems from the *Cross Currents* article that even the continental goose was posthumously delivered of an egg though it bore the radical defect of being an "ism," i.e., "democratism . . . made religious pretensions and assumed absolutist tendencies" (p. 17).

[21] Cf., e.g., *C.T.S.A. Proceedings*, 1948, pp. 33–38.

process itself, because these forms embody the most ultimate of all values, freedom,"[22] they destroy the medieval and Christian roots out of which constitutional democracy has sprung. They do so by denying authority, in terms of a substantive, supra-human truth and law, in favor of an unlimited exaltation of freedom. But it was precisely the creative tension generated between these two poles that issued in constitutional democracy.

But Murray attempts to do more. Since some Catholics were evidently embarrassed by a theoretical commitment to a Church-state relationship possible only in some sort of imitation of a Bourbon regime, he set out to see whether the Church-state relationships possible in a constitutional democracy might not actually be better than those of the old regime, as well as of those of antiquity and the Middle Ages. And this leads to the element of progressist chauvinism in his thought. Ignoring the important contribution of ancient philosophy,[23] he depicts antiquity as utterly englobing the concerns of the spirit within the political order, a perversion that was cured by the Catholic Church which gave birth to the medieval polity. That polity suffered from political immaturity and was cured by worse medicine: royal absolutism and nationalism. But the essentially right developments of the medieval adolescence reëmerged after the absolutist interlude to give us our pride and glory, constitutional democracy. This is, no doubt, heartening to all who are fortunate to live in an "Anglo-Saxon" country in our blessed days, and Murray is hardly inclined to detract from anyone's rejoicing over it. Indeed, he hints that this development corresponds to the eternal order and objectives of the cosmos, and, presumably, of its Maker. "Democracy today presents itself with all the force of an idea *whose time has come*."[24] Indeed the "substance of the [democratic] development, as likewise in the case of the

---

[22] *We Hold These Truths*, pp. 51–53; 205–215.
[23] Cf. *supra*, pp. 16–20.
[24] "The Problem of State Religion," *TS*, vol. XII (June, 1951), p. 162.

nation-state, has been increasingly revealed as corresponding to an intention of nature." That is a statement of heroic dimensions, and one might expect an equally heroic effort at revealing the structure of the "intentions of nature." The only evidence seems to be that "Pius XII has cited this view with evident approval."[25]

But, having annulled the marriage between the Church and the *ancien régime,* from which point of view all other church-state relations appeared as useful liaisons at best, Murray is not prepared to rush her into another marriage, this time with democracy. On the tactical level, he does not want to bring down on his head the Spanish clergy, or any proponents of Bourbonism.[26] On the theoretical level, he wishes to ensure the freedom of the Church from permanent, inextricable commitment to any particular kind of regime as against all others. That includes democracy. Inspection of Murray's historical argument shows that, although democracy is "an idea whose time has come," there is no reason to suppose that other, new regimes may yet have a "time"; and, even though democracy may correspond to "an intention of nature," Murray is careful not to be borne away on the general enthusiasm to such an extent as to say that it corresponds to *the* intention of nature.

To begin with, "America has passionately pursued the ideal of freedom, expressed in a whole system of political and civil rights to new lengths." Furthermore, "a subtle alteration of the tradition had already commenced" prior to the founding of the Republic. It may be that American democracy will turn out to be

[25] *Cross Currents,* p. 17, citing the Pope's famous Christmas Radio Message of 1944.

[26] He repeatedly assures the Spaniards that they alone can adequately judge which set of arrangements best fits their circumstances, provided they don't assert the universal validity of their conclusions. He likewise defends the concordatory union of throne and altar as the best that could be done under the imperfections inherent in the old regime. Cf., e.g., "On Religious Freedom," *TS,* vol. X (September, 1949), pp. 426–432; *Cross Currents,* pp. 46–50.

a "flat majoritarianism, which is no mansion but a barn; perhaps even a tool shed in which the weapons of tyranny may be forged."[27] He even goes so far as to say that "the American constitutional system exaggerates the distinction between Church and state by its self-denying ordinances." Yet "there are times and circumstances . . . when some exaggeration of the restrictions placed on government is necessary in order to insure freedom."[28]

Thus, Murray makes clear that to describe the American Republic is not exactly the same thing as describing the "Ideal Republic of Truth and Justice."[29] As far as he is concerned, "the adjective 'best' when applied absolutely to a concrete political system is meaningless."[30]

Still, he is not content to defend only the rights of Americans for Americans. His notion of democratic government has a broader relevance. "There can in fact be no popular share in power . . . without those constitutional means for the vindication of rights and interests and for the direction of the political process which are known as the democratic institutions—freedom of opinion, of association, of speech, of the press." As for religious freedom, it has a special relationship to these foregoing: "It is now judged not politically possible or just to except out of the guarantee of these freedoms the freedom of religious association and a constitutional right to the free expression of religious opinion." He argues that such an exception is not just inasmuch as it implies a violation of the basic equality that the citizens "may justly claim as a basic civic right." Neither is it "politically possible," for "all the democratic freedoms form an organic whole." This is true to such an extent that "it is not . . . possible within this system to make exceptions, without endangering the

[27] "Pluralism," *Thought,* vol. XXIX (Summer, 1954), p. 174–179.
[28] *Ibid.,* p. 201.
[29] "Leo XIII on Church and State," *TS,* vol. XIV (March, 1953), p. 25.
[30] "The Church and Totalitarian Democracy," *TS,* vol. XIII (December, 1952), 552 n.

185

political system itself." This is obviously a decisive point in the whole argument, and, as such, demands a careful, theoretical grounding proportionate to its importance. He does not develop a full argument, but his instinctive perceptions are sure. There is an all-enveloping "political mood" of democracy. It is "the mood of freedom—the idea that freedom is the citizen's highest right, that freedom is the highest political end, and that the function of the state itself, which is the function of ordering, is the ordering of freedoms into an *ordo legalis,* and the maintenance of the processes of freedom whereby order itself is kept alive and active, and developed to meet the developing needs of society."[31]

It is at this point in the over-all structure of his argument that a deep ambiguity in Murray's position comes to light. On the basis of his perceptions of the workings of democracy in the modern nation-state, he is led to a formulation of its inner dynamic and essential features that is virtually the same, with the exception of its evaluative tone, as Aristotle's treatment of the fundamental roots of democracy in the ancient city-state.[32] Democracy for both of them is a system of freedom based on equality. But for Aristotle it is one mode of political community among others that are, furthermore, all understood by him to stand in a hierarchy determined by the degree to which they realize the fulness of human capacities.

But, to situate a constitutional type in a structure determined by functional capabilities as Aristotle does, it is necessary, among other things, to discern a basic typology of constitutional systems in terms of their fundamental psychic structures and the institutional armatures and instruments of those psychic structures. In turn, the elaboration of such a typology demands that one at-

[31] *C.T.S.A. Proceedings,* 1948, p. 63.

[32] The substantive congruence between Murray's scattered remarks and Aristotle's treatment (in *Politics* vi. 2. 1317a40–1317b17) is remarkable (cf. Plato, *Republic* viii. 557–558).

tempt to limn a regime that will serve, at least provisionally, as a standard of maximum functional performance in terms of which other regimes can be assessed and situated to produce the typology. But Murray both denies that such a typology and standard can be articulated and at the same time rhetorically accepts a primitive typology and some of the elements of a maximally functional regime[33] in his chauvinistic remarks about Anglo-Saxon democracy as the "adult" state.

In order to ensure the Church her freedom, in order to guarantee the Church against enfeoffment to any particular form of government, in order to prevent the emergence of a new "thesis," he denies the possibility of a philosophical typology of regimes. The reason for this "is the changing character of 'the state.' " This is not to say that there are no "absolute principles of politics, universal in their application; but their application is relative to complex historical factors, and even the theoretical statement of them is subject to revision in the light of enlarged political experience." As an example of such a principle he notes: "the idea of the political relationship ('governors–governed') is permanently valid as an idea, a necessity of nature and reason." Nevertheless, "its institutionalization, and the concept held of it, shows enormous variations."[34] Political philosophy historically accepted the task of discovering the order among the variations, and that required the adumbration of the best regime. But Murray eschews the work of discerning the structure of the "*optimum genus reipublicae.*" The "notion of the optimum" is "perilous."[35] And it is hardly congruent with the "sound Anglo-Saxon, and basically Catholic, principle of

[33] Of course, it would be more civilized to say: "best regime simply." But, as things stand, that would almost inevitably be misunderstood.

[34] "The Problem of State Religion," *TS* vol. XII (June, 1951), pp. 156–160.

[35] "Leo XIII on Church and State," *TS*, vol. XIV (March, 1953), pp. 24–25.

the relativism of political forms."[36] Thus, though adhering, "with all the conviction of intelligence, to the tradition of natural law as the basis of free and ordered political life,"[37] he bids goodbye to a great part of it by abandoning what had always been considered integral to it: a theory of regimes.[38]

Precisely because he fails to attempt to work out the *optimum genus reipublicae,* he is unable to say whether the particular "intention of nature" that democratic nation-states realize (whatever it is) is in any functional relationship with other intentions of nature, whatever they are. As far as I can tell, his intentions of nature are abstract formalisms such as freedom, authority, equality, self-government, the governors-governed relationship which he supposes are rooted in the nature of things, and, in that sense, trans-temporal, "necessarily exigent in all temporal situations."[39]

Naturally, if one takes them singly, any regime can be found to realize some "intention of nature" or other. But on turning to the next one, one is likely to find that the same regime slights it. Murray repeatedly finds that this is the case, in fact, with the

[36] "The Church and Totalitarian Democracy," *TS,* vol. XIII (December, 1952), p. 552 n. Rhetorically, the brilliance of the conjunction of "Anglo-Saxon" and "Catholic" (a conjunction he makes elsewhere as well) is altogether delightful, but theoretically it is not particularly clear that its tribal appeal adds any more weight to his principle than might have accrued to it had he called it a basically "white" principle.

[37] *We Hold These Truths,* p. 41.

[38] Since the natural-law tradition to which Murray adheres is rooted in Aristotle, it might not be foolish to note that, of the two major works that contain his natural right teaching, one of them, the *Politics,* is almost wholly concerned with a theory of regimes.

[39] To take only one of them, Murray regards the "governors-governed" relationship as "the political relationship." There is, however, nothing specifically political about it since it may evidently exist in the family, in the army, in the sheepfold, between God and men, between master and slave, employer and employee, and, etymologically more precise, between pilot and the ship with its crew. In his peculiar understanding of political theory as consisting of such abstract formalisms, Murray almost presents a caricature of the defects attributed to St. Thomas Acquinas by a student of Leo Strauss, Harry V. Jaffa, in *Thomism and Aristotelianism* (Chicago: 1952).

democratic nation-state. Of course, there are those who question any natural teleology, who regard it as a *deus ex machina*. But the point here is that Murray and many others with him set up not one, but a whole olympus of *dii ex machina* without any Jovian thunderbolt to keep them in order.

Denying the possibility of a theory of regimes leads to a number of curious consequences. It prevents the Church from being wedded to any specific regime and thus frees her to preach the gospel under all regimes. But at the same time, it excludes the possibility of the rational articulation of prophetic judgment on any regime. Or to put it another way, it excludes the possibility of any attempt at a comprehensive critical approach to any regime. Specific criticisms on the basis of specific values or intentions of nature are, of course, possible. Similarly, it is possible to cry "huzzah" for almost any regime on the basis of some value or intention of nature that it especially realizes. But there is no way of placing those elements of praise and blame in a context as comprehensive as the responsibility that men inescapably bear for the whole shape and thrust of their common life.

There are other consequences. It is, no doubt, true that the problem of subsidiarity and the dangers of totalitarianism are especially pressing in our vast nation-states; and Murray thinks that such is the case. Thus, to deny not only the historical existence, but even the noetic possibility of an ideal Republic of Truth and Justice seems to avert both reactionary and progressivist utopian fanaticisms that would force everyone to enter their republic or be killed. At the same time, it tends toward a curious demoralization of politics. Fearing the dangers of a totalitarian monism that are involved in any polity that organizes a regime for the common pursuit of great human aims, this position, by denying the possibility of a relevant comprehensive standard, continually tends to reduce the concern of politics to mere housekeeping functions. Even though it may recognize that the end of politics is a moral good, it regularly minimizes the degree to

189

which a polity ought to attempt the common realization of moral ends through its instruments of common action: the institutions of the state and the actions of governing.[40]

Nevertheless, in some cases, notably in the face of nineteenth-century threats to what Murray calls the "traditional substance of Western society" or the "human heritage,"[41] he is prepared to say that the principle of limited law and government might legitimately give way to other concerns of human communities. But again, it is impossible to articulate a standard of typical regimes and circumstances in which such shifts in emphasis are more or less appropriate.

In short, it may very well be true, as Murray argues, that the canonists' "thesis" is but an arbitrary, reactionary, and gilded distortion of the existential realities of the Church's experience with the absolute monarchies. But his "smashing attack on the bright and brittle illusion of utopianism" in its canonist variety wins "its victory under the banner of an opposite illusion that is marshy and murky but no less an illusion."[42] Murray's "Anglo-Saxon, and basically Catholic, principle of the relativism of political forms" is on the constitutional level a comprehensive counterpart of the situationalism that he condemns in narrower contexts.[43]

This danger is particularly important since many European prelates at Vatican II seem to look to America for a new initiative within the Church on the whole issue. Aware of the progress of the Church in America, tired of the sterile and sterilizing struggles with the militant secularism that have characterized so

[40] Cf., e.g., *Cross Currents*, pp. 28–29; *C.T.S.A. Proceedings*, 1948, p. 73; "The Church and Totalitarian Democracy," *TS*, vol. XIII (December, 1952), pp. 551–554; "Leo XIII on Church and State," *TS*, vol. XIV (March, 1953), pp. 24–26.

[41] "Leo XIII on Church and State," *TS*, vol. XIV (March, 1953), p. 29; "Government and the Order of Culture," *TS*, XV (March, 1954), pp. 16–17.

[42] *We Hold These Truths*, pp. 284–285.

[43] *Ibid.*, ch. 12.

much of Church history since the French Revolution, increasingly concerned at the irrelevance of the ossified Church-state formulae of the seminary manuals on public ecclesiastical law, many seem to hope that the American experience may provide grounds for a theoretical reconciliation between the Church and the modern state. Murray's writing and influence seem, insofar as one can tell from afar, to be one center of such hopes. The question, here as well as in some other areas, is whether the price of liberation from the dead hand of a sclerotic scholasticism is situationalism, here on the grand scale of historical millennia and of the fundamental, constitutional articulations of man's public life.

Theory and History

Democracy and the Norms for Church-State Relations

No doubt there is considerable diversity in the attempts to provide a solution of the Church-state problem limned in the foregoing chapters. Nevertheless, it seems that reflection on them permits one to distinguish certain permanent elements in the problem, elements that must be considered in any systematic treatment.

Of course, in different historical contexts the avenues whereby the problem is entered may differ. For John of Paris, it is a question of the relative powers of king and pope. For contemporary Americans, the general rubric under which the problem arises is "religious freedom." That rubric, in turn, covers two general notions that are related to but broader than the religious clauses of the First Amendment. The first is the freedom of individual citizens from governmental pressure either to conform to or to omit the affirmations and actions of any religious belief. The second is the freedom of religious as well as anti-religious organizations from governmental interference in their internal affairs or harassment in their activities. At first, it seems that these questions are fundamentally different from the concerns of one so far away as a John of Paris or a Giles of Rome. But as the American argument proceeds, certain issues are raised that are seeen, on reflection, to converge with medieval issues toward more general problematic formulations permanently and inherently part of the Church-state problem.

Obviously, it is not possible to begin at those convergences. It is necessary to begin a discussion at the outside, as it were, where the divergences are more visible. And, since that is the case, it is best to begin with what is most familiar and proceed to what is less so. Therefore, I have chosen to begin at the Church-state problem as it presents itself in the context of American democracy. That is to say, I have chosen to begin at the point that gives rise to the dispute between Murray and his opponents.

Before saying anything else, it is necessary to note some objections. It will be said that the United States is not simply a democracy, that its size compels it to be a representative democracy if it is to be democratic at all. That is true enough, and its relevance will become clear presently. But it will also be said that the United States is not a democracy at all, representative or otherwise. It will be said that, although its constitution includes an important democratic element, it is in fact a republic. That is to say, it includes a number of non-democratic elements, the most obvious of which are the Senate and the Supreme Court, as well as some elements of the presidency. That is a serious objection, but it is necessary to see how far it goes.

Beginning with the presidency, it is clear that its originally aristocratic cast was rather swiftly undermined. Although there are some anachronistic remnants of the old system still existing at the fringes (elements that might become decisive under unusual circumstances), the electoral college has been largely abolished in reality in favor of an electoral procedure that is democratic in its thrust and spirit as well as in the perceptions of the voters. The election campaign is fundamentally the simple democratic procedure of an appeal for an arithmetical majority of the voters of the adult citizens. This is so even though the professional politician must also look to the technical complication introduced in the vote by states which may be of decisive importance in a very close race. It is, of course, technically possible that a president

193

can be elected in spite of having been decisively beaten in the popular vote. However, it is difficult to imagine that such an event would not precipitate a formal constitutional amendment of the presidential electoral system in the direction of greater democracy, a change that is already a subject of widespread discussion and agitation.

The partial democratization of the Senate has already been accomplished by the Seventeenth Amendment. Until recently, the remaining arithmetical inequity inherent in each state's having been allowed two senators was justified by democratists on the ground that the House of Representatives, for a variety of reasons not envisioned by the Founding Fathers, had become grossly unrepresentative of the increasing urban majority. However, since the Supreme Court has, in effect, overruled *Colegrove vs. Green* and required the equalization of congressional districts,[1] it is not at all clear how the undemocratic character of the Senate's electoral base will be justified now. It will, of course, be noted that the United States is a federal regime and that the senators represent the states. However, a host of reasons have conspired to make the states increasingly irrelevant and even opposed to the natural lines of community and interest that exist within the nation. I need only mention a few to indicate the depth of the irrelevance. Their jurisdictions were frequently drawn arbitrarily on a map of the wilderness. But the developments of population, industry, and commerce have been such that state boundaries are often as much a hindrance as anything else to the direction of the immense urban complexes that straddle their borders. Even in the old states where there are a few remnants of a distinct form of culture and civilization, successive waves of immigration have swept over and through them, tending to reduce or submerge the old differences between them. Finally, the rationalized structure of our nationwide economy

[1] *Wesberry vs. Sanders,* 84 S. Ct. 526 (1964); and cf. *Colegrove vs. Green,* 328 U.S. 549, 66 S. Ct. 1198 (1946).

194

has begun to produce a nomadic people. The symptoms are discussed everywhere: mobile homes, frequent home sales, regular shifting of executives who would otherwise provide one of the obvious sources of community leadership, etc., etc. Obviously, we are in a transition stage. It is still usually relevant to ask, "Where are you from?" since most people are still "from" somewhere. But one increasingly meets young people who are not "from" anywhere and who, a bit uneasily, respond to that question with a list of a half-dozen or more places where their parents have pitched their tents. They are not "from" any of them in the identity-revealing sense that was meant by the question. In short, the movement toward new forms of sociality and isolation is such that the political meaning of the states cedes, more and more, to arbitrariness. Given the history of democratic developments in our country, it is unreasonable to suppose that the states will continue to retain their undemocratic representation in the Senate on the basis of what support will be left them: antiquarian sentiment.

As for the Supreme Court, it has clearly become a modern tribunate that takes as its special concern the defense of the people against invasions of democratic principle by their government. This is clearly revealed in the decision on congressional districting, as well as in a host of other places. The point here is not whether that is the function that the Court ought to perform if it is to carry out its constitutional obligations. The point here is not whether the Constitution, either as written or as amended, envisages a democratic regime. The point is simply that that is the tendency of all our political development, as well as the reality of the Court's own self-interpretation.

On what grounds, then, might a republic be based among us if the states have begun to lose meaning? Could the property qualification be reintroduced as a structural element of one house of Congress? Merely to raise the question is enough to reveal its unreality. Hamilton, not to speak of John Adams, is hardly likely to be adopted as the theoretician of a new American republic.[2] A popular edition of Adam's writings has even been bowdlerized in part on this issue.[3] And if not money, which holds such high honor here, will noble birth be alleged by anyone as a claim to rule?

Is it conceivable that Jefferson's aristocracy of merit become the basis of a new body of *patres conscripti?* The defender of the rights of man and the founder of the University of Virginia might be surprised that the former are now alleged as grounds for admission to the latter and its imitations.[4]

Still, this is not to say that the present American regime is wholly democratic. No one has yet proposed that, insofar as it is necessary for the people to be ruled by a separate ruling personnel, those persons should be chosen by lot, given extremely short terms of office, and that the office they hold should be collegial rather than personal, and that the offices should be fragmented, each independent of the other rather than in a hierarchy, lest the people be compelled to do any great thing against their will. For a variety of reasons, the American regime remains a mixed regime in which the democratic element is most important and growing more so.[5]

[2] This is sadly acknowledged even by that gentle and learned partisan of Hamilton, Clinton Rossiter, in his *Alexander Hamilton and the Constitution* (New York: 1964).

[3] See George A. Peek, Jr., ed., *The Political Writings of John Adams* (New York: 1954), pp. 99–100.

[4] The depth and intensity of Jefferson's hope for a true *aristoi* is as moving as its naïveté is, for a statesman, repulsive. See his great letter to John Adams of October 28, 1813, in *The Adams-Jefferson Letters, 1812–1826,* ed. by Lester J. Cappon (Chapel Hill, N.C.: 1959), p. 387.

[5] It should by now be clear that I am using the term "democracy" in its etymological, and thus classical, sense where it refers to a particular distribution of ruling power. Modern usage is here altogether worthless, since in its new meaning it refers to an astonishing variety of regimes provided they include or are alleged to include an important element of popular participation. And within regimes that are so styled, "democratic" becomes virtually identical with the morally good, or, at least, with the only legitimate form of government. Scientific analysis then becomes impossible.

It is within the context of this heavily and increasingly democratic constitution that the problem of religious freedom arises. The special form that it takes for Catholics makes it a matter that is inextricably intertwined with freedom of speech, taking "speech" in the very broad sense of any expression or manifestation of ideas. This is not so because the canonists are concerned, in their thetic Catholic society, to punish heretics or to prevent them from worshipping God in the way they think He required. It is so because they are concerned to suppress the *public manifestation* of heterodoxy.[6] What is inescapably involved in their objective is an elaborate scheme of censorship, either before or after the fact, of words and actions tending to spread religiously heterodox ideas. Their position, therefore, necessarily carries with it profound opposition to certain essential elements of a democratic regime.

In a city-state democracy each citizen must obviously be granted freedom of speech within a wide latitude, at least when he is in the ruling assembly. Otherwise, the assembly would be quite unable to conduct its affairs, since a city in which any word might at any moment become a cause for punishment by the majority would be a city about to plunge into anarchy or civil war. Nevertheless, it is not impossible for such a democracy regularly and legally to exclude certain kinds of speech from its public places. There is no reason to suppose that a city would be any less democratic for having taken steps to exclude from its midst public blasphemy or violation of the laws of the gods respecting sacrifices, prayers, and the like. It may be foolish thereby. It may be vicious thereby. But there is no reason to say of that city that it is not democratic thereby, since the notion of democracy does not evidently contain within itself the notion of particular limits beyond which the rule of the people, the *demos,* may not extend.

But the case is quite different in the representative democracy

[6] Cf. *supra,* pp. 164–165.

197

of the nation-state. Given a bit of intelligence and a bit of luck, the people of a city-state democracy may preserve their full ruling powers against a host of usurpers. There are a variety of well-known devices whereby they ensure their continued dominance. Wherever possible, they conduct their affairs themselves, in assembly. Where execution requires the designation of some special personnel, they make every effort to render that personnel innocuous to the democratic constitution. They make the executive offices collegial. They divide the tasks as far as possible among a multiplicity of colleges of officials. The colleges are filled by lot and the term of office is of very short duration. In short, every effort is made to prevent the performance of political tasks being placed in the hands of a separate governing group, and, where that is necessary, every effort is made to keep that governing group virtually indistinguishable from the people as a whole. The threat of usurpation by the officials can be contained, since they are in office for perhaps a single month and are responsible for performance to a regular accounting before the democratic assembly.[7]

But the citizens of a representative democracy in a nation-state can adopt no such expedients. The size and complexity of their body politic is such that they cannot conduct the most important part of their affairs for themselves. They must have a separate governing personnel that necessarily has great power. The size and complexity of the body politic is such that even the leaders of that separate governing personnel must be given terms of office running for longer than a month or so if they are to retain control of the subordinate officials over whom they are set. Therefore, they are necessarily in a position in which they are ordinarily far freer of subordination to the popular will and fancy than their counterparts in the city-state.

[7] Cf. Aristotle, *Politics* vi. 15. 1299b30–1300a5; vi. 2; *Constitution of Athens* 42–69. The chief military officers were, for obvious reasons, not chosen by lot but by show of hands (*Constitution of Athens* 61.).

198

Furthermore, the popular will and fancy is far weaker and vaguer in most ordinary cases in the nation-state due to the enormously difficult problem of communications. The fact of the nation-state's great size and complexity issues in a quantity of important decisions so large that no one can know them all. And the communication of even one important matter to all or most of the people is a problem of the first magnitude. Public-opinion polling on political issues regularly reveals that the people have only very sketchy notions of their public affairs. The remoteness of events and decisions from the activity of their ordinary life tends to produce in the citizen the spirit of the relatively bored spectator, if he pays any attention at all.

Nevertheless, the maintenance of the democratic element in the constitution evidently depends on the maintenance of multiple sources of information to the citizens as to basic directions of government and the persons who determine them. If the sources of political information on a mass scale are reduced to one under a unified control, it is clear that the people, absolutely dependent on the information given them, have become potential subjects of a systematic manipulation, rather than rulers.[8] Most dangerous of all, plainly, is the case in which the separate governing personnel have in their own hands control over the content of mass communications. Then the likelihood of maintaining the democratic element in the constitution is almost nil, since the maintenance of the conditions for free popular decision is a gift at the grace of the governors. Every large democracy has, therefore, been singularly cautious about permitting the setting up of any governmental censorship apparatus, even if the apparatus were to be concerned with a subject to the communication of which the majority was thoroughly opposed. Naturally, the threat increases as the number of controlled

[8] Obviously, the media of mass communications subject the people to a considerable variety of systematic manipulations by control of images and information. But the fact of the plurality of manipulative attempts reduces their effectiveness.

199

media increases, and as the media covered are more political in their ordinary scope.[9]

The threat posed by public censorship to the democratic elements of the constitution is so great that the notorious "camel's nose argument," though logical nonsense, reflects considerable practical wisdom. The canonists do not argue that all expressions of opinion ought to be subject to censorship, but only expressions of heretical or blasphemous opinion. But even though the decision were made by the overwhelming majority of the citizens, and even though the field of control were limited to those subjects, the threat to the constitution would still be very grave precisely because it aims at what is inherently one of the most vulnerable spots of a large democracy. To suppress such speech effectively in the modern nation-state would plainly require an enormous governmental apparatus with great power of inquisition and enforcement.[10] It would be singularly difficult to cut out only the proscribed opinions without damaging the vulnerable fabric of communications. What could one do with *The Christian Science Monitor*, for example, if its publisher declined to remove its religious references? What could one do with a book in which, out of two hundred pages of political argument, six were found heretical? Refuse it publication? Burn it? Remove only the offending pages? How would the people assure themselves that only heretical material had been deleted? What would one do with material in which the religious and political content were inextricably intertwined? These are but illustrations, yet the consequence is already clear. Democracy in a large nation-state is permanently faced with the inherent

[9] Thus newspapers, radio, and television are more sensitive areas than films, for example.

[10] If it be objected that no such apparatus is envisaged, the inescapable rejoinder is that then the legislation would prove ineffective in fact, which tends to undermine the whole legal fabric by inducing disrespect for the law. No one can reasonably propose that a legislator lay down a law that has as its net effect the undermining of law.

weakness of having to concede a great deal of genuine ruling power to a political élite. It nevertheless attempts to retain a fundamental control over the basic directions of policy and over the chief persons who specify and execute those general policy directions. But the censorship inherent in the canonists' position would place in the hands of those whom the people wish to control an instrument whereby they can systematically suppress the information on the basis of which popular control rests. The canonists' line of argument carries in its train consequences that threaten fundamentally to subvert a democratic constitution.

This whole response to the proponents of censorship, religious or otherwise, is well-known, even a commonplace. It is also relatively superficial, since it refers only to the logic of external relationships in the operation of a particular kind of governmental structure. But there is a deeper stratum of relationship joining democracy and free speech (including religious speech).[11] Murray suggests this in his analysis of Pope Leo XIII. His line of argument is that the regimes that Leo XIII had in mind were paternal regimes in which a father-king ruled over a childish multitude. But the modern democratic regimes present a quite different aspect. They are adult states. Their citizens have grown up, i.e., they are literate and take a responsible share in the conduct of their affairs.[12] The use of the term "adult" in this connection is very suggestive. It points to the more fundamental connection between democracy and free speech.

Children are subject to their parents and are not only told what to do and not to do, but they are also told what they may say and what they may not say. But when they grow up, when they

---

[11] Permit me to repeat that, since it is not the thinking of heretical thoughts nor worshipping in heretical forms that the canonists wish the law to suppress but only *public manifestations* of heterodoxy, the legal problem is a problem of public speech in the broad sense of manifestation of thought.

[12] Cf., e.g., J.C.M., "Leo XIII: Two Concepts of Government: II. Government and the Order of Culture," *TS*, vol. XV (March, 1954), pp. 1–33.

become adults, then it seems that they may do and say what pleases them. Then they need not tolerate being told what to do and say. Naturally, it turns out that there are still limits: internal ones, learned in childhood, and external ones in the form of enforced laws, as well as subtle social pressures. But in the adult state, the external limits are only such as the grown-ups place on themselves. It is precisely here that the democratic character of the "adult" state becomes clear. The requirements for becoming a peer of the democratic society are scarcely more demanding than those for becoming an adult. To become the latter it is only necessary to have been born and to have lived long enough to grow up. To become a citizen of a democratic society the additional requirements are few. Some degree of citizen parentage is ordinarily required, or, failing that, some period of residence followed by an application for membership. One must ordinarily not be mentally defective in a massively obvious way. And one must not have been convicted of a felony. These are usually the main requirements for citizenship, that is, for becoming a peer, a ruling equal, in a democracy. Thus, with the exception of madmen and gross criminals, all that the ordinary citizen needs to show by way of attainments justifying his claim to an equal share in rule is that he was born of a citizen parent and has perdured the process of biological maturation to the age of eighteen or twenty-one. Perhaps he will be required to know his letters, perhaps not;[13] but, since almost everyone knows them, the requirement is only relevant in special cases or when it is systematically abused by the citizens with a view to excluding some special group from the society, as in the case of the Negroes in parts of the United States.

Well, since this has not always and everywhere been the standard for participation in the rights and powers of a society,

[13] I have spoken of the citizen as "he." That, of course, is a relic of an undemocratic past. One finds that usage more and more frequently replaced by "he or she."

since other societies have had diverse standards such as noble birth, sex, wealth, education, public service, virtue, wisdom, and so forth, since other societies have had different grades of citizenship and not one only, it is necessary to ask what are the peculiar characteristics of a regime in which only growing up is the standard for citizenship. The first thing to be noticed is that, in the matter of imposing external restraints on themselves, the citizens cannot be expected to go very far in this regard. Such restraints constitute a sort of collective self-discipline. But in a society based on the egalitarian principle of one-man-one-vote, the degree of public self-discipline can hardly be supposed to go far beyond the level of human self-mastery characteristic of the ordinary citizen, that is to say, the statistically average citizen. To take an obvious example, the expansion of public education in Britain could hardly take the form of duplicating the style of the great public schools. I am not here concerned with the peculiar merits and defects of the spirits that inform the life of those schools; the point is that they are directed to the formation of a highly disciplined and coherent *style* of life in all of its ramifications, and that the mass of the citizens could scarcely be supposed to be prepared to send their sons to such a training. Indeed, it is likely that most of them would suffer unbearably in the transition.

But so far, the question has been approached on the tacit assumption that equality, expressed in the formula one-man-one-vote, is the primal reality around which everything else centers in a democratic regime. There is a certain truth to this on the level of institutional structures. Yet it is not at all clear that it is the psychic spring of democracy. Reflection reveals that the argument made earlier about the reason for democratic aversion to censorship does not correspond to the full range of grounds for rejection. It is, of course, perfectly true that an elaborate censorship apparatus would further increase the political in-

203

equality between the mass of the citizens and the separate ruling personnel in a large state with a democratic principle. But the rejection of censorship is clearly based on other considerations as well. Censorship is regarded as an intolerable interference in the citizen's liberty.

Although equality is an integral part of the "democratic way," it is deeply rooted in a spirit of liberty. Inequality is obnoxious in the measure that it also imposes limits to liberty that do not seem necessary. This last qualification is very important. The democratic citizens are not anarchists. They are not so stupid except perhaps in momentary excitements, as to suppose that reality imposes no limits whatever on their desires. In general, they are not prepared to tolerate among their public officers such obvious incompetents as would periodically be thrown up by the fully equalitarian system of the lot.[14] By using the system of election by vote, they clearly recognize that every citizen is not, in fact, to be regarded as competent to hold public office.[15] Our foregoing emphasis on equality, seen from the point of view of citizenship, must now be counterbalanced by some element of recognized inequality with respect to holding elective offices. Might it not be that, as Jefferson hoped, an aristocracy of merit, however rough in approximation, has in fact grown up? Is it not necessary to admit that, however democratic in spirit, the citizens are sufficiently aware of the complexity and difficulty of the tasks that face the principal public officers in our large political units, so that they would laugh down a proposal that such officials be chosen in a lottery or in rotation (as they do not laugh down such procedures for jury duty, for ex-

[14] Given the lot system, the Athenians wisely used a collegial system in their public offices. They were thus able to minimize the problem posed by the choice by lot of a fool for public office. He would be offset by a number of others. The net effect, thus, would tend to approximate a random sample of the citizenry.

[15] Cf. Aristotle, *Politics* iv. 9. 1294ᵇ10–13.

ample[16])? This clearly seems to be the case, and the question, therefore, must be asked whether it does not require that some new terms such as "representative republic" be applied to the American regime. In short, is it not necessary to say that the relatively pure democracy possible to the Athenians is not possible for us because of the size and complexity of our societies, that we recognize that fact, that the consequence is a political hierarchy that amounts to an aristocracy of merit combined with a democratic electorate,[17] and that, finally, it is therefore foolish to call our regime a democracy even when qualified by "representative"? The seemingly inexorable progress of the argument is, however, spurious, because the "aristocracy of merit" has a peculiar character that makes it quite different from Aristotle's notion of aristocracy[18] and thus cannot lead to the Aristotelian conclusion. For it is clear, beginning with Jefferson himself, that it has become increasingly more difficult for us to admit a political hierarchy in terms of moral worth.

The merit that Jefferson had in mind was utilitarian merit. The University that was to be the training ground for his "veritable *aristoi*" was to be devoted to "all the useful sciences," at the apex of which stood agriculture.[19] To be sure, we are hardly

[16]Tocqueville's arguments for the democratic jury system are still powerful in America even where the competence of lay juries is open to serious question, as in civil suits, where the fact of almost universal insurance has led to the charge that juries regularly betray their trust, and in civil suits involving the extraordinary complications of modern corporation law and practice that are usually beyond lay comprehension. See *Democracy in America*, vol. I, ch. 16, and cf. Aristotle's *Constitution of Athens* 63–69; Bernard Botein, "A Judge Votes for the Jury," *The New York Times Magazine*, September 11, 1960, p. 30.

[17] Cf. Jefferson's interesting reflection on this question in Saul K. Padover, ed., *Thomas Jefferson on Democracy* (New York: 1946; orig. ed. pub. 1939), pp. 21–22, 25, 39.

[18] *Politics* iii. 5. 1278ª18–20; iii. 7. 1279ª 35–38; iii. 15. 1286ᵇ 5–8; iv. 7; *Nicomachean Ethics* viii. 10.

[19] Cf. the letter to Adams cited *supra*, p. 196, n. 4, and the letter of 1803 to David Williams quoted in Padover, ed., *Thomas Jefferson on Democracy*, pp. 88–89.

prepared to admit the primacy of rustic excellences, however scientifically grounded, as anyone can see from the history of our agricultural and mechanical colleges. But it is also clear that most of us are almost unprepared to tolerate useless disciplines. This is true for the great free universities as well as for the state universities, which need to justify their appropriations to democratically elected legislatures. Even the students who are enrolled in what are still called "liberal arts" are seldom prepared to suppose that they are to be studied as accomplishments appropriate to the activity of a free man. And who will say that our universities are in any serious sense centered on a theoretical contemplation that is pursued quite for its own sake, and that is regarded as the highest of human activities?[20] There may, of course, be individuals who still have a spiritual home in the Academy or the Lyceum, but the pressures of finances, students, and society at large are such that the activities of the university, even for its full members, are seen as inherently useful or practical. This is so much the case that the pressure for immediate results often threatens to destroy the goose that lays the golden eggs.

The whole structure of the modern view of knowing and the knowable has excluded the possibility of science centered on a contemplative activity, since it has excluded the knowability of a contemplative object. This has been commonly accepted since Kant. It was already seen by Hobbes, Locke, and Rousseau. All of them understood that the scientific destruction of the religious and metaphysical traditions of antiquity and the Middle Ages carried with it a profound threat to public order. In different ways, all of them sought to reëstablish public order on a basis of generally valid, inalienable, individual rights. The inescapable consequence, for all of them and their successors, was that pub-

---

[20] I have here omitted, for obvious reasons, any consideration of the special, mystical contemplation of Christianity, even though it is partly in the same tradition.

licly relevant virtue could only be understood in terms of utility to a collection of equal, irreducibly separate, but identical ends actually willed in some way by metaphysically isolated individuals. Precisely because reality no longer appeared as a hierarchy of analogous communions, political activity could no longer appear as an imaging forth, on one level, of the infinitely creative abundance of the self-knowledge of the first cause, and, for Christians, of the salvific super-abundance of the divine love which encompasses not only the creation, but also the redemption of the world in Christ. In the new circumstances of an opaque reality beyond each knower (in which knowing has the character of ideational construction rather than contemplation), and thus of the radical isolation of the knowers from each other, since only the appearances and not the depths of being of their concrete individuality are mutually accessible,[21] it is impossible to admit as a ground for holding public office superiority in substantive moral virtue or worth. Under the new circumstances, political authority is indistinguishable from coercive power, and this becomes a central problem for modern political thought in a way inconceivable for antiquity or the Middle Ages.[22]

On the level of practical politics, this development always involves a democratic element in that the ends of the state are always vulgar. They are the univocal objects of the overwhelming mass of citizens.[23] In its moderately democratic, Lockean versions, such as the American, the object of political action is comfortable self-preservation.[24] That is to say, the discipline pe-

[21] An artistic realization of this very opacity is Albert Camus' *The Stranger* (New York: 1946).

[22] J.L. Talmon has made this brilliantly clear in his book, *The Origins of Totalitarian Democracy* (New York: 1960); cf. especially the first three chapters.

[23] Thus even Hobbes understood that Leviathan is justified because and only because it satisfies the vulgar demands that are expressed in inalienable rights.

[24] Cf. *The Second Treatise*, para. 95.

culiar to and implicit in the acceptance of the pre-modern notion of aristocracy is radically repudiated by democratic politics. That is not to say that the citizens of the representative democracy will accept no discipline whatever; but it means that they will accept it only in terms of a utilitarian aristocracy that claims only a special competence in securing vulgar rather than aristocratic ends.[25] The citizens will accept considerable discipline in great crises such as a war or a clear and gross threat to economic survival.[26] Indeed, they may be prepared freely to make greater sacrifices than the citizens of any other regime in such crises.

But there is scant evidence that they are prepared freely to take upon themselves the ascetic moment inherent in great enterprises when the object is the realization of some profound moral or spiritual style, or formation, or character of soul. Both the ancients and the moderns agree on this peculiar taste for liberty characteristic of democratic regimes. Some praise it and some blame it, but they agree on the fact. It may take the form of an unreflective but powerful demand for the liberty to "live as you like," as Aristotle puts it. Or it may take one of the many ideological forms of libertarianism. In our time, it evidently takes both forms, and they mutually reinforce each other.[27] It is

[25] Consider the implications of the following election appeals published by the British Tories asking for popular support in the 1964 general election of the old Etonians and Oxbridge graduates who lead the Conservative Party: "Standards for Living—1000 new homes a day with the Conservatives," or: "Conservatives give you a better Standard of Living—don't chuck it away!"

[26] Examples are plentiful. One might mention the rigors of economic life under the post-war Labour government in Britain; the wage restraint of German workers during the so-called *Wirtschaftswunder*. Even the Athenians abandoned the lot when it came to picking generals (Aristotle, *Constitution of Athens* 61).

[27] Authorities might be multiplied almost indefinitely. A few will have to suffice. Plato, *Republic* viii, 556–558; Aristotle, *Politics* vi. 2. 1317ª 40–1317ᵇ 17; Thucydides, *Peloponnesian War* ii. 6. Funeral Oration of Pericles; as for the moderns, cf. T.L. Thorson's summary of the "mainstream of American democratic thought," in his *The Logic of Democracy* (New York: 1962), p. 154; H.B. Mayo, *An Introduction to Democratic Theory* (New York: 1960), pp. 218–241; W. Ebenstein, *Modern Political Thought* (New

clear that the great civilizational and cultural seedtimes have not been characterized by democratic politics. Neither the Homeric roots of Greek civilization and culture nor the regal and republican foundations of Rome, nor again the early medieval foundations of Western European civilization, symbolized in Charlemagne, were democratic. And it is obvious that a democratic Exodus is inconceivable. The refusal of discipline implicit in the democratic denial of hierarchy inescapably excludes the *public* realization of those sharp excellences of the spirit that, although not themselves ascetic, always demand an ascetic moment in their process of realization.[28] Only by virtue of some hierarchical articulation can a people pursue such objects.

Naturally, there are times in which there is a brilliant blazing forth of spiritual glory in regimes more or less democratic on the level of institutions. It would be intolerable to have written the foregoing paragraph and then to have failed to deal with the light of glory that still streams on us out of fifth-century Athens from the democratic reform of Cleisthenes to the Melian dialogue. The democratic reforms initiated by Solon and brought

---

York: 1960), pp. 127–272; Padover, ed., *Thomas Jefferson on Democracy;* as for the problem of freedom in a scientist version of democracy, cf. K. Mannheim, *Freedom, Power and Democratic Planning* (New York: 1950); R. Horwitz, "Scientific Propaganda: Harold D. Lasswell," in H.J. Storing, ed., *Essays on the Scientific Study of Politics* (New York: 1962), pp. 292–300; the classical relativist version of democracy is in Hans Kelsen, *General Theory of Law and State* (Cambridge, Mass.: 1945), and "Science and Politics," *American Political Science Review,* vol. XLV (September, 1951), pp. 641–661. Perhaps better than any authorities might be a day spent in an average, big city high school.

28 José Ortega y Gasset pointed this out as clearly as anyone in *The Revolt of the Masses.* Nevertheless, since his experience was chiefly of the continental European regimes of his time, he failed to notice that in many situations the mass man in the moderately democratic regimes of Lockean cast is prepared to accept the discipline necessary to the satisfaction of his objectives, as I have already suggested. The post-sputnik educational developments in the United States were often of this type. The discipline of a more demanding course of studies was often accepted in the name of military and security concerns, whereas an equivalent effort in the name of high culture and civilization is hardly likely on any considerable scale.

209

to completion by Cleisthenes cut away the sclerotic remains of an old patriarchal aristocracy, hardened into a self-centered oligarchy which, by virtue of regarding the masses as a mere means, fundamentally broke the moral unity of the city. That liberation permitted a generation's attempt to in-form the life of city and citizens with the psychic discoveries of a new *aristoi* who had transformed the virtues of the Homeric aristocracy.[29] Thus, although it is true that the democratic reform issued in the encounter at Melos, it is also true that it was the condition of Aeschylus, of the tragedy as public cult.

Neither would it be permissible to ignore the hopes for and intimations of Roman virtue (how quickly dashed!) that everywhere shaped the American and French revolutions. But Washington struck no deep resonance in the American spirit. He was unable to articulate a symbolic structure to form his people after the image of Cincinnatus. His memory chiefly lives in the sentimental legend of the cherry tree, the rigor of his virtue diminished to child's scope so as to be comprehensible. And what else is left of the *virtus* and glory of the first, and last, of our kings and consuls? the pseudo-Roman façades that camouflage indiscriminately the temples and the public counting-houses of the city that bears his name.

The French, compressing the blood of centuries into a torrent between narrower walls, sped from Junius and Lucretius to Caesar in a decade and a half.

Furthermore, it must be pointed out that, in terms of external structure, the modern nation-state need not confine itself to the democratist immobilism of modern France.[30] The representative democracy may leave enough space for an aristocratic element in the form of a powerful chief-executive office with enough free-

[29] Cf. Eric Voegelin, *The World of the Polis* (n.p.: Louisiana State University Press, 1957), part III.

[30] Cf., e.g., Philip Williams, *Politics in Post-War France*, 2nd ed. (London: 1958); David Thomson, *Democracy in France* (New York: 1946).

dom to realize a pontifical leadership. However, the conditions for the realization of such leadership are rare. It not only takes a soul capable of such divine heights as are revealed in Lincoln's second inaugural; it also requires a people formed enough after heaven's image that to build a bridge between man and God is conceivable. Both are necessary.

With Lincoln gone, Andrew Johnson could not bring it off. The suffering of the people issued in the fury, hate, spoliation, and corruption of the Reconstruction that still festers in our midst. Perhaps even Lincoln would not have succeeded in transforming that suffering into the price of a nation's spiritual regeneration and unity. There can be no point in arguing that. But there is another point that can be made. Had Lincoln been faced with a people such as we are now, there is far less likelihood that he could have succeeded. Not that we are incapable of having imposed a more moderate peace on a beaten South. That might or might not be the case. But Lincoln sought something far deeper than that.

His speech articulates the trans-historical meaning of his people's recent history, and by doing so seeks to transform their struggle and suffering from a source of division as long as memory shall last into an expiatory sacrifice in accordance with the divine judgment. It is his hope that, if he can persuade them to turn "this mighty scourge of war" into a divine purgation, cleansed by a divine self-knowledge they can transform the memory of the war into a spring of reconciliation whence would issue a citizenry reunited in the communion of "charity for all." But a people of whom it is conceivable that they might respond to such a vocation must be a people who are deeply attuned to the "bits of Hebraic poetry" that inform Lincoln's last speeches.[31] They must be a people deeply enough attuned to the biblical

[31] Cf. Vernon Parrington, *Main Currents in American Thought* (New York: 1930), vol. 2, pp. 158–159, making allowances for Parrington's uncomprehending sentimentality.

tradition in all the most important facets of their existence so that they might discover their history as an epiphany of a universal salvation history. Only of such a people can one reasonably suppose that they might be capable of the spiritual depths necessary to understand and follow a prophetic voice through the purifying fire of the divine judgment, a demand that the fire of the battlefield be reconstituted and understood at the depths of the soul. That such a people may have existed in Lincoln's time must be attributed to the Reformation's liberation of Christians from a Church organization that had grown sclerotic (a parallel on a different level, to the Solonic and Cleisthenic reforms of Athens). Indeed, it is to this fact that the Protestant nostalgia for a Protestant Christian America harks back.

It is a hearkening back because that is no longer the spiritual discipline and milieu of our society. Those "bits of Hebraic poetry," that awesome structure of biblical salvation history, are no longer the core of our public communication and self-understanding. One need only spend a day at a fair or public meeting, listening to the flow of symbols, to know that.

Perhaps more revealing would be a reflection on the moral perception of the Second World War by Americans. Our treatment of post-war Germany and Japan may be argued to have been far more enlightened than the Reconstruction of the defeated South. But on the level of our spiritual perception of the war's meaning, it is necessary to note that it seems never to have occurred to our leadership to propose an objective higher than the inhuman and totalitarian formula of unconditional surrender. I do not wish to suggest that the Germans and Japanese did not need to be thoroughly conquered on the level of military action. What I wish to suggest is that it never occurred to us or our leadership that by making unconditional surrender our sole objective for our enemies, we insisted on reducing both them and ourselves to that very level of inhumanity and totalitarian mass force which we ostensibly opposed in them. No man with a soul can help but weep when he sees that there was once a time when we might have realized in ourselves that trans-tragic salvation history whereby our suffering of divine justice might have issued in the reconstitution of the human community.[32]

Such a reflection leads to a consideration of the spiritual limits of our century's versions of representative democracy. Aristotle finds it reasonable to speak of democracy as the rule of the poor. He supposes that they are not only easily distinguishable from the rich, but that the distinction is politically relevant in such a way that the poor and the rich are inclined to fight with each other for control of the constitution. The latter attempt to erect an oligarchy and the former attempt to erect a democracy. Within this tension, it is the peculiar genius of demagogues in democracies to whip up the poor to an attack on the rich, and Aristotle regards such attacks as the cause of revolutionary changes within democratic regimes.[33] Under the economic conditions of the pre-modern world, the only ways to pander to the jealous avarice of the poor were to attack the rich or to press for the conquest of an empire. But the technological style of the modern, democratic nation-state's economy is such that everyone can expect an income that continually expands at a considerable rate. There are breakdowns, of course, but they are naturally regarded as matters of technical adjustment that will submit to proper engineering.[34] Revolutionary class conflict on

[32] If laughter as well as tears may augur wisdom, then there may yet be slight cause of hope in the laughter that greeted Bob Newhart's satire on Lincoln's conversation with his press agent about the Gettysburg Address. Nevertheless, it is not at all clear that most of us would appreciate the magnitude of the politico-spiritual gap that is manifested by a comparison of views of the meaning of war and peace expressed by Lincoln and Roosevelt. Cf., e.g., H.S. Commager, *Documents of American History* (New York: 1948), doc. nos. 229, 230, 234, 235, 236, 238, 239, 243, 244, 557, 569.

[33] Cf., e.g., *Politics* iii. 8; v. 5.

[34] Clearly, this is a simplification. There are the so-called "pockets of permanent poverty" within our states. But they are chiefly composed of people who have not been integrated into the modern economy, and who

213

an economic base is, therefore, not only unnecessary, but it positively threatens our continued success with our less-frustrating Midas-touch. We seem only to need to be foresighted enough to cooperate, rather than to make war on one another, in order to turn everything into anything that pleases us. Indeed, lest our desires flag, we have turned the impulse of our sexuality, via advertising images, into another motor to maintain the ever-expanding circle of our frenzy of transformation-consumption. Thus, by means of cooperation through the secrets of scientific technique, we have managed to constitute ourselves a collective and more cautious version of the pleasure-haunted Midas, bastard son of the Great Goddess, promoter of the worship of Dionysius and cultivator of the roses of Aphrodite.[35] In short, we have far surpassed Aristotle's hopes for stabilizing a moderate democratic regime.

It is at this point that it is nessary to ask what could possibly be the significance of a publicly enforced religious orthodoxy such as is involved in the canonists' position? Whence could such a policy spring in the midst of a society characterized by "the victory of the *animal laborans*"? What could be the roots of such a policy for a society in which the central and normal object of the common life had become the unlimited expansion of "the laboring metabolism of man with nature,"[36] a society in which the public good had become substantially co-extensive with the security of mere life, security against external and internal enemies who threaten the continued functioning of the

---

exist in a milieu quite outside the world of the majority of their fellow citizens. So the problem is now regarded as being one of engineering their incorporation into the ever-expanding, mass-production economy, rather than a matter of the redistribution of a rather inflexible national income. It is interesting to note how, having added the new dimension of an ever-expanding, machine economy, Aristotle's recommendations about the best policy for a "war on poverty" are still immediately relevant; cf. *Politics* vi. 5.

[35] Cf. Robert Graves, *The Greek Myths* (New York: 1959), p. 83.

[36] Hannah Arendt, *The Human Condition* (New York: 1959). Cf. especially chs. III and VI, pp. 292–297.

Midas-ritual in terms of which all activities are supposed to find their meaning and immortality?

In such a spiritual milieu, a publicly enforced religious orthodoxy could only spring out of a desperate attempt to smash by violence the visible evidences of a public homelessness, rootlessness, and meaninglessness. It could only mean a desperate, and pathetic, because impossible, attempt to abolish the nausea at being in danger of radical dissolution and disappearance that is the consequence of being without natural limits and inner structure. Ordinarily, the masses escape those terrors by virtue of the crushingly vulgar sentimentalism that also pervades the mass media of communications. That sentimentalism is the last resort of common sense in the masses who cannot afford and are not stupid enough to suppose that the problem can be solved solely by "analysis," i.e., by nothing but individual psychic manipulation. But sentimental religiosity is a palliative behind which lies a dread awareness of being surrounded by an ungovernable and seemingly meaningless environment. Given the economic transformations which I have already mentioned, the revelant elements of the environment are mostly human and not natural.[37] As long as the system functions successfully, the pit of arbitrariness and meaninglessness over which it hovers can be sufficiently hidden from view to prevent mass hysteria. The seeming orderliness of day-to-day facts is enough for most men. Under these circumstances, only the so-called fringe groups are deeply enough affected by the immanent disorder (of intelligence turned wholly to the support of mere biological process) to seek radical solutions. Naturally, most of them are altogether unable to elaborate and articulate a spiritual-civilizational alternative of sufficient comprehensiveness to arouse even idle curiosity. Thus, their ordinary solution is the discovery of some "enemy" on

[37] Jefferson clearly understood the importance of such a shift in his celebrated preference for the yeoman farmer over the city dweller. Cf. Padover, ed., *Thomas Jefferson on Democracy*, pp. 68–71.

215

whom the whole burden of modern terror is blamed. He or they become scapegoat for the mass ignorance of order and meaning. It is only necessary to stamp out the enemy in order to return to or to establish for the first time the full reign of human order. Naturally, a "white" or "blue" or "red" ideological orthodoxy on simplistic, fighting lines is adumbrated as a radical alternative to that of the enemy. The whole encounter, then, is envisaged as the decisive battle between the forces of good and evil.[38]

Of course, there are enough amateur and professional psycho-analysts throughout our society to point out the aberrational character of the fringe-group orientations, and thus provide the masses with an excuse to persist in the maintenance of their il-lusions. That, of course, assumes that the general public is not confronted with crude evidence of gross disorder or the threat of it, most obviously war or its threat and economic collapse or its threat.[39]

But when the mass of the citizens sees such threats and is

[38] In this respect, it might be noted that, contrary to superficial appear-ances, Nazi ideology was more reasonable than its Marxist competitors. Unlike them, it grasped the fact that if man were to take the place of God he not only had to be both creator and judge, but also he would have to perform those functions *continuously,* without end, since man's temporalness compelled him to replace the divine eternity with a limitless future. Thus the process of selective breeding (i.e., man's self-creation) has no end point. And neither does the process of genocide have an end. When the Jews have all been consigned to the fires of a man-made hell, the nether regions cannot simply be closed and those who remain in the upper world sit down in beautiful fellowship. The very endlessness of man's manifesta-tion of himself as god-the-judge and thus as *rector mundi* depends upon his continual discovery, indictment, conviction and infernal punishment of *untermenschen.* Besides Jews there are Slavs, the mentally retarded, the physically unfit, the aged, and so on forever, since the categories themselves are pure constructs of the creative and law-giving wills of the *Übermenschen.*

[39] It is no mere accident that the extremists of the right link the military and the economic threat. It heightens the tension by putting the two per-ceived threats into a single bloc. Furthermore, many of them claim that the threat of internal, politico-economic subversion is far greater than the mili-tary threat. This permits them to have an enemy who can be fought at once whereas, even if they advocate a so-called preventive war, they can have no immediate hope of starting one.

216

deeply touched by them, then are the citizens most likely to be caught up in a collective hysteria great enough to demand and obtain a systematic attempt to enforce conformity with any set of doctrines, religious or otherwise. It is precisely at such moments when the spiritual devitalization of modern mass-men becomes significant and dangerous. There are always demagogic intelligences present in such a society. Their instincts respond to the symptoms of emerging fear and excitement. Whether they will seize upon a more or less religious formula in contrast to which the enemy is defined will be an accidental function of particular demagogues and the situations within which they move. But in any case, the psychic function of the ideological formula devised by the demagogue is the radical simplification of the disorder so as to point out a cause that the spiritually devitalized *demos* can imagine itself removing by destroying. Naturally, the action involved must be in the form of some crude smashing, or burning or other violence, since that is the means of liberation available to everyone and most simply corresponds to the gross forms of terror it is meant to harness.

Under such circumstances, the action of the masses is always demonic whether the banners under which they move are ostensibly religious or not. That is, however, what churchmen as well as others can forget, or even hide from themselves in their hopes for this or that ideal. But the reality with which one is likely to be confronted in a democracy under these circumstances is some form of hysterical pseudo-conversion to a counterfeit of order characterized by typical vulgar hopes for quick and easy salvation through some magical and violent tricks or technique.

Of course, the canonists will object that what they have in mind is not any such neo-totalitarian Catholic and democratic hysteria. They will say that they have in mind a peaceful, orderly, sane, calm, judicious, prudent population of good Catholics who live under a democratic constitution and who use their overwhelming majority to set up a procedure for suppressing heretical manifestations that would disturb their Catholic, sane, and civilized existence. They can only base such an argument on the assumption that democracy is some sort of superficial organizational scheme that can be fitted to almost any political milieu. But such a view is controverted by our recent experience, by the history of the Western world in which there have been, so far, but two democratic periods (the first rather brief, and the second?), and by theoretical considerations.

To take only the last, it is plain that the radical equality implicit in the one-man-one-vate principle already involves the reduction of the people to the level of massness insofar as the majority-rule principle genuinely determines political action, i.e., insofar as the specifically democratic political institution dominates the action of the community.[40] But one cannot assume that

[40] I do not assume that the people, even in their massness, are either politically irrelevant or devoid of virtues. What I have not assumed is that, as ruling masses, as seen under the dominant aspect of one-man-one-vote, they exhaust the politically relevant or the sphere of virtue. Thus it is clear that what I have written has no relationship to the new literary genre called "democratic theory," in which it is assumed that democracy is the political good thing (and thus the task is only to describe an altogether agreeable version of it which usually turns out to be the very one we have; cf., e.g., Robert Dahl, *A Preface to Democratic Theory,* Chicago: 1956), or in which the problem is to prove that democracy, at least in some version, really is such an altogether good thing as has been assumed *a priori* all along (cf., e.g., Thomas L. Thorson, *The Logic of Democracy,* New York: 1962). Inevitably, so narrow a view of things leads to the ridiculous, as, for example, the utterly bizarre question raised by Thorson: *Plato: Totalitarian or Democrat?* (Englewood Cliffs, N.J.: 1963). But, since most of the college students to whom such philosophical nonsense is directed were never in any danger of becoming Platonists anyway (totalitarian or otherwise), there is not much harm in it. Indeed, such ideological tracts may have the value of reaffirming for the thoughtless an obvious truth. They proceed on the assumption that the only alternative to democracy is some sort of "authoritarianism," more or less totalitarian. They then make clear that only a scoundrel or a fool would refuse to risk his life, his fortune, and his sacred honor for the democratic alternative. In our circumstances that is no small truth and in spreading it abroad they may perform a useful service. At the same time, they increase the anti-philosophical and anti-Christian dualism

a society will order the central institutions of its common activity on such lines unless something of profound significance has already occurred in its deepest internal relationships to make the citizens perceive one another in this way, i.e., as radically opaque units that are potential integers in an aggregate mass.

It seems that, at the origins of both of the democratic periods in the West, there had been a great collapse of a shared sky of meanings that had certain consequences. As long as it stood, this structure of meanings ensured the availability of a commonly accepted standard of political hierarchy (though, of course, there could be disputes about almost all the details), and, at the same time, it provided a public and inescapable (since it was not regarded as man-made) standard for judging and resisting tyrants. In Athens, there was a decline and corruption of the fabric of religiously sanctioned, patriarchal-constitutional rule over a gentilic structure. That decline threatened unlimited civil chaos. The response to it was the reforms of Solon and Cleisthenes, broken by tyrannies.[41] In the modern West, one also finds a collapse of the typical political constellation of the Middle Ages (king, people, and parliament), as well as of its symbolic underpinnings: a shared faith and theology and a shared philosophico-scientific view of an intelligible universe. Both were finally broken by the Reformation and nominalist philosophy, not to mention the accompanying rise of the *scientia nova*. Here, too, the crises in political order were met by tyrannical absolutism and democratic counter-developments. Both were distortions of single elements of the previous "mixed regime." Hobbes, who shared in the demolition of the roots of the medieval regime, clearly understood the magnitude of the

---

that is involved in the progressive gross simplification of American political discussion into "liberalism" and "conservatism" where one set of childish revolts begets another, all masquerading under the banner of political philosophy.

[41] Cf. *supra*, p. 16, n. 2, and Eric Voegelin, *The World of the Polis*, especially chs. 3–7.

problem for civic order that was posed by the collapse of the old symbolic structure. In the absence of a shared perception of an objective sky of meanings, and in the absence of a shared and infinite end for man, the problem is to keep men from one another's throats.

In the old order, everyone stood within a higher structure of meaning that he had not made and that he could only acknowledge. Meanings had not become human constructs. In the old order, the end of human activity was an infinitely intelligible and thus communicable object of contemplation. Therefore, it was simply absurd to suppose that the true object of human inclinations gave rise of itself to human conflict, however much human perversity might occasion it nonetheless. Now, in the absence of such a shared and infinitely sharable end, each man discovered a world in which he occupied the center of meaning, and of which he and he alone was the end. Unfortunately, other men are also discovered, each of whom also seems to wish to regard himself as the successor to the old God. The bare existence of two men thus becomes for each a seemingly intolerable affront and unlimited threat.

Hobbes' solution to the threat of the war of all against all was, as everyone knows, hardly a thoroughgoing defense of democracy. His solution was to structure a system of absolute sovereignty on a doctrine of inalienable rights[42] and alienable rights. One of the forms which the absolute sovereignty of Leviathan might take was that of democracy, although Hobbes thought monarchy had fewer technical defects.[43] His successors developed the line of argument resting on the radical equality and ultimate mutual opacity and "otherness" of fellow citizens

---

[42] Which amount to: life, liberty, and the pursuit of happiness; cf. *Leviathan,* ch. 14 and ch. 6, "felicity."

[43] *Leviathan,* ch. 19.

into a systematic majoritarianism limited by constitutional defenses of natural rights and the necessary means to them.[44] To be sure, there is clearly no consensus today (if ever there was one) in America on a doctrine of natural rights or inalienable rights. As a philosophic position, classic natural-rights doctrines are scarcely in fashion in either the courts or the universities. But the problem of the threat of unlimited aggression and attempts at tyranny that spring out of the loss of a shared sky of non-man-made intelligibility remains with us, and the attitude of our courts has been to expand the scope of constitutionally guaranteed rights wherever possible, since it now seems that every exercise of authority is an arbitrary exercise of force or power, and thus to be limited as far as possible to those that are inescapably necessary.

Not only are the canonists unaware of this deep connection between forms of government and certain spiritual formations, but for that very reason they also fail to see the enormous value under such circumstances of a block of constitutional guarantees that is as broad and as inviolable as possible. Such guarantees are, of course, not enough to turn back, with a handful of court orders, a passionate and desperate majority. But the point is that they habituate the citizens systematically to refrain from gross assaults on their fellows. They habituate the citizens to a set of limits behind which they are all the more easily kept in moments of excitement precisely because of the habitual nature of the limits and their quasi-sacred and ancient character.

The canonists may regard such limits as nothing but the simultaneous incarnation and defense of the notorious and papally condemned modern liberties, the *conscientia ex lex* of

[44] Compare, e.g., Willmoore Kendall, *John Locke and the Doctrine of Majority-Rule* (Urbana, Ill.: 1941), Edward Dumbauld, ed., *The Political Writings of Thomas Jefferson* (New York: 1955), pp. 54–60, 126–128, and *The Federalist*, no. 78.

the continental Liberals. With lapses,[45] as presently understood in our courts and society, they are none other. But it should be clear that we are most likely faced for the present with a choice between them and the demonic and murderous insanity of one after another totalitarian terror. Nor will it do to reply that what the canonists have in mind is a Catholic population rather than a spiritually degenerate mass. Perhaps it is still necessary to repeat that the reality of civilizational decay in the West has been profound enough so that the predominantly Catholic populations of Bavaria and Italy were hardly conspicuous in refusing to have a hand in the patently Satanic schemes of Hitler and Mussolini.[46] In short, the Syllabus of Errors is not only not enough, it is today positively dangerous. There are always stupid or naïve activists who are attracted by such reactionary blasts, and who will use them to pull down whatever bulwarks of political order may exist in the name of some idiotic scheme of social engineering. In day-to-day politics, the institutions of representative democracy may be able to withstand their assaults. But in a crisis, their enmity may prove to have eroded enough of the state's supports to prove fatal. The canonists need to wonder about the experience of that part of the French hierarchy which bore a share of the burden of historical responsibility for the Gestapo's work in France in consequence of their having helped weaken the Republic in a long series of actions toying with and even pandering to the anti-dreyfusard reactionaries, the *Action Française,* and their spiritual kin. However much the "modern liberties" may have had a hand in pulling down the remnants of

[45] E.g., Justice Douglas' famous dictum: "We are a religious people whose institutions presuppose a Supreme Being." Students of Pius IX or Leo XIII will, no doubt, be interested in the sentences that follow. *Zorach v. Clauson,* 343 U.S. 306.

[46] One of the reflections stirred up by Rolf Hochhuth's *Deputy* is that even had Pope Pius XII taken a firm public stand against Nazi genocide, there is scant evidence that it would have made much of a dent in the support of the Catholics for the Hitler regime and its activities. Cf. Gordon Zahn, *German Catholics and Hitler's Wars* (New York: 1964).

the old, seemingly Catholic, order, they are now the bulwark against far more infernal depths. Only a criminal irresponsibility would try to cut out of the bloc of constitutional guarantees a large segment that can not be easily limited or defined in law, and that opens up to the pressures of mass frenzy or systematic manipulation a vast and central area of our public communication.[47]

The inherent defect of the formalistic and legalistic terms in which so many churchmen have approached the Church-state question is that it reduces the multi-colored and mysterious coat of history to an almost Manichaean black and white. Such an approach does not notice that the abstract, external, and mechanically conceived standard of right order that it holds up may be an occasion of monstrous sins for the deracinated mass-men of

[47] At this point, perhaps, someone will raise the objection that I, too, am guilty of the crime of the canonists, that my critical remarks have endangered the representative democracy, that, if what I say about the canonists is true, then I ought to join the ranks of the democratic ideologists. It is necessary to say, first, that I have purposely written a book that will not be widely read, surely no college textbook. But a more important point might be suggested this way: I live in an old house, by midwestern American standards. It has some major failings and many minor ones. After much work, there are still many parts of it that are in need of major restoration or reformation. It is not difficult for me to imagine another house, more spacious, without defective parts, more convenient, less expensive to heat, with a more gracious and systematic style whether ancient or modern. But my house has my sweat and money in its floors and walls. Its high ceilings and rooms with doors on every opening suit my person. And more than that: it was built by my University in the peculiar style of decaying-French-Indiana-Victorian that marks its older buildings. It was built for one who followed my vocation, for one who represented my country in the country of my forefathers, who died where I was born. It was built with a view of the great, golden-domed, Victorian fantasy in the precincts of which I am to live out my calling and thereby, hopefully, have a hand in saving myself and my fellows with whom Providence has joined me. It is, in short, *my* house. Nevertheless, I should be an ass were I to fail to recognize that the kitchen floor is sagging, will never be wholly level, and needs unusual support if it is not to fall into the cellar. On the level of political theory, a similar honesty may be required if one is to avoid falling into the cellar as well as to avoid supposing that every floor needs identical arrangements for a fit existence. Sometimes there are painful truths that cannot be faced at first, but they must at least be seen, if only out of the corner of the eye.

223

our time. It is not enough to be concerned to protect the *simplices in fide* from the corrosive skepticism of Weimar democracy when the alternative is the integral self-affirmation of the masters of the gas chambers and crematories. For talk about an ideal order to be other than an occasion of sin, it must be so guarded as to avoid the ever-present human hope for salvation by magic, by some trick that forces reality. Even a step toward the approximation of an ideal structure requires a genuine *aristoi* of the spirit and of action, capable of profound spiritual experience, capable of giving it a symbolic and political expression accessible to their countrymen, and capable of mastering both in themselves and in their fellow citizens the uprush of the demonic forces of pride that threaten to convert every greatness in man into yet another murderous oppression. And, as if that were not unlikely enough, there must needs be a set of circumstances that permit such a step toward an approximation, and such circumstances cannot be manufactured.[48]

But if history cannot be ignored, neither ought it to be adored. To the dangerous abstractionism of the canonist's legalism there are historicist and democratist reactions, sometimes separate, sometimes together. Both find a degree of manifestation in the work of Murray, among others. Reacting against an intelligence that has lost touch with the earth and that mistakes the symmetry of a legal construct for the ultimate structure of Providence, the historicist renounces intelligence, surrenders to the flux of time with the tiredness of a whole civilization that has lost its way, and contents himself as best he can, if at all, with our mushrooming empire over matter, the vulgar replacement of the vice-regal vocation in time and eternity which he no longer hears. Less able to face the limitless abyss of a history without a hint of form (and, therefore, perhaps more healthy), the democratist attempts to convert meaninglessness itself into a

---

[48] One need not be a Platonist to appreciate the hesitancy and caution of Socrates when speaking of such matters in *Republic* v. 471-vi. 502.

value by making radical ignorance of all intimations of the absolute the precondition of human brotherhood, the political manifestation of which is democracy. Blindness thus becomes a virtue, the blindman being unable to view the grounds for oppressing or killing his brother. Indeed, his blindness becomes the occasion of a profoundly complacent self-congratulation, it being called the root of democratic amity, the freedom of brothers to do as they please without murdering or oppressing one another.[49]

If that is our situation, then the Church today is faced with a double rather than a single problem as is often thought. It is, of course, necessary for her to defend the human conscience and the human personality from the violations that everywhere threaten. It is especially necessary for the Church to defend the human conscience and the human personality against assaults and threats that are launched in the name of Christ by Christians, even well-intentioned Christians. It is necessary for the Church clearly to dissociate herself from that primitivistic legalism that discovers in the gospels only a warrant for the construction of a kingdom of God resting on the military superiority of the believers, who relentlessly put down and drive from the face of the earth every poor sinner who has not yet found it possible to recognize or to shoulder the true cross of orthodox and catholic religion. But that is not all that is necessary.

It is necessary for the Church not to do those things at the price of subjecting the due freedom of the Christian in philosophizing and in statesmanship to a new and powerful clericalism. There is a great deal of agitation in the Church today for the hierarchy to express the mind of the Church in the language of the day so as to make it comprehensible to contemporary hearers. No doubt, any other course would be absurd. But the question is hardly so simple. In the past, the clerical hierarchy canonized or seemed to canonize Aristotelian scholasticism and the *ancien régime*. Today the Church is in danger of imposing or

[49] Cf. Jacques Maritain, *Truth and Human Fellowship* (Princeton: 1957).

225

seeming to impose on her thinkers and statesmen a set of pseudo-theoretical formulae representing the vulgar detritus of philosophical and political initiatives that were already growing sclerotic a century ago. In the sphere of politics, one would have to expect formulations rooted in the popular platitudes left in the wake of Locke and Rousseau, of the Declarations of Independence and of the Rights of Man and of the Citizen.[50] It is not enough to object that such formulations must appear to the world as belated, opportunistic, and embarrassed rehabilitations of things that failed to burn up in the fire of Pius IX's anathemas. That may be true, but it is beside the main point.

The enormity of the clericalism of this position is made fully clear in Murray's article, "The Problem of Religious Freedom,"[51] a summary of his previous work and of what amounts to his advice to the Council. As such, it concentrates in an admirable fashion the peculiar weaknesses of his approach. Murray insists that the question at issue in contemporary disputes about religious freedom is a constitutional question rather than primarily a theological one (p. 570), a view that accounts for the utter absence of any scriptural element to his argument save two brief paragraphs inserted as if in afterthought at the very end of a long, seventy four page article. Nevertheless, the new "personal and political consciousness of contemporary man" on this constitutional question (p. 516) "ought to be approved by the authority of the Church" (p. 522), i.e., by the ecclesiastical hierarchy in the Council, thus continuing the work of Pius XII, who had begun to effect "a badly needed *aggiornamento* of the official political philosophy of the Church" (p. 545).

Reflecting on the experience of Socrates, one may well wonder what, exactly, an "*official* political philosophy" is. Can such a thing really exist? The last attempt at one was made by Gio-

[50] Cf., e.g., J.C.M., "On Religious Liberty," *America,* November, 1963, pp. 704–706.
[51] *TS,* vol. XXV, December 1964, pp. 503–575.

vanni Gentile. Are the Council and the pope to take his place, formulating and authoritatively approving their version of mass political consciousness at this or that moment of historical "growth"? Are we to believe that the bishops, by virtue of their special graces, are constituted a philosophical council, or a constitutional council? The bishops themselves make no such claims. Are we to believe that the function of the Council is to approve or disapprove of the popular consciousness of either today's or yesterday's world? Is it not, rather, to illumine it with the gospel and thereby to place it in the purifying fire of the divine judgment? Must it not, rather, be the task of Vatican II to give voice to the ultimate spiritual orientations of the gospel that must control any constitutional arrangements concerning religion? Is it not the whole significance of the ecclesiology implicit in the recent liturgical reforms that "the Church" is not to be understood as merely the ecclesiastical hierarchy, but as the people of God, and that there are diverse gifts and offices in the Church and that none should usurp another's place? Is it not a consequence of this that Christian philosophers and statesmen (and not the hierarchy) must be responsible for evaluating and structuring, in the light of the gospel preached to them by the bishops, the popular consciousness in its political and constitutional dimensions? And what, after all, would be the force of a conciliar statement in interpretation and validation of today's popular consciousness? Would it not be open to statesmen in a few years to invalidate the Council's pronouncements on the grounds that it is out of date and no longer corresponds to a new political situation and a new popular consciousness, just as Murray correctly shows the political thought of Leo XIII, except in its vaguest generalities, to be irrelevant to our situation?

Murray's advice to the council is designed to relieve the Church quickly of a host of old, unpleasant, and often true charges of intolerable and sinful pressures on the consciences of non-Catholics. But it does so at the price of reinforcing the grounds for another set of old, unpleasant, and often true charges that the Church has become distorted by a deep-rooted clericalism that is ultimately responsible for much of the radical secularization of the modern world. In this case, as in so many others, the clericalist short-cut will likely prove just another well-intentioned illusion.

As an alternative, the Council might develop and adopt a profound and fully elaborated theological formulation of the scriptural arguments mentioned in the two brief paragraphs at the end of Murray's article, arguments that are, without the requisite depth and scope, the basis of the last chapter of this book.

At the heart of the matter is the question whether it is the proper function of the ecclesiastical hierarchy to pass judgment or to seem to pass judgment on the theoretical issues in dispute between political philosophers on the one hand, and historicists and democratists on the other. Can the ecclesiastical hierarchy be expeced to decide whether a theoretical science of regimes is possible? Whether and on what grounds one can determine if democracy is the best regime, or even best for our time, or even inescapable for our time? Can it be said that the special graces of their offices specially fit popes and bishops to awe the world of the mind with the splendor of unmatched theoretical depth and brilliance? Or to bring order to the world of action by an awesome display of a cogent and constitutive statesmanship as was attributed to ancient law-givers? Not only theology, but the history of Italy mocks the thought. It may well be that such questions will remain unanswered in our time and that no new law-givers will be ours, but, in any case, there is no reason to believe that the locus of solution is in any institution, still less in the institution of the ecclesiastical hierarchy.

Nevertheless, the Church may still judge, correct, and direct the world of speculative thought and the world of action. She may do so if she brings forth from the womb of baptism re-born thinkers and statesmen who can ransom the times. To hope for that means also to hope for an ecclesiastical hierarchy that has shorn itself of false pretensions, that has rediscovered its far greater powers to judge, correct, and direct the whole universe of man's civilization not on the level of the imperial ukase, but at far deeper levels, at the roots of the soul. For that, the hierarchy does not need the voice and style of our moment, nor that of a stilted Renaissance Latin, nor that of scholasticism. Rather, the hierarchy needs to rediscover how to live and speak to our time by adapting for our time the prophetic, mystically pregnant, parabolic, and authoritative mode of the gospels.

What we need to rediscover is that the whole voice and action of the Church is not, contrary to the clericalism of the eternal Giles of Rome, simply the voice and action of the hierarchy. But neither are they, contrary to the anti-clericalism of the eternal Marsilius, simply the voice and action of laymen who refuse to acknowledge that "the burden of the priests is heavier."[52] Until we discover how properly to value and relate both, we shall have to stumble tragically through further repetitions of the Condemnation of 1277,[53] and of the assault on Boniface VIII at Anagni in 1303.

It cannot be the object of the magisterium either to make the world safe for democracy or for the *ancien régime*. But is it too much to hope that it discover a mode whereby it might give new birth and sustenance to statesmen who could speak with such a voice as spoke in Lincoln's Second Inaugural? Is it too much to hope that it discover a mode whereby it might give new birth and sustenance to a people that could hearken to such a voice?

[52] *Epist.* xii. 2 in Migne, *PL,* vol. LIX, p. 42.
[53] See Gilson, *History,* pp. 402–410.

The Relationship
of Ecclesiastical
and Political Structures

ONE way of viewing the contrast between the medieval and the contemporary relationships of Church and state is to speak of the medieval arrangements as appropriate to a "sacral society" in which, furthermore, the political aspects of the common life are relatively underdeveloped as compared with the religious and ecclesiastical. This overshadowing of the political by the ecclesiastical may be said to occur at "the moment when the supremacy of the spiritual order is publicly recognized." It is in consequence of this first public recognition that, "on account of the extra-ordinary power of attraction inherent in spiritual values, they will inevitably begin to envelop, enwrap, and embrace all values of the temporal order, so that these latter will seem in a way to be based on them, or, more exactly, withdrawn behind them, hidden in them, renouncing all ambition for the time being to assert their difference and emphasize their originality." This is the explanation of Charles Cardinal Journet.[1] To it may be added Murray's argument to the effect that in the chaos of the Dark Ages, the Church alone was the bearer of the insti-

[1] *The Church of the Word Incarnate*, vol. 1, p. 219. Cf. Jacques Maritain, *True Humanism*, trans. M.R. Adamson, 5th ed. (London: 1950), pp. 137–147; *Man and the State* (Chicago: 1951), pp. 157–165.

tutional heritage of Roman order. Therefore, it fell to the ecclesiastical hierarchy to be the tutor of the barbarians, and to substitute its juridical structure in places where there should have been a political one, but where none was in fact, or only a grossly defective one.[2]

From this point of view, the tendency represented by Giles of Rome is toward the extreme form of that sacralization of society. John of Paris and those like him appear as representatives of a moderate form of the reassertion of the rights of politics. Finally, Marsilius of Padua begins, on the level of theory, the thoroughgoing reassertion of the comprehension of religion by politics. On the practical level, that reaction took the form of divine-right absolute kingship in most of Western Europe except Italy. It is against this seeming return to the ancient world's political tradition that Cardinal Bellarmine fought when he attacked royal absolutism. Royal absolutism, in turn, was attacked by rationalistic liberal ideology on the level of thought, and by democratic revolutions on the level of action. For all the defects of liberal ideology and liberal democracy, the order of free persons toward which they work is seen, from this general point of view, to be fundamentally right, natural, reasonable.[3]

No doubt there is a great deal of truth in such a view, but it fails to notice a major element in the whole development. There is a sense in which the whole development may be viewed as a dispute about the nature of priestly power, rather than a dispute about the limits of priestly authority vis-à-vis political authority.

[2] There is, of course, also the view that all history, at least since Moses, is one grand march toward the First Amendment's religious clauses. However absurd such poster eschatology may be, it is interesting to note how it forms a part of the noble lie that legitimizes the U.S. Constitution by modern sacred myth. Cf., e.g., Leo Pfeffer, *Church, State, and Freedom* (Boston: 1953).

[3] Cf. Jacques Maritain, *True Humanism*, pp. 147–204. Murray, too, has his criticisms of these developments, but he is far more guarded in pointing them out than Maritain, who is less limited by relatively narrow polemical objectives.

The politico-religious background out of which both the ancient and medieval civilizations sprang was that of sacred kingship. Both the Homeric and the Germanic warrior tribes were centered on a father-king whose title to rule and whose ruling function were profoundly religious. Although the system was not always that of simple patrilineal primogeniture such as reconstructed by Fustel de Coulanges, it seems almost always to have followed some system of blood or kin right.[4] In that case, the people or the *patres* or the warriors, or their captains, had a hand in electing the king from among those with a right to the office by blood.[5]

But, whatever the details of any particular constitution, in all cases the significance of the blood relationship was religious, and the office itself was decisively religious. The king was a priest in that it was his task to enunciate the divine judgments about the problems of human action faced by his society. By virtue of his blood-line, the king was in contact with the sacred ancestors, and most especially with those heroes, demi-gods, or gods who founded or refounded his line and, with it, the society which is centered on it. That is to say, by virtue of his special contact with the great ancestors through whose knowledge of the divine order of things the society's order was established, the king made present again and again the only real basis of existence: the divinely ordained order.

By virtue of his ancestors and, perhaps, of his election by the other chiefs who also headed family cults, he alone was competent to determine whether a course of action was in accordance

---

[4] The principal references for this discussion may be found *supra*, p. 16, n. 2; p. 58, n. 1; p. 114, n. 62; p. 124, n. 77; and see Eric Voegelin, *The World of the Polis.*

[5] Cf., e.g., the description by Widukind of the election of Otto I in 936. Here three elections occur: designation by his father, election by the military chieftains and enthronement by them outside the church, and, finally, the acceptance by the "people" assembled inside the church under the presidency of the Archbishop of Mainz. *Res Gest. Sax.* ii. 1–2, *M.G.H.*, Ss.R.G. vol. 59, pp. 63–67.

with the divine, and thus real, order of things. He pronounced the judgments and he performed the rites whereby the tribe or city was restored to the purity of existence in the divinely established way after periodic deviations from the path of real existence.[6] Fundamentally, real law was made by the god or gods. It was the special function of the king to know the sacred formulae. And, since the rituals involved belonged to a family cult, only a member of the family could be fully initiated to them. Only a member of the family could perform the religious acts of consulting them, interpreting their significance for the specific problem at hand, and commanding action in conformity with them. Only later, when there was some fundamental break in the kingly rule, were the laws even written down. So profound was this ancient notion throughout the Western world that, when monarchy was reëstablished anew under the Empire, it was only natural that the Emperor should become more and more god-like. It was only natural that the emperor should take up the ancient royal function of pontiff, i.e., to build a bridge between heaven and earth, to root the human, political structure in the divine and eternal structure of reality. In less monarchical regimes, various means were resorted to in order to accomplish the same basic religious objective along with a different distribution of power and responsibility. But the notion of the political society as an integrally religious organization was everywhere characteristic of antiquity as well as of the barbarian tribes who invaded Western Europe in the Dark Ages. Quite aside from the accuracy of Gregory of Tours by modern standards of historiography, it is not in the least fanciful to imagine a Clovis at the battle of Tolbiac crying out to Christ: "If thou wilt give me victory over my enemies and I prove that power which thy followers say they have proved concerning thee, I will believe in

[6] The decisive importance for many societies of ritual restorations to a pure existence in the divine way has been brilliantly pointed out by Mircea Eliade in *The Myth of the Eternal Return*.

233

thee and be baptized in thy name." Nor does it require any great stretch of the imagination to conjure up the subsequent mass baptism of Clovis and his victorious host. Such events, in one form or another, took place as far apart as the host of Constantine and Prince Vladimir I of Kiev as late as 989.[7]

But the baptisms had a variety of effects in addition to their supernatural ones. It may be perfectly true, as Kern argues, that even in the Christian Middle Ages old law was good law and the older the better.[8] Nevertheless, old law was no longer sacred law obtained from the gods by the ancestors of the king who were the heroic, quasi-divine founders of a people. The waters of baptism washed away the old gods, and with them the king's special claim to authority: his mystic connection with the divine sources of order. The consequences of that fact were symbolized when Childeric, Clovis' descendant, was deposed and shorn of his sacred long hair by a tonsure, all under the religious sanction of the pope.[9]

A number of different stages were passed through in the process. To replace the religious foundations of pagan royal government, the quasi-sacrament of royal anointment was developed. Under Charlemagne there was even danger that the king would develop a new religious status higher than the pope as well as the other bishops of the Empire. But the Church managed, by and large, to reduce the sacramental character of the coronation ritual to the point at which the participation of the bishops signified that the king was commissioned, perhaps revocably, as the secular arm of the Church. The danger of the purely sacramental approach was that it seemed to involve an irrevocable grant of authority in that it imprinted forever on the soul of the king the character of *rex et sacerdos* whence he might

---

[7] Gregory of Tours even calls Clovis a new Constantine. *Historia Ecclesiastica Francorum* ii. 30–31. *M.G.H.*, Ss.R.M., vol. I, pp. 91–93.

[8] *Kingship and Law in the Middle Ages*, pp. 146–166.

[9] Cf. *supra*, pp. 113–115.

lay claim to an authority deeper than that possessed by the *sacerdotium*.[10]

But the other solution carried with it a profound danger of its own. It tended radically to secularize the function of the king. This has been obscured by the fact that, in reaction against the clerical, and particularly papal, absolutism, the kings of Europe subsequently claimed a divine-right absolutism of their own. But they never succeeded in working out a satisfactory theological grounding for it.[11] They did not manage to turn back the clock to the days when the chief ruler was also the chief priest. Kingship and priesthood had been too successfully distinguished by that time to admit of a pre-Gelasian king-priest. And it is a commonplace to note that one of the really remarkable civilizational changes in the West was the distinction between politics and religion effected by the Christian distinction between *rex* and *sacerdos*. But what is not understood is that the price of that achievement so far in the West has been the radical secularization of politics. The question is whether it is the necessary price.

If the religious function of the king is merely to be the secular arm of the Church, if his task is merely to perform those brutal and bloody tasks with which the clergy do not wish to be soiled, then his religious significance is at an end the moment he asserts his independence of his clerical masters.[12] If, in short, the religious significance of political action is simply that it creates an order of external peace, including the silencing of heretical voices, within which the clergy carry on the religiously important work, then a politics free of clerical domination is a

[10] Cf. Ernst H. Kantorowicz, *The King's Two Bodies* (Princeton: 1957), especially ch. 3.

[11] Indeed, they were driven to such ludicrously desperate expedients as Sir Robert Filmer's *Patriarcha*.

[12] There is certainly a tendency in this direction in St. Augustine, although he is far too subtle to be reduced to nothing but that. Nevertheless, it is no accident that Giles of Rome was an Augustinian.

235

politics devoid of religious significance. The divine-right kings tried to produce a substitute but failed.[13] Their place was taken by regimes that denied any religious dimensions or significance to their action.[14] That is all commonplace enough, but there is another aspect of the development that is not noticed.

The absolute kings by divine right are ordinarily regarded as political centralizers, and rightly. They are ordinarily regarded as unifiers of political and religious authority, and rightly. But, with respect to the latter, it should be noticed that below the king religious and political authority remained for the most part in separate hierarchies. Although they were in reaction against papal domination of both politics and religion for all of Christendom, although they were reasserting the pre-Christian unification of politics and religion on the level of a newly emerging set of *gentes* rather than on the universal level of the pope, yet the divine-right kings never were confronted with a divine-right aristocracy. The secularization of politics by the Church seems to have been so effective that it never occurred to the European aristocracies to try to reclaim the priestly authority that anciently lay in the sacred ancestry of great chieftains, even when they recognized another as overlord.

Since the papacy had become deeply involved in a major political struggle—the effort to build a Christendom at the apex of which would stand the pope with his penitude of power, political and religious, a veritable *rex et sacerdos*—the kings of

[13] The divine-right kings were probably doomed to failure for a number of reasons. Perhaps not the least of them was the fact that they retained enough of the Catholic tradition so that they never claimed to have the power of orders, however much they may have interfered with and even exercised ecclesiastical jurisdiction. To have done so would have been a major victory of antique religion over Catholicism. Even Marsilius, in another line of thought, did not claim the power of orders for the people.

[14] However, in many cases they provide an absolute standard of meaning by preaching some futuristic myth that purports to reveal a perfect society toward which the secular sphere itself moves. Specific actions, in such a context, have meaning only in the measure that they tend to produce movement in that direction.

the emerging national states understood that the politics whereby they could extricate themselves from the papal political power must be a religious politics. In this they were at one with Marsilius, who saw that clerical political power could only be broken by relocating the center of religious authority from pope and clergy to the politically organized people. But the divine-right kings instinctively grasped that their counter-papal religious politics must be monarchical even aside from other considerations of political centralization. With the exception of the monarchs themselves, none of the lay orders of society was seen as exercising a priestly and sacred office.[15] The lords temporal were distinct from the lords spiritual, and the commons likewise had no priestly role.

There was another consideration that impelled the nations of Europe to resist papal political domination in the way of royal absolutism, rather than in the Marsilian way of relocating ultimate religious authority in the whole Christian community, however organized politically. The very centralization of ecclesiastical power in the hands of the pope who could act through a far-flung apparatus of officials directly subject to his jurisdiction, imposed on the opposition the need for a similar stripping away of articulations of authority appropriate to a state of lesser tension. By a sort of natural law of conflict, the compression and centralization of the power of initiative in one party tends to encourage the like in the other. Faced with papal centralization of authority, the kings naturally attempted to reduce the clergy in their kingdoms to as complete an obedience to

15 Of course, in the narrow sense of priesthood, it had long since been clear to theologians that the royal anointment and coronation and enthronement did not constitute an ordination. But popular wisdom is too deep to be confused by such distinctions or to suppose that they capture anywhere near all that needs to be said. Anyone could see at Rheims or Westminster (where one can still see) that the coronation puts the king in a priestly and sacred office of some sort. Cf., e.g., P.E. Schramm, *A History of the English Coronation* (Oxford: 1937), and E.C. Ratcliff, *The Coronation Service of H.M. Queen Elizabeth II* (London: 1953).

themselves in matters affecting action as that claimed by the pope. By a principle of parity, as it were, papal absolutism tended to produce a royal absolutism. If the pope can coerce at whim a host of politically important figures within the king's domain, and if those magnates accept the directions of the pope as coercively binding for political action, then is the king overturned and his whole constitution with him, because there is one great structure within his realm that is politically irresponsible and that can act with the coherence of a disciplined body. The king has two tactics open to him. He may employ both. He can tighten the discipline over his own, non-ecclesiastical, subjects in order to be capable of equally controlled counter-action. And he can attempt to cut the line of command and communication between pope and bishops, placing the latter in a position where they are dependent on the king, through whom they must go to reach the pope. In such a case, the pope's last card is the power of deposing the king. By the time of the divine-right kings, the popes no longer held that card in political fact.

Perhaps it should be pointed out that such a centralization tends in the long run to dry up both the spiritual vigor of a church and the political vigor of a country. Nevertheless, some degree of it is inescapable in time of conflict, and all the more so when the opponent has already undertaken a martial simplification of his regime. That is natural enough and perhaps even wholesome. But what is dangerous is that it be long protracted, and that, during a great span of years, the multifarious vitalities and virtues that in less trying times express themselves in a more decentralized authority suffer the loss of exercise, of avenues for growth, or are perversely turned to accidental uses and, in the end, shrivel up. Then the conflict is a disaster for all, for victor and vanquished alike if there be victory, and for both still if there can be none. Perhaps that was the worst irony of the concordatory age. Not only were hearts seldom really together, but the parties to the concordats had become heartless. That, of course, does not prevent the mind from calculating.

John of Paris seems to understand at least some element of this descending spiral when he advocates a mixed regime in both Church and state. He attemps to avoid final and catastrophic showdowns in which all forces have been aligned behind one or the other of two combatants: the king threatening to march on Rome with all his allies, and the pope marshalling his defensive forces and threatening to excommunicate half the world. John of Paris argues that both pope and king ought to be moderated by some aristocratic senate: for the king, the magnates; for the pope, the cardinals and, ultimately, a council of the episcopacy. All of this, in turn, ought to rest on popular election.

However moderating an influence such a double structure might have, John of Paris does not have an adequate theological ground for his prudential construct, as was pointed out earlier.[16] It will be necessary to return to this question after some other structural considerations have been noted.

To this point, the pressure toward a duplication of ecclesiastical centralization in political structures has been viewed largely as originating in the Church and pressing the political structure to conform to the ecclesiastical pattern. However, the thrust goes both ways.

When the Church is confronted with a powerful and unified political regime (and especially when that unity is being forged or recast in a new image), then the political pressures attempting to use the prestige and influence of the clergy (or, in other cases, to neutralize or destroy it) are extreme. The natural tendency is for the Church to simplify and centralize her structure in order to retain some freedom of action. The most systematic expression of this tendency is the organization of the

16 Cf. *supra,* pp. 120–123.

hierarchy under an irremovable primate who holds considerable power over the rest of the national episcopacy, whose appointment comes from Rome alone without interference by secular authority, and who, together with the pope, determines the appointment of the rest of the national episcopacy. Finally, major decisions are made by Rome or confirmed by Rome prior to publication.

There is a double thrust to such an arrangement. First, it sets up a reliable chain of communication through which the voice of the Church may be heard, and heard saying the same thing at the same time everywhere in the country in question. Second, it locates one of the centers of decision outside the sphere of direct control by the political authorities. It is far more difficult in most cases to bring effective pressure on a unified episcopacy than on individual bishops. And it is far more difficult to control the voice of the Church if the major appointments and decisions are made or confirmed in Rome, that is to say, by the pope, who is outside the immediate jurisdiction of the political authorities. Evidence of such an organizational strategy by ecclesiastical officials faced with powerful political pressures is abundant from the Middle Ages to the present day.

Naturally, the secular regime in such a case will use a variety of well-known tactics to defeat such a system. Aside from a great number of specific pressures that can be brought to bear on individual clergymen, the basic strategy will be weaken or sever the supra-national tie to Rome and to capture the episcopacy as a unified body, or to isolate the bishops from one another and capture them individually. The means are well known: veto on episcopal appointments, the power of nomination, channeling all communications between bishops and pope through a governmental agency with power to prevent transmission, the setting up of a national church not in communion with Rome. The completion of the process (short of complete eradication

240

of organized Catholic religion) is the reduction of the hierarchy to a mere organ of the state administration.[17]

In a democratic regime, on the other hand, the structural problem is quite different from that in monarchical or oligarchical polities. Under the latter, the centralization of power in the hands of one or a few in either Church or state encourages a similar organization in the other. However, the liberal, modern, nation-state democracies of the West are confronted in the Catholic Church with a different problem. In greater or lesser degree, the Church retains in those countries organizational elements that were historically rooted in the conflict with absolutism, and with the secular, totalitarian democracies inspired by the French revolution. The central feature of this remnant of former times is a concentration in Rome of the power to appoint bishops and to make a vast number of important and unimportant decisions.[18] In this case, the very fact of such concentration

[17] Obviously, even a review of such situations of conflict cannot be attempted here. The number of cases is enormous, and, furthermore, quite diverse, depending on the character of the political impetus that initiates it (e.g., forging of a national unity leading to separatist national churches as an integral part of the distinct national identity, erecting a universal empire on a caesaro-papist basis, developing a totalitarian regime in which the object is to capture the church, first because no autonomous bodies can be tolerated, and secondly with a view to the ultimate weakening and destruction of religion altogether).

[18] As for the element of national episcopal unity, conditions vary. Some states have no primate, nor national synod or council, nor even a national episcopal conference. The United States in the early part of the nineteenth century had the *de facto* equivalent of a primate and synod (until 1846), during which time the Archbishop of Baltimore was the sole metropolitan in the country, and thus the synods of his province constituted the equivalent of national councils. In mid-nineteenth century, this arrangement was followed by national or plenary councils (in 1852, 1866, and 1884) under the presidency of an apostolic delegate (i.e., a papal representative). This was followed by a thirty-five year lapse of external episcopal organization on a national level. Finally, there was established a national episcopal conference which can speak in the name of the hierarchy, but which cannot juridically bind any of its members to any course of action (as can a synod or council). Cf., e.g., Peter Guilday, *A History of the Councils of Baltimore* (New

seems inherently subversive of the political regime, quite aside from any specific policy conflicts.

The external, legal manifestation of this concentration of power centers on a set of provisions of the Code of Canon Law. There the Church claims the right to impose both spiritual and *temporal* penalties on delinquents under her jurisdiction, and that by divine right. She has the power to excommunicate, including the cutting off of profane communication between the faithful and one class of excommunicates. Such penalties, temporal and spiritual, may be imposed not only for doctrinal faults, but for public ecclesiastical crime, and anyone who gives aid or comfort to one condemned to the most serious form of excommunication is himself excommunicated *ipso facto* if the aid and comfort is given in regard to the delict for which the original excommunication was incurred. Finally, and of the greatest political significance, the decision in questions of this nature lies with ecclesiastical authority, at the apex of which is, of course, the Holy See.[19]

Naturally, there is considerable dispute among canoists as to: the range of specific acts that may be penalized; the status of temporal penalties (e.g., are they to be understood, as John of Paris argues, as lesser penalties imposable on condition that the subject voluntarily accepts them in lieu of a greater, spiritual penalty?); the scope of profane communication permissible between the faithful and the excommunicate; the obligation of laymen in secular offices of authority to enforce the judgments of ecclesiastical authority by force of arms if necessary; etc. But there is one important school of interpretation, represented in the curia of the Holy See, that holds to a scope and binding power of ecclesiastical jurisdiction that is virtually as

York: 1932), and *The National Pastorals of the American Hierarchy* (Washington, D.C.: National Catholic Welfare Conference, 1923), pp. xi–xii.

[19] Cf. the following canons of the Codex: 2214.1; 2267; 2195–2198; 2331; 2338.2; 1552–1554; 1556–1559.1; 1569–1570.

great as that advocated by Giles of Rome, although the basis in the direct power theory is dropped for a Bellarminian statement of the indirect power.[20] And, although this is surely not the only interpretation of the sacred canons, it is just as surely a common one, perhaps also the most influential one prior to Vatican II. It is, in any case, a possible one and a likely one, since it conforms to the tendencies of canonists from the Middle Ages to the present. And it is just this possibility that threatens the democratic political structure.

Of course, no one supposes that Alfredo Cardinal Ottaviani would assert the Church's right in the United States to invoke the "secular arm" to suppress heretics. Churchmen of his opinion on these matters are far too prudent and circumspect for any such nonsense. What some persons are concerned about, however, is the inherent tendency of this Bellarminian reading of the Code. In the measure that Catholics accept the clerical authority contained in such a reading, they become irresponsible agents of a state within a state who, by virtue of their organization, have an enormous tactical advantage over their fellow citizens. From a political point of view, they pose a threat to democratic institutions tactically similar to that of the large Communist parties of Western Europe: a bloc of votes absolutely disciplined to act in unison in accordance with directions from a professional leadership. They are not free to act as they see fit, but as they are directed. Therefore, the consequence appears to be that, while non-Catholic citizens have one vote each, the leader of the Catholics may not even be a citizen and yet, in political fact, have millions of votes in his hand. The tactical advantage of such a situation is obvious. It is also obvious that Catholics in such a situation are not citizens of a democracy, but simply agents of an enormously powerful magnate. And the indirect power as developed by Bellarmine and Ottaviani even

---

[20] Cf., e.g. Alaphridus Ottaviani, *Institutiones Juris Publici Ecclesiastici* (Rome: 1935), 2 vols. And cf. *supra,* p. 161, n. 9.

goes so far as to demand of those agents the execution by military force of the policies formulated by the ecclesiastical hierarchy.

It is perfectly true that the foregoing is almost a caricature of the persistent nightmares entertained by leaders of such fright groups as Protestants and Other Americans United for the Separation of Church and State. It is perfectly true that in no Western democracy is any such political power really in the hands of any cleric, not to speak of the pope. It is perfectly true that there is no clear evidence that Italian Catholics, for example, have been anywhere nearly so disciplined as to vote unanimously against the Communist Party in spite of excommunicatory fulminations from their bishops. It is perfectly true that it has been a long time since a pope could put an army in the field almost anywhere in Christendom.

Nevertheless, it is also perfectly true that, whatever the situation with respect to lay obedience in contemporary fact, it is easy to read the sacred canons in a way, traditional with canonists, that demand such obedience as a matter of right, that asserts the rightful power of the ecclesiastical hierarchy to issue binding directives in every area of human existence that is morally charged, and to enforce those directives with spiritual and temporal penalties, including the sword of the secular arm.[21] And, although the hierarchy cannot *de facto* exercise so broad an authority, the political reality is more subtle. It could scarcely be regarded as a singularly perverse suspicion if one were to suspect that such an interpretation of the canons would be accompanied by an extraordinarily heavy emphasis on obedience

[21] It may be objected that the hierarchy cannot directly attack with the sword, that it can only employ military force "indirectly" through laymen. Aside from the fact that it makes precious little difference whether one is killed by the bishop himself or by soldiers acting in consequence of his judgment (however circuitous the line of consequences), the question is whether the infamous papal "nod" of St. Bernard (*Pat. Lat.* clxxxii. 776) is binding *de jure,* so that the pope "demands that which is owed him" (Ottaviani, *Institutiones,* vol. 1, p. 378).

to clerical authority in the widespread educational work of the Church. Thus, although the nightmares of members of P.O.A.U. would be seen scarcely to correspond to the reality of the day, their further suspicions would not seem wholly unfounded.

It must appear to them that the hierarchy cannot in fact exercise so broad a power because of the weakness of Catholic religion in the laymen. It must appear that it is only because the laymen are partly assimilated to a non-Catholic society that they are not prepared to accept the order erected by Canon Law. It must appear that if the bishops were ever in a position to secure a high degree of isolation of Catholics from non-Catholic influences and systematically to indoctrinate them, then the *de facto* authority of the hierarchy would begin to approach the scope of the canonists' dreams.

Aside from the scientifically primitive form of the argument (it is plain that the problems of obedience and indoctrination are a lot more complex than the fright groups suppose), and from its historical myopia (even at the height of medieval clerical power, there was no lack of Catholic armies to fight the pope), there is an important element of truth in its roots. The canonist's ordinary interpretation of a handful of canons manages to produce a psychic and political structure in which "the Church" stands for the priesthood, and "the priesthood" stands for the hierarchical priesthood, and the laymen are the mere objects of priestly attention and the thoughtlessly obedient tools of the priests who, alone, really act. That is clearly a caricature, but it is not an outrageous caricature. There is enough reality to it to be politically important. In a democracy, where numbers count, the caricature may be the reality for the politically important majority who have neither the time nor the intellectual training for too subtle distinctions. In a religiously pluralistic democracy, the potency of the caricature leads toward a split between Catholics and their fellow citizens who see the Church as an enormously dangerous power-structure. In a pre-

dominantly Catholic country, the element of truth in the caricature tends to expand and tends to summon up an anti-clerical
reaction. In either case, the tendency is away from democracy
and toward a more or less overt struggle for power between two
groups, at least one of which is monarchically or oligarchically
run, solidified and disciplined for action. That struggle may even
manifest itself in the collapse of the state in civil violence or
war.

Naturally, that is only a tendency flowing from one set of
circumstances. There are other matters of great significance.
When, as in the United States, the bishops are not organized
in a national synod that can reach decisions that bind all the
members as well as the rest of the faithful, the possibility of
imprudent political decisions sanctioned by anathemas is, on
the national level, greatly reduced. Such an exercise of clerical
power can only take place on the diocesan level, where it might
be decisive in local or state politics. Thus, the larger the political unit involved, the more difficult it would be for the bishops
to act in this way, since everything depends on coordinating the
actions of a great number of bishops each of whom is free to
cooperate or not as he sees fit. Since a prudential decision is
involved, it may be difficult to obtain universal cooperation
even from a small group of bishops.

Thus, lack of a national synod greatly reduces the likelihood
of effective use of canonical coercion on a national level. But
a qualification must be added. The above applies only insofar
as there is no attempt by Rome to secure a coordinated line of
action from a national episcopacy. Then the very fragmentation of the bishops and their dependence on Rome in a variety
of ways makes it more difficult for them to resist Roman direction.

Since the likelihood of an attempt by the clerical hierarchy to
control political action by the use of canonical coercion must
vary not only according to these considerations, but also ac-

cording to national and local traditions and the circumstances of the specific case, the nature and severity of a political counter-thrust of anti-clerical or anti-Catholic nature will likewise vary. But any exercise of this claimed power of jurisdiction is likely to produce both a deep split in the body politic and the beginnings of counter-moves in defense of political autonomy. In the event that the movement of politics has already been in the direction of state control of ecclesiastical affairs, the process is likely to be speeded up under cover of a defense of legitimate political autonomy against arbitrary clerical interference.

In a democracy, the political solution to the threat of an ecclesiastical monolith is to democratize the Church or crush it. But, from the point of view of the Church, the former is just a particular version of the latter. She cannot accept an ecclesiastical polity on congregational lines because she regards the powers and mission of the hierarchic priesthood as deriving not from man, however organized, but from Christ via the apostolic succession. Even the Marsilian regime, which lodged the power of jurisdiction in the hands of the whole community of believers, cannot be accepted by the Church because it lodges the full control over the exercise as well as the reception of the power of orders in hands that are not in the apostolic succession. This, by itself, was enough to procure the condemnation of Marsilianism in spite of the fact that he did not necessarily envisage this principle as operating solely in democratic forms.

Thus, short of an impossible transformation of Catholicism into some sort of neo-congregationalism, the only likely *modus vivendi* would seem to be that of continued clerical claim to rights of domination that cannot in fact be exercised, and continued lay disinclination to accept such claims (not to speak of overt disobedience in crisis situations) with no acceptable articulation of grounds for the disinclination or refusal. Because of the severe strain sometimes placed on the consciences of Catholics by such a situation, it cannot be viewed as being a

247

satisfactory ground for a politically stable solution, and every success of Catholic education or preaching must seem to non-Catholics as an increase in the danger of subversion of their regime. But perhaps another line of solution is open.

If every Catholic Christian shares a priesthood by virtue of his baptism and confirmation, then the question arises whether its exercise is under the jurisdiction of the hierarchical priesthood, and, if it is, whether it is so in the same sense that members of the hierarchic priesthood are under a jurisdictional control.

No one doubts that a member of the hierarchic priesthood is properly subject to a jurisdiction that can tell him when he may exercise his power of orders, in what way he is to exercise it (i.e., according to what formulae and after what rubrics), and to or for whom he is to exercise his power of orders. The power or orders is not his in the sense that the power to speak is his. Rather, it is given him under commission and in such a fashion that one might say of him that he gives himself to his priestly power, making of himself an instrument of a divine power. But it is not his in the sense that it depends on his virtues beyond the bare ability to intend to do his work and to say the appropriate words and to perform appropriate actions. And no one doubts but that the exercise of that power, both in the sacraments properly so called and in the sacrament of the word in the official teaching voice of the Church, is rightly subject to a jurisdictional authority. Nor does anyone doubt that even when laymen, on occasion, exercise some part of that jurisdiction, they do it by delegation from the papal or episcopal primacy, as the case may be.

But there appears to be another kind of priesthood. There appears to be another way of making Christ present among men: the way of personal witness, the way of the saint who shines with the glory of the divine presence in him. To be sure, this ought not to be understood as an alternative to the sacramental priesthood as some argue. Indeed, it depends on the sacramental priesthood in that the official teaching and sanctifying action of the Church are its roots. Nevertheless, they are not enough to constitute the fullness of this kind of priesthood. The baptized and confirmed believer must also place the whole of his personal depths and natural powers under the transforming influx of the Holy Spirit. Thus, the precise nature of this priesthood inescapably varies in terms of three things, none of which are under the control of the hierarchic priesthood as such: the particular grace and calling given by God to each person or community, the natural powers and talents of the person or community, and the degree to which the persons in question have been transformed by the divine grace. What is involved is the utterly intimate and total spiritual condition of an existential human whole. Consequently, there can be no question of organizing its manifestation in the same way as the work of the hierarchic priesthood. The saint is responsible for the whole of his action because the whole of his action proceeds from his person and its efficacy is dependent on his prudence. But the bishop does not have to be prudent to confer the power of orders, nor need the priest be prudent to receive or exercise it.

To attempt to reduce that sort of priestly action to a necessary obedience to the ecclesiastical hierarchy is patently absurd, since the ecclesiastical hierarchy does not make a claim to a special prudence. When it is a question of public, personal action in witness to Christ the saint and not the hierarchic priesthood must be the standard. When, on the other hand, it is a question of the discipline of the administration of the sacraments or of the authoritative preaching of the word of God, both in its dogmatic and in its moral aspects, then obedience must be given to those whose power derives from apostolic succession, and especially from the commissions given to Peter.

Of course, so far I have only been speaking of abstractions. The categories of saint and cleric are obviously not mutually exclusive. It is the prayer of every Catholic that God raise up in the Church holy priests and bishops.[22] In such cases, there accrues to the priest or bishop or pope an authority not inherent in his office.

But whether in layman or cleric, it is precisely the sanctified powers of the holy man that the present canons seem to fail to recognize. It seems as if the power and vision of the saint are put under the direction of a jurisdictional structure that has no claim to such powers or vision. That is the situation in which the jurisdictional structure of the hierarchic priesthood is set over the whole sphere of personal action, including the political,[23] as if it were not only infallible in its teaching office, but impeccable in the leadership of personal action, which is obviously historical nonsense.

As a counter to this deformity, there are reformers who call for the democratization of the Church. But the Church is not and cannot be a democracy. Christ rules the Church. In her there can be no claims to human sovereignty, for it is at the very heart of the Church's call to man that he lay down his claims to sovereignty and fall down to adore God alone, Lord of peoples and of hosts, as well as King of kings and Lord of lords. That lordship finds necessary expression in the apostolic succession, with the primacy of Peter at its center. Man neither preaches the gospel to himself nor does he make his own sacraments. Christ preaches the gospel and establishes sacraments. And if we hear the gospel from the mouths of men and if we receive the sacraments from the hands of men, it is only from men who do those things not of their own accord or of their own inter-

---

[22] Everyone knows that an unholy priest or bishop gives especially grave scandal because of his proximity to sacred things. It is also true that the difference between the structures of personal and sacramental or hierarchic priesthood can be especially painful when a saintly man is also a member of the hierarchic priesthood and finds himself under the jurisdiction of a vicious bishop or pope.

[23] This is explicitly the intention of Giles of Rome at *D.E.P.* 1. 2–3, where he treats the famous Pauline text on the spiritual man in 1 Cor 2:15.

pretation of the gifts of the Spirit that they have received, but because they were picked out, empowered, and commissioned by Christ or by others who, in turn, were chosen, empowered, and commissioned by Him. Any organizational reform that would obliterate or hide this essential manifestation of the Church's dependence on the divine initiative would be thoroughly false.

By the same token, neither can there be a Marsilian reform: reduction of the action of the hierarchic priesthood, in the sacrament of the word or in the sacraments proper, to merely ministerial actions done under the command of a sovereign human community. Not only is man's salvation dependent on a divine initiative in Incarnation, Death, and Resurrection, but that initiative is utterly gratuitous. There is no sovereign human community that can command the Word to become flesh, that can command the Christ to offer His life, that can bring Him forth from the tomb. And, therefore, there is no human community that can command the ordained ministers of that saving initiative, Peter with the other bishops and their assistants, to preach or not to preach the gospel, or that can command them concerning what the gospel means, or that can command them to administer or not to administer the sacraments.

But, having said these essential things, it is also necessary to call for adequate institutional manifestations of the untransferable responsibility of each of the baptized before the divine tribunal, a responsibility that each person bears for his personal action, a responsibility that is greater before the divine tribunal than before any tribunal of the hierarchic priesthood. Only then can the hierarchic priesthood seriously call out to all believers to affirm the unavoidable, direct, and absolute responsibility of each man in his conscience to the works of manifesting Christ Incarnate by the transformation of the whole of their personal depths and interrelationships so that the whole of their public actions is that of an *alter Christus*.

251

And the world of public, personal action is preëminently the world of politics. At the heart of all politics is a dramatic confrontation of men testing, in word, gesture, and action, the image of each for a revelation of the true mimetic standard of genuine, public, human perfection. And this is true for the most sordid as for the most sublime encounters in public life.

It can hardly be said that the direct, personal responsibility of the priesthood of the baptized for the sphere of human action, especially politics, is adequately represented in the present organizational structure of the Catholic Church. The matter of excommunication is, in a way, an external key to the whole problem, because it is the gravest penalty of the Church. To know when and how the solemn anathema[24] may be pronounced and what are its consequences is to know the limits and the ways of ecclesiastical jurisdiction. This is true despite the fact that it is relatively rare, nowadays, in political contexts, and despite the fact that under present law only Rome can impose the highest form of excommunication, which breaks not only sacred, but also secular communication between the faithful and the excommunicate.[25]

In the doctrine of Bellarmine, the Church has sought a middle way between the extremes of Marsilianism on the one hand, and, on the other, the radical clericalism of Giles. But, as Cardinal Ottaviani's work makes clear,[26] the Bellarminian solution supposes, and is understood to suppose, that, if worst comes to worst, the hierarchic priesthood can still demand an obedience in which the personal action of the non-hierarchic priesthood is turned on and off from the outside as if by a switch. The evident reality has been a good deal more success in turning it off than in turning it on.

The first prerequisite of a more satisfactory solution does not

[24] Cf. canon 2257.2, and *supra,* p. 242, n. 19.
[25] Cf. canons 2258, 2267, and 2338.2.
[26] Cf. *supra,* pp. 242–244.

seem to be the much-called-for "theology of the layman." The problem is deeper than that. It seems that a renewed and deepened theology of the Holy Ghost is needed. No doubt, it carries with it many dangers connected with excesses of all sorts of chiliasm or millenarianism. Nevertheless, only in such a context can one reasonably expect a renewed ecclesiology of sufficient depth adequately to limn the scope and responsibilities of the baptized and confirmed Christian for the public order of action.

Even from our present position, it is possible to outline some of the major lines of institutional alignment appropriate to a due recognition of the inalienable responsibility of the baptized and confirmed for the sphere of human action. Three main objectives in this connection ought to be secured by any reform of ecclesiastical structures.

In actions of the Church that directly affect the sphere of human action, for which the Christian bears an inalienable responsibility rooted in the moral unity of the human person, the prior assent of the laity ought to be required.

In actions properly proceeding directly from the power of holy orders, the hierarchic priesthood must remain ultimately free of lay control. That is to say that the authoritative public proclamation of the gospel and the administration of the sacraments ought not to be subject to the command of laymen.[27]

Finally, the institutions through which lay assent is to be

---

[27] There are different approaches to the much disputed ecclesiological questions concerning the priestly character of laymen and their relationship to the hierarchic priesthood even as concerns the administration of the sacraments and the preaching of the gospel. However, I have purposely avoided involvement in those arguments by the use of formulations that cover only the free jurisdiction of the hierarchic priesthood over the acts proper to it. I think that such limited formulations are adequate to the political dimension of the problem with which I am concerned, and I think that they will be satisfactory both to a more scholastic approach to priesthood and to a more historical one. Cf., e.g., Charles Journet, *The Church of the Word Incarnate*, vol. 1, pp. 1–192; Yves M.J. Congar, O.P., *Jalons pour une théologie du laïcat*, pp. 146–313, 367–453.

expressed must conform to the extra-ecclesiastical structure of the common life of the people concerned.

Put more concretely, the first objective means that the hierarchic priesthood as such should lay no claim authoritatively to produce political effects without the prior assent of the laity. That restriction obviously must include the power to cause the crucial political effect that is the cutting off of communication between fellow-citizens, i.e., excommunication in its broadest sense.

Nevertheless, as a balancing principle, it must be equally clear that the hierarchic priesthood must remain ultimately free to perform or not to perform its properly sacerdotal acts of authoritatively and publicly proclaiming the gospel and administering the sacraments. Obviously, between those two principles there lies a great, grey area. Thus, for example, anyone sensitive to the dynamic of human action cannot fail to see that for a bishop publicly to refuse to give communion to a statesman following a line of policy opposed by the ecclesiastical hierarchy is not only an act of priestly judgment, but also may be a powerful political act. With the qualifications that necessarily flow from the third principle, it seems that disastrous arbitrariness on the part of the hierarchic priesthood can best be avoided in this area if lay assent were also required for the refusal of the sacraments to individuals, provided, however, that the hierarchy always remains free to withdraw the ministrations of the priesthood from a whole community that obstinately insisted on protecting a course of action judged intolerably evil by the hierarchy.

The advantage of such an arrangement is not only that it prevents the hierarchy from engaging lightly in arbitrary political action, but also that it compels the hierarchy to take notice of the moral climate of the community for which it is responsible. In the case of a morally degenerating community, the hierarchy would be confronted with a clear public manifestation of the magnitude of its spiritual problems, and be unable to delude itself as to the efficacy of a handful of actions against some prominent individuals. In other cases, the regular encounter between the prophetic voice of the hierarchy and the moral sense of the community would tend to the benefit of both in diverse ways.

But, it may be argued, while such a precedure may avoid arbitrary and imprudent political action by the hierarchy, while it may avert some of the descending spirals of disaster growing out of the hierarchy's ignorance of the true spiritual climate of the community, still such an arrangement does not avert the most profound clashes in which the whole community is organized in defense of an indefensible line of conduct in the face of the solemn condemnation of the hierarchic priesthood. No doubt, that is the case. It cannot be avoided without distortion of the human condition between the first and second comings of Christ. Marsilius avoids such clashes by reducing Peter's voice and action to dependence on the commands of Caesar. Giles of Rome avoids them by giving Peter the imperial scepter. The first, like Herod, tries to annul the divine freedom to burst into man's history and summon him on a new path, and therefore it attempts to prevent the divine initiative from entering the lists in the great moral crises; in the name of man's freedom and of the freedom of the city, it attempts to still, at the moment of decision, the prophetic voice of Peter lest he cry out to Jerusalem: "Turn ye unto the Lord thy God!" The second, in the name of the divine freedom, attempts to deprive man and the city of their freedom lest in the hardening of their hearts before the divine summons they seem to defeat God Himself. The problem, however, is not to avert the great spiritual encounters that are an inevitable part of the double freedom of God and man. Ultimately, such encounters cannot be averted, but only driven to assume other, less appropriate manifestations. The problem, rather, is to avert false, arbitrary, unnecessary, confused, and confusing clashes insofar as that can be done by a wise institutionalization of the inescapable realities of our common life.

However, no one institutional structure can perform such a task *semper et ubique*. That is the import of the third principle. It is absurd to suppose that a regular and free representation of the mind of the laity could be obtained under the conditions imposed by a totalitarian tyranny, for example. It is equally absurd to suppose that the same structure can serve to represent the laity of a society organized by a feudal aristocracy, that of an absolute monarchy and that of a representative democracy, to name but a few of the alternatives. Different problems accompany each of them. One extreme case may serve to illustrate the dimensions of the difficulty. In a totalitarian tyranny that has not yet managed to establish its grip on the country firmly enough to risk suppressing a primate and the connection with Rome, it may well be that the primate, as a man, finds himself obligated to act as a center of resistance to the full elaboration of the totalitarian objectives of the ruling apparatus. The objectives protected by such a resistance may well be political as well as religious. Under such circumstances, no formal constitutional structure could guarantee genuine representation of lay opinion at any national synod. Under such circumstances, if concerted resistance is to be undertaken at all (not even to say prudently), it must be largely under the unfettered direction of the primate, who will have to rely on the tacit assent of the laity. Perhaps it will be asked: what if the primate is a political fool? No doubt, that is possible, and in that case the people will either follow him or not in his folly. Either way, they are likely to suffer bitterly for their sins, and there is no place for saving them from it by ecclesiastical constitutional engineering; there is only place for prayer that may convert their suffering into purification.

But in other circumstances, the complications are not so great. In a representative democracy, for example, it is quite possible for lay opinion to be formally represented at both the diocesan and national levels by bodies springing directly or indirectly from an electoral choice on a basis of formal personal equality (i.e., one man, one vote). It would then be quite possible for such a representation to grant or refuse assent to all canonical legislation respecting political questions, either by virtue of its content or by virtue of the nature of the penalty. Similarly, the judgment of individual cases of political import ought also to include a balance between panels of lay and clerical judges.

Obviously, the democratic election of laymen to such positions under present circumstances could hardly produce a lay representation in which any thoughtful man could repose confidence. It is absurd to expect laymen to bear high responsibilities when they are largely excluded from low ones. If the three principles I have suggested are valid for great temporal affairs, surely they are valid for the less. Indeed, their application in the less will prove necessary if lay representation in great affairs is ever to be an expression of an even minimally informed, articulate, responsible, and devoted body of the faithful. In short, the ordinary diocesan and parochial administration of those matters involving temporal values should rest on an institutional structure providing for the mutual consent of pastor and flock. Clearly included are matters of finance, building, social services, and school policy, staffing, and administration.

There are times when the social and political situations of the faithful make such suggestions plainly inappropriate. Groups of poor immigrants, for example, existing on the fringes of a society, have a necessarily simplified structure. They rightly centralize their common life in their educated leader-priest. But when, as in America, they are no longer on the fringes of society, new structures are necessary. In a representative democracy, anything less than a full equality of laymen in the government of matters involving temporal values will, in the long run, lead to another sad history of anti-clerical apostasy. Then all of Peter's powers are for naught when Caesar has no "ears to hear" (Mt 13:9).

Obviously, I have not touched directly on lay representation at the court of Peter. But the three principles are relevant here, too, and the third one most immediately. The existing confusion and lack of decisive institutions in international politics make a universal system of lay representation impossible. With respect to international affairs, it is, furthermore, strictly speaking, unnecessary under our circumstances, since no one recognizes, *de facto,* any authority in the pope to compel the breaking of secular communication between nation-states or their leading statesmen. However, as long as lay assent to the political dimension of the Church's action can only be achieved on the level of the nation-states, it seems that with respect to their internal political affairs the pope ought to be bound by the same limits as the national hierarchies.

The Wheat and the Tares

THE medieval writer on Church-state questions had, of necessity, to be concerned with the problem of the symmetry of regimes. It was necessary for him to compare the roots of the authority and the structural order of papal and regal power. This was true of the medieval writers studied earlier (and of Bellarmine, who preserves a good deal of medieval thinking), even though they differed radically in their substantive views. But this problem is almost completely ignored by the American Catholics. The center of their problem is religious pluralism.

To the medieval writer, it is perfectly clear that if the ecclesiastical and political structures are symmetrical, and if they are both ultimately controlled by the same individual or group, then important Church-state clashes can be prevented. In this context, the peculiar political genius of John of Paris was to try to maintain a diversity of ultimate authorities in Church and state, while reducing the chances of unnecessary conflict by recommending some symmetry in structure which would tend to check extremists on either side. But this aspect of the problem is quite missed by the Americans. Murray can dismiss John's advocacy of a mixed regime in the Church as well as the state on the ground that is a quite accidental, and separable, element of John's doctrine.[1] To some extent, this difference can be charged to difference in situation.

Medieval society was religiously homogeneous. But in a reli-

[1] Cf. *supra,* p. 120, n. 69.

259

giously pluralistic society, the situation is otherwise. The ecclesiastical structures of the diverse religious groups may be quite different. Even among groups with the same or similar church polities, there may be great differences in political orientation, both because of doctrine and because of decisive differences between the characters of the dominant group in each. Thus, for example, two congregationally ruled churches may take, on religio-moral grounds, strongly opposed views on politically important issues (e.g., the long history of well-known differences between northern and southern congregationally organized churches in the U.S. on the questions of slavery and racial equality). Even symmetry between the organizational lines of a church and the state in a religiously pluralistic society is no guarantee against the likelihood of conflict. If, for example, both are structured on a base of majority control, there is nothing to prevent the majority in a church from being quite different in character and objectives from the political majority in the pluralistic society.

Under such circumstances, there may be clashes between the objectives of ecclesiastical and political structures, but they may be politically tolerable. In the United States, they have usually been rendered tolerable by two important facts. The pluralistic structure of society has been very great. Not only is the believing citizenry split into a great number of denominations with separate church polities, but the believers belong to a vast variety of other politically relevant groupings that encompass the non-believers as well. The tendency of each group is, therefore, to moderate its actions sufficiently so as not to alienate permanently those among the opposition together with whom one hopes to constitute a majority on the next issue.[2] Secondly,

[2] Cf., e.g., Alexis de Tocqueville, *Democracy in America*, I, 15. The same insight was raised to the level of a universal explanation of politics by Arthur F. Bentley in *The Process of Government* (Chicago: 1908). Bentley's simplification has been repeated in modern dress by David B. Truman, *The Governmental Process* (New York: 1951).

this has been reinforced on the institutional level by outlawing, by constitutional provision, the possibility of one religious group capturing the state and using it as an instrument to suppress or disadvantage the others. Removal of that threat[3] makes it all the easier to keep religio-political conflict within the moderate bounds laid out by a politics of ever shifting majorities.

In this context, the relatively monarchical structure of the Catholic Church may be inherently distasteful to non-Catholic Christians, as well as to others. But it only becomes an important issue when the Catholic citizenry reaches such a size that it presents the possibility of a Catholic majority as something to be weighed seriously. But the possibility of a great Catholic majority is also apprehended as posing a deeper threat to each of the other religious groups (and non-believers as well). The Catholic Church is seen as fundamentally opposed to religious pluralism. This opposition is seen, sometimes clearly and sometimes very dimly, as being rooted at theological depths that cannot be abandoned by Catholics. Furthermore, those same depths have as another manifestation the ecclesiastical structure of the Church. Thus, the asymmetry between the Catholic Church's organizational structure and that of the United States is seen as connected with the Church's opposition to religious pluralism. Moreover, the latter is regarded as a theoretically deeper stratum of Catholic belief than the matter of ecclesiastical structure, even though papal infallibility has been declared a matter of faith.

It could be alleged that the concentration of American writers on the problem of pluralism rather than the problem of or-

---

[3] Actually, the threat is not wholly removed, but only made more remote insofar as the amending procedure of article five requires a special majority. That applies directly to the federal government. American federalism complicates the reality legally. For that history, cf. Anson Phelps Stokes, *Church and State in the United States* (New York: 1950), 3 vols. Now the religious clauses of the First Amendment are applied to state governments by the courts via the Fourteenth Amendment since *Murdock vs. Penna.*, 319 U.S. 105, and *Everson vs. Bd. of Education*, 330 U.S. 1.

261

ganizational symmetry is, thus, a product of twin facts: the American society is religiously pluralistic whereas the medieval was not, and debates about ecclesiastical structure have been especially dangerous in America.[4] To this could be added the fact that modern European Catholicism, from which American Catholicism is but newly sprung, is still deeply marked by the struggles with the reformers by a faith once universal in Western Europe. And the largest groups of American Catholics brought with them as heritages a structure of customary relations and ways of thinking about the relationships between religious and politico-social realities that were developed in countries that were traditionally "Catholic," that had never integrated dissenting sects into their national life in a stable form of religious pluralism. They could hardly be expected, in their circumstances, to have developed a new view of these affairs in a generation or so. Nor could they, least of all the Irish, be expected to build on the experience of that little body of English Catholics who had been in America from the days of Colonial Maryland.

But, after all the situational qualifications are made, there is a far deeper ground for the concern with religious pluralism as a political problem. And it may be well to begin to indicate its nature by quoting a brilliant passage by a Protestant Christian who has thought deeply on these matters.

Man's search for unity is unconquerable, and the Christian has a special reason for seeking integrity because of his fundamental faith in the God who is One. When he has realized, in consequence of experience and reflection, that he cannot be at one with himself if he denies nature and culture in the effort to be obedient to Christ, or that such denial itself involves a kind of disobedience to the commandments of love, since the social institutions are instruments of that love, then he must

---

[4] The struggle in the American Church over the trustee system made American bishops and pastors especially disinclined to admit laymen to any positions of ecclesiastical authority. Cf., e.g., Theodore Maynard, *The Story of American Catholicism* (New York: 1949), pp. 185–196, 235–237.

seek some sort of reconciliation between Christ and culture without denial of either. The drive toward moral unity in the self is mated with the urgent quest of reason to discover the unity of its principles and the unified principle of the realities toward which it is directed. . . . With the drives toward moral and intellectual integrity the social demand for the unity of society is inseparably connected. Society itself is an expression of the desire of the many for oneness; its ills are all forms of dissensions; . . . The union of church and state, of state with state and class with class, and the union of all these with the supernatural Lord and Companion is the ineluctable desire of the believer.[5]

It is a desire that in some degree informs all who have heard the gospel. But it is especially pressing for Catholics who do not, as does Niebuhr, question the validity as instruments of their unification in Christ of the sacramental, magisterial, liturgical authority of pope and bishops.

Firmly rooted in the doctrine of the Incarnation, it gives rise to that peculiar thrust which is found at different times among all sorts of Christians, but which has been especially characteristic of Catholicism, where it is often called integrism or integralism. The American canonists express, in the relatively narrow terms appropriate to legal obligations, the center of that position when they launch their assault on the legitimacy of legally recognized public religious pluralism. At the heart of their argument is the question of public worship, and everything flows from that.

With the canonists, it is only a matter of the legal obligation of religion, i.e., the obligation of every society to perform acts of worship of the source of its being and prosperity. But that legal point is a remnant of a far deeper perception of the character of human community that finally shapes the moral elements of the integrist's Christian hope.

Understanding that political community is a shared structure of action, the integrist at his best perceives that the archetypical

[5] H. Richard Niebuhr, *Christ and Culture* (New York: 1951), pp. 141–142.

263

human action is liturgical worship. He perceives that liturgical worship establishes the ultimate pattern of active communication and community. In the liturgical drama he notes the element of divine self-revelation, followed by grateful self-offering of the Christian people. The latter, in turn, is divinized so as to make the response proportionate to the initial revelation. The revelation and the response, thus divinized, are then the source of such profound reconciliation and union between God and man that they manifest themselves in a communion feast in which believers are united to one another in their transformation into "other Christs." And this, in turn, calls forth and regenerates the depths of that civil amity which "seems to hold states together, and lawgivers care more for it than for justice; . . . [for] when men are friends they have no need of justice, while when they are just they need friendship as well, and the truest form of justice is thought to be a friendly quality."[6] Pope John XXIII understood that when, speaking of Catholic social doctrine, he said that the "objective is justice . . . [the] driving force is love."[7]

The integrist at his best notes that great law-givers of every age have required the citizens of the states they shaped to share a common table at least at some great feast. Perhaps only in representative ritual or perhaps in great abundance of food, the citizens have been summoned to feast together with the gods. Such feasts, among other things, emphasize to men the reality of their being sharers of a divine abundance. And this is accomplished by way of a powerful, symbolic victory over the very nature of the root act of the feast: eating. The nature of eating illuminates the limitedness, insecurity, and otherness of men. When a man eats, he testifies to his limitedness: he is dependent for his continued existence on repeatedly recharging himself by appropriating to himself things that are not himself.

---

[6] Aristotle, *Nicomachean Ethics* viii. 1. 1155ª22–25.
[7] *Mater et Magistra*, 226.

Furthermore, in doing so he is, on the level of mere eating, radically alone: two men cannot eat the same thing; what is termed "sharing" is in fact a division into portions, each man, and he only, eating his own. But not only are men confronted, when eating, with their dependence on that which is other than themselves, food, and not only are they isolated each with his own piece, but they are frequently confronted with the inadequacy of the food supply to fully satisfy all of them. And that symbolizes men's ever-recurrent discovery of the limitedness of the means of satisfying their desires, of the unlimitedness of their desires, and of the consequence: what *he* takes *I* may not take. That discovery has regularly led to war. Worse still: in the experience of hunger, men sometimes are driven to the awareness that they may eat even their fellows. The civic banquet recasts that whole experience in the limitless abundance of the divine solicitude. Not that material abundance is magically procured thereby, but in the civic banquet the citizens are introduced to a communion and a solidarity in which the neediness that isolates each one from his fellows is overcome in that each becomes capable of material self-sacrifice for the sake of the communion in spirit with his fellow citizens.

The Christian integrist sees in the ubiquity of such practices a testimony to the depths of man's natural search for fellowship by relating himself to the divine source of creation.[8] He adds to it the good news of Christ in Whom God takes on humanity and archetypically establishes the way to god-likeness for man through sacrificial suffering. He adds to it the good news of Christ with Whom men join the communion of the brothers of Christ. He adds to it the good news of Christ through Whom they are joined with one another under a common Father. The Christian integrist, dizzy before the fact of the In-

[8] Even we Americans, who can hardly be expected, in our puritan depths, to be comfortable at a great Dionysia, nevertheless have our Thanksgiving Day. And even with our short history, there is a small start in the cult of heroes with the celebration of the birthdays of Washington and Lincoln.

carnation and its overawing significance, sees revealed before him a divine response to the sadness of Aristotle, who, in this context, appears as the most perfect of natural men. Aristotle was the philosopher of friendship who wrote that "no one would choose to live if he had no friends even though he had everything else." But Aristotle is torn. He strains every nerve to be god-like, yet he cannot wish his friend to be a god. Then he would lose his friend, for a god is "too far away." And so the philosopher of friendship is compelled to say that, like the gods who are far away and who do not turn from their perfections to answer man's cry, "it is for himself most of all that each man wishes what is good." That divine isolation enfolds him even when he lays down his life for his friend. He gives them his life, as it were, but takes for himself a greater good, a noble act that transcends the narrow compass of its brief time. And that is to the advantage, though not to the nobility, of the subjects of a true king.[9]

For the Christian integrist, the fact of the Incarnation makes it no longer necessary to tell Plato's noble lie[10] to hold the citizens in brotherhood one with another. Rather, his task and spirit are essentially missionary: the transformation in Christ of the whole of creation which now labors under the burden of sin.

It may seem unusual, not to say perverse, to speak of the essential task and spirit of integrism as missionary. Integrism is nowadays more commonly seen as fundamentally inward-looking and conservative, if not reactionary, whereas the missionary spirit is seen as directed outward, adaptive, progressive. There is a truth to that in our historical perspective, but it is not the whole truth, and it refers to an integrism grown sclerotic, in which nostalgia has replaced Christian hope. In our time, missionary activity is seen primarily as an extensive phenomenon.

---

[9] *Nicomachean Ethics* viii. 1. 1155ª5–6; 7. 1159ª3–12; 10. 1160ª31–1160ᵇ10; ix. 8. 1168ª27–1169ᵇ2; x. 7. 1177ª11–1178ª8.
[10] *Republic* iii. 414–415.

But there are civilizational moments when the missionary thrust is just as much, if not more, intensive as extensive. In such moments of civilizational-cultural youth, when the whole order of life and meaning is being established for a long time, when the seeds of the brilliance of later centuries are being sown,[11] the energies of faith are directed to the Christian transformation of the new patterns of life: of art, love, and thought that are being elaborated out of a flux. The objective then is not so much the preaching of the gospel to new ears, though that is not forgotten, but rather the penetration of the gospel beyond the ears to every fibre of being and action.

In the world of the spirit as in the world of nature, it is not possible to direct all energies outward. No sane religious superior expects to send men to mission lands without having first devoted the missioner's energies to a long and difficult self-transformation. Nor should it be surprising that cities, nations, and civilizations sometimes devote more energy to intensive missionary self-transformation at one time, and at another time they cross every sea and desert in the search of new souls. It is conceivable that the two be balanced, but it is unlikely. The tides of human affairs are not found in charts and tables, and, even when known, few peoples are wise enough to heed them in their steering. And even when they do, their situations change, and with the changes new tasks and new perspectives are thrust on them.

When, on whatever occasion, a people has given itself to such a movement of self-transformation, an effort of *in*tensive missionary energy, it is not and cannot simply be a matter of private, spiritual transformation. Not that that is not involved, but by itself it is both unnatural and un-Christian. Inevitably involved is the structure, the style, of its common action at

[11] The organic metaphors are metaphors only. I do not wish to suggest a civilizational cyclicalism in strict analogy to the cosmic cycles of birth, growth, decay, and rebirth.

267

every level. To take but one example, the Carolingian renaissance encompassed a wide range of secular and sacred reforms that were intimately and inescapably interconnected.

More than a millennium later, those who hoped and hope to create a new Western Europe have found it impossible to avoid reflecting on the Carolingian struggle, achievement, and failure, so profound is the impress still. In the Holy Empire that has haunted Western Europe since those days, even war itself was to be brought within the ambit of the Prince of Peace. No one who has heard the Song of Roland or of the Crusades can help but be moved by the spiritual depths of the struggle— for all its pride and folly. The world of government no less than the world of war was subjected to that hope. Thus Bellarmine, who reflected, as Murray notes,[12] the common assumptions of the Middle Ages though their death knell was ringing, regarded both ecclesiastical and political power as functioning within one body, the Mystical Body, the Church. And it is a matter of course for him that when kings and princes become Christians, they subject their sceptres to Christ.[13]

Yet hidden amid all this flaming hope are two profound and related dangers. The attempt to transform all things in Christ involves a powerful lure toward an illegitimate externalization (which regularly leads, by way of reaction, to iconoclasm, puritanism, the attempt at wholly spiritual and inward religion). The integrist hope rightly demands the Christianization of every aspect of man's life, rightly regards a religious-secular schizophrenia as abnormal. But the difficulty of the task and man's weakness conspire to lure him to accept appearances for reality, to accept formalities for genuine form. In lieu of the immense and never-ending struggle to Christianize politics, he is tempted to accept the externals: obedience of kings to the pope. In lieu

---

[12] "Bellarmine," pp. 506–508.   [13] Cf. *supra*, pp. 131–136.

of the terribly difficult task of discovering and structuring a Christian use of the chthonic forces let loose in war, he is tempted to accept an externally religious objective, such as the reconquest of the Holy Land. When he capitulates to such lures, he sins by idolatry; he pursues and serves the works of his own hands. (This seems to be the discovery of the Reformers, who were so suspicious of works.)

One step further in the experience of the difficulty of the hoped-for transformation and the integrist is prepared to admit that his hopes were inordinate. With Giles of Rome, he is prepared to admit that the mass of men have hardly been Christianized in much more than appearances. The appearances are useful in maintaining order and in securing the peace and leisure of a spiritual élite of contemplatives. But he knows that even the appearances are preserved against heretics and schismatics by threats of brute force, expropriation, and radical exile from the whole world of man, even by death.

But, whether in milder or more extreme forms, the perversions of integrism give rise to a revolt of nature. To give one's life for Christ is one thing. To lose a saintly king of France in a marginally religious and politically absurd crusade is quite another. To try to Christianize the Germanic warrior bands is one thing. To suppose that a solution is limned in the high-flown, glorious military nonsense of Roland at Roncevaux is quite another. To attempt to Christianize politics is one thing. To do it by the centralization of political power in the hands of popes, some of whom turn out to be knaves or political fools or both, that is quite another thing. The revolt of nature may at first take the mild form of the tendency toward Semi-Pelagianism of John of Paris in the world of thought,[14] or of King Philip the Fair in the world of action.[15]

[14] Cf. *supra*, pp. 97–99.   [15] Carlyle, *HMPT*, vol. 5, p. 375.

But things had gone too far by the end of the thirteenth century to be amenable to the mild correctives of John of Paris. Italy had had enough of papal politics, even if it yet had five hundred years more of it in store. Marsilius turned the tables on hierocratic integrism by reducing the clergy to dependence on lay political authority. Machiavelli and his successors openly dropped all Christian concerns, and launched an assault on Christianity as a perverse enemy of political order, of freedom, and of genuine human virtue. From then on, integrism appears largely as a reactionary defense of one after another crumbling entrenchment of Christian privilege. Integrists, with greater or lesser enthusiasm as they are more or less tired and resigned, are left with the legalistic argument for public political suppression of the spread of heresy as the center of their jejune reflections on the obligation of religion.

Nevertheless, it would be absurd to suggest that this line of development exhausts the Christian orientations to the relationships of grace and nature in politics. There is always, more or less fully developed, another spiritual style in these matters that is also profoundly Christian. It is the vocation to prophetic criticism of the existential reality of man and his works. More eschatological than incarnational, it continually points out that the Second Coming is not yet. It repeatedly recalls men to the Christian truth that none of their kingdoms are the kingdom of Christ. Its task is to point out that our time is still a time of hope, and therefore not a time of perfect fulfillment.

To the integrist, prophetic criticism cries out to beware lest he confuse his own activity with the final ordering that is the prerogative of Christ. To the Christian kings, prophetic criticism cries out that their thrones are not identical with the judgment seat of the Lord Who will come to judge the living and the dead. To societies engaged in the work of transforming the structures of their common life in accordance with the new law of Christ, prophetic criticism warns them lest what they really

270

seek to build is a Tower of Babel. Prophetic criticism finds it necessary again and again to recall man from his presumption and pride, to point out the vices, the crimes, the impurities, base metals, and moral stenches that hide behind the integrist's gilt and incense. The prophetic voice cries out that in our time the kingdom of God is "within you," and is the word of divine grace and not of the pride of men who build.

Ultimately, the prophetic voice challenges the unities of the integrist as out of due season. For the prophetic voice, our time, the time between the first and second comings of Christ, the time of hope, is inescapably a pluralistic time. It is the time of testing between good and evil. The prophetic voice refuses to permit the integrist the illusion that a victory over evil can be won by such simple expedients as baptizing a whole people in the river, reworking its legal structure in accordance with Christian principles, repressing heretical opinion, and subordinating political authorities to the pope. The prophetic critic does not deny the centrality of worship, but he points out that societies that have celebrated profoundly moving liturgical services filled with music of great power and beauty have also been capable of enormous crimes and hidden infidelities.

The prophetic critic points out that the integrist may be able to suppress public expression of heretical opinion, but he seldom manages to suppress it altogether. The integrist in his necessary concern for externals may be able to suppress the public communication of heretical formulae, but the roots of heresy are far deeper than that. They are at the very heart of our time of testing. Suppression of the verbal formulae of heresy in no way assures its genuine abolition. To take one example: it is quite possible to live the life of a Pelagian without ever having heard any Pelagian doctrines. What is worse, it is the more dangerous for being hid behind the public façade of orthodoxy. Generation can succeed generation undisturbed in their pride, never

271

forced to face the issues and choose, lulled by a superficial sense of Christian orthodoxy.

But, like integrism, prophetic criticism has its peculiar lures, its special temptations. It can cloak a flight from responsibility. Pointing out the difficulties and the dangers of the integrist thrust, pointing out the illusions and temptations of integrism, the prophetic critic easily forgets the Incarnation and Resurrection. Denouncing the externalism of the integrists, he easily flees his own task of making the Word become flesh in him and his. He easily mistakes the cleanliness of his own hands for a reason to congratulate himself, whereas the absence of mortar and gilt from his fingers is the sign of his sterility and even of a despair hidden only by the fact that attention is directed primarily to others.

Neither integrism nor prophetic criticism by itself is wholly Christian. The Christian community needs both spiritual styles in order to be fully itself. On occasion, a man appears in whom the grace of God has brought both to a balanced fullness. Most of the time it is necessary for the Christian community to include men who embody both, some one and some the other. Each needs the other by way of a corrective for his peculiar weakness.

But it is also necessary to seek a balance between those two spiritual styles on the level of public institutional structures. The Roman communion has been particularly susceptible to the integrist's temptation to accept external appearances of the kingdom for the reality and the consequent temptation toward an institutionalized violence designed to protect the kingdom by driving heretics from the world. For Giles of Rome, they were driven from the very material world. In contemporary Spain, they have been driven from the human world of public visibility. Thus, the Church needs to protect herself against this temptation by a formal recognition that the way to the kingdom of heaven is not through assuming the prerogatives of the last

272

judgment by driving the deniers of the kingdom's unity out of the world. The problem of heresy needs to be situated within the context of the coexistence of good and evil prior to the last judgment. The Church needs to repeat to Christ's servants the words of the householder concerning the wheat and the tares, to remind them that they are not the angels of the last judgment (Mt 13:24–30, 36–43, 47–50).

As I write this, it seems likely that Vatican II will take some action in this direction, and it is long overdue. But it also seems that it may well be at least partly clothed in some of the language of rationalistic individualism characteristic of early American natural-rights doctrines.[16] This is the announced objective of Murray, who is a conciliar expert in this field.[17] Even in that language, a conciliar statement may be valuable for our immediate situation. But in the long run it will create new problems. It is not only that natural-rights doctrines have undergone such devastating philosophical critiques that their use today can only cover an absurd and ultimately reactionary attempt by American Catholics triumphantly to reply to the doubters of their patriotism. There is a far deeper difficulty. Such language may leave room for the mustard seed and the leaven, but it is too narrow to accommodate the mustard tree and the leavened lump that grow up between the two treatments of the wheat and the tares (see Mt 13:31–33).

If the voice of the Council adopts the rationalistic language of absolutized individual rights, then the Council will have postponed for the indefinite future the achievement of a creative balance between the voice of prophetic criticism and the voice of the integrist who hopes for some reconciliation of Christ and culture, and who knows that such a reconciliation, however

---

[16] Lest there be any confusion, it may be permissible to belabor the obvious by calling attention to the well-known distinction between doctrines of natural right and natural law on the one hand, and of natural rights on the other.

[17] J.C.M., "On Religious Liberty," pp. 704–706.

provisional, must have a part of its being in the public world of social and political institutional structures. But the language of absolutized individual rights has no room for public and institutional manifestations of a spiritual unity inasmuch as that language was structured out of a denial of the possibility of such unity, beginning with Hobbes and Locke.

However, in the moments when a people has been moved to transform itself in any fundamental way, a considerable degree of unity about ultimate objects is indispensable if the transformation is to have any prospects of success. Even shallow revolutionaries know that. What is necessarily involved is a transformation of the shared psychic structure whereby a people has an identity. That, in turn, requires a transformation of the public and institutional expressions and symbolizations of that identity.

If a people sets out on the long path of an attempt to achieve a shared tranformation in Christ, that obviously requires an external religious unity. Only then can they hope to elaborate a common life and common institutions that are both profoundly their own and profoundly Christian. Is it the task of the Council to teach them that that is an illegitimate hope? To teach them the new doctrine that human community is not deep enough to be transformed in Christ? To teach them that such transformation is only relevant to individuals and not to natural human communities? Is it not rather the task of the Council to teach them that if that is their objective, they must find a way to do it without driving out of the world those who cannot or will not join them on that *via dolorosa?* To teach them that they must find a way of doing it without usurping the divine judgment seat and playing a blasphemous game in which the lives and human dignity of their fellow men are the counters? Is it not the task of the Council to teach them the replies of Christ to Pilate (Jn 18:36–37), and that the crown they have chosen is made of thorns?

The Council Fathers cannot be expected to know all the political solutions any more than the Bible can be expected to teach geometry. The problem is singularly complex and antedates Christianity. In the ancient world, it manifested itself in the tendency to exclude from the realm of law (and thus from the "world" and into exterior chaos) all non-citizens. The non-citizen was such by virtue of having no share in the religious structure that shaped the city.[18] The *jus gentium* was a partial solution to the problem of order in the politico-religious pluralism of the ancient world. It gave way to the imperial unification of the *gentes* at the price of their freedom and of a clearly inadequate religious syncretism.

To its everlasting shame, medieval Christendom failed radically to solve the problem. Symbolic of its failure are the Crusades and the extermination of the Albigensians. The French, at least, should have known better. They possessed at Paris what was said to be Christ's crown of thorns. Though Christ's mission cost Him His life, the Most Christian King would not part with Languedoc in witness to the mission France claimed for herself. Pope and bishops might have reminded the French that Christian crowns draw blood on the brow.

The magisterium needs to teach that religiously homogeneous communities have a special obligation to work out political means to affirm their specifically human solidarity with communities that do not share the faith. Still, the Council Fathers cannot be expected to be experts on those matters. If the mean between a scarcely enforceable *jus gentium* and imperial uniformity is some form of federalism, the forms are exceedingly diverse and the experience not self-explanatory.[19] Solutions, if

[18] Cf., e.g., Aristotle, *Constitution of Athens* 55.3.

[19] Compare, e.g., the diverse developments in the realm of religio-political federalism in Switzerland and in the early import of the First Amendment to the U.S. Constitution. Cf., e.g., Christopher Hughes, *The Federal Constitution of Switzerland* (London: 1954), and Anson Phelps Stokes, *Church and State in the United States* (New York: 1950).

there are any, will have to be worked out by statesmen and political thinkers.

However, much of the modern Western world is no longer characterized by religiously homogeneous political communities. The modern West has committed itself to technological objectives that break up such communities. That commitment is partly a product of a revulsion against religious fanaticism and the wars and massacres to which it led. That revulsion led to a powerful tendency to secularize political society radically by directing it to the maximization of exclusively private and/or pre-political goals. And the technological objectives that have come to dominate so much of our lives seem integrally to involve the regular shifting and mixture of individuals as interchangeable units in the perpetual and kaleidoscopic transformations of the economy. For the semi-nomadic populations produced in Europe and America by these forces, the religious pluralism inherent in this time before the harvest takes the form of religiously diverse individuals living in close proximity. Here the task of the magisterium is not only to teach the faithful that the gospel does not authorize them to oppress others in any way, but also to teach them that the gospel must in some way inform the structure of their public lives.

Again, the practical solutions are by no means obvious. To take only the schools question, the Church in America has erected a whole set of quasi-public educational institutions as an alternative to the formally public schools which, depending on locality, may be secularistic, or formed by a *de facto* Protestant establishment. But the Catholic schools are charged with being divisive, and it may well be that they fail to develop in their students an ability to affirm existentially their solidarity with their non-Catholic fellow citizens except in a schizophrenic way. While they are thrown together repeatedly with non-Catholics in a great variety of situations as individuals, they do not, or seldom, experience the sharing of a common life between their

276

diverse communities. Here again, a solution would seem to depend on a creative elaboration of public educational institutions. But the Council Fathers cannot decree that either.

It seems to me that any serious attempt at an educational policy in accord with the religious pluralism of our society would envisage experiments in multi-denominational public schools— not non-denominational, but multi-denominational schools.[20] I am hardly in a position to say what the difficulties might be. They would, no doubt, be great. Such schools might prove to be expensive. They would require, and this would be among their virtues, the responsible participants to discover modes of co-operation that forced no one's conscience, that neither slurred over doctrinal differences with a false irenicism nor built up walls where none need exist. It is not inconceivable that such experiments could effect a release of long pent-up constructive forces of religion that might re-inspirit a sick civilization to sing a new song unto the Lord.[21]

Obviously, that is not necessarily a recipe for every society and for every age. Different civilizational moments pose the pluralistic problem in different ways and require a different dialogue between integrist and prophetic critic.

So perhaps someone will say: "There! At the very end you, too, have come to Murray's historicism." But that is to miss the point. It is, no doubt, true as he argues that no historical realization is the Ideal Republic of Truth and Justice. That is a valid expression of the voice of prophetic criticism. But it may also be true that no Christian action in public affairs is possible without

[20] I would here include non-believers in whatever groupings they might elaborate as denominations.

[21] Obviously, no such experiments can be undertaken by public authority as long as the whole subject is burdened by a banal constitutional jurisprudence proceeding in a simple world of rationalistic absolutes that would bring a blush to the cheeks of even so shameless a sloganeer as John Stewart Mill. But perhaps the crisis of our civilization has become deep enough that we may be able to go beyond Victorian superficialities. After Auschwitz, Mill is irrelevant.

277

the pole star of the apocalyptic vision of the City of God. And no serious reflection on the significance of that vision for action in this world can avoid exploring the human possibilities for realizing crude images of that vision, as well as the dangers inherent in such attempts by men who are both bathed in grace and flawed by sin. And it would be absurd to pretend either that they are not arranged in a hierarchy—as are the states of individual life—or that any particular realization is possible or prudent as an objective for a given society.

It may not be an easy task to begin again, and there may be danger in it, but every Christian who is in the world must, at the level of his competence, ask the question how the structure of the common action in which he moves can be conformed to the archetypal Christian action. In it, the integrist's truth and the prophetic critic's truth are both present, and the tension symoblizes our time: to stretch out the arms to embrace one's brothers—and to receive the nails.

278

Index of Names

279